Conversations with W. S. Merwin

Literary Conversations Series

Conversations
with W. S. Merwin

Edited by Michael Wutz and Hal Crimmel

University Press of Mississippi   Jackson

www.upress.state.ms.us

The University Press of Mississippi is a member of the Association of American University Presses.

First printing 2015
∞
Library of Congress Cataloging-in-Publication Data

Merwin, W. S. (William Stanley), 1927–
    Conversations with W. S. Merwin / edited by Michael Wutz and Hal Crimmel.
        pages cm. — (Literary conversations series)
    Includes index.
    ISBN 978-1-62846-222-7 (hardback) — ISBN 978-1-62674-619-0 (ebook) 1. Merwin,
W. S. (William Stanley), 1927-—Interviews. 2. Poets, American—20th century—Interviews.
3. Poetry—Authorship. I. Wutz, Michael, editor. II. Crimmel, Hal, 1966– editor. III. Title.
    PS3563.E75Z46 2015
    811'.54—dc23
    [B]   2014039427

British Library Cataloging-in-Publication Data available

Books by W. S. Merwin

Poetry

A Mask for Janus. New Haven and London: Yale UP and Oxford UP, 1952.

The Dancing Bears. New Haven: Yale UP, 1954.

Green with Beasts: Poems. London: Hart-Davis, 1956. New York: Knopf, 1956.

The Drunk in the Furnace. New York: Macmillan, 1960.

The Moving Target. New York: Atheneum, 1963.

Collected Poems. New York: Atheneum. 1966.

The Lice: Poems. New York: Atheneum, 1967. London: Hart-Davis, 1967.

Animae. San Francisco: Kayak, 1969.

The Carrier of Ladders. New York: Atheneum, 1970.

Writings to an Unfinished Accompaniment. New York: Atheneum, 1973.

The Compass Flower: Poems. New York: Atheneum, 1977.

Opening the Hand: Poems. New York: Atheneum, 1983.

Regions of Memory: Uncollected Prose 1949–82. W. S. Merwin. Edited by Ed Folsom and Cary Nelson. Urbana: University of Illinois Press, 1987.

The Rain in the Trees: Poems. New York: Knopf, 1988.

Selected Poems. New York: Atheneum, 1988.

The Second Four Books of Poems. Port Townsend: Copper Canyon Press, 1993.

Travels: Poems. New York: Knopf, 1993.

Flower & Hand: Poems, 1977–1983. Port Townsend: Copper Canyon Press, 1996.

The Folding Cliffs: A Narrative of 19th-century Hawaii. New York: Knopf, 1998.

The River Sound: Poems. New York: Knopf, 1999.

The First Four Books of Poems. Port Townsend: Copper Canyon Press, 2000.

The Pupil: Poems. New York: Knopf, 2001.

Migration: New & Selected Poems. Port Townsend: Copper Canyon Press, 2005.

The Shadow of Sirius. Port Townsend: Copper Canyon Press, 2008.

The Collected Poems of W. S. Merwin, 1952–1993. 2 vols. Edited by J. D. McClatchy. New York: Library of America, 2013.

The Collected Poems of W. S. Merwin, 1996–2011. 2 vols. Edited by J. D. McClatchy. New York: Library of America, 2013.

The Moon before Morning. Port Townsend: Copper Canyon Press, 2014.

Prose

The Miner's Pale Children. New York: Atheneum, 1970.
Houses and Travellers: Prose. New York: Atheneum, 1977.
Unframed Originals. New York: Atheneum, 1982.
The Lost Upland: Stories of Southwest France. New York: Knopf, 1992.
The Mays of Ventadorn. Washington D.C.: National Geographic, 2002.
Summer Doorways: A Memoir. Washington D.C.: Shoemaker & Hoard, 2005.
The Book of Fables. Port Townsend: Copper Canyon Press, 2007.

Translations

The Poem of the Cid. London: Dent, 1959.
The Satires of Persius. Bloomington: Indiana UP, 1961.
Medieval Epics. 1963. Translated with William Alfred and Helen M. Mustard. New York: Modern Library, 1998.
The Song of Roland. New York: Vintage Books, 1963.
Selected Translations, 1948–1968. New York: Atheneum, 1968.
Products of the Perfected Civilization: Selected Writings of Chamfort, by Sébastien Roch Nicolas Chamfort. New York: Macmillan, 1969.
Transparence of the World, by Jean Follain. New York: Atheneum, 1969.
Twenty Love Poems and a Song of Despair, by Pablo Neruda. London: Cape, 1969.
Voices, by Antonio Porchia. Port Townsend: Copper Canyon Press, 1969.
Selected Poems, by Osip Mandelstam. Translated with Clarence Brown. New York: Atheneum, 1970.
Asian Figures. New York: Atheneum, 1972.
Sanskrit Love Poems. Translated with J. Moussaieff Masson. London: E. Alkazi, 1977.
Iphigeneia at Aulis, by Euripides. Translated with George E. Dimock. New York: Oxford UP, 1978.
Selected Translations, 1968–1978. New York: Atheneum, 1979.
Vertical Poetry, by Roberto Juarroz. San Francisco: North Point Press, 1988.
Sun at Midnight: Poems and Sermons, by Musō Soseki. Translated with Soiku Shigematsu. San Francisco: North Point Press, 1989.
Gacela of Unforeseen Love, by Federico García Lorca. Washington: October Mountain. 1993.
Blood Wedding and Yerma, by Federico García Lorca. Translated with Langston Hughes. New York: Theatre Communications Group, 1994.

East Window: The Asian Translations. Port Townsend: Copper Canyon
    Press, 1998.
Purgatorio by Dante Alighieri. New York: Knopf, 2000.
Sir Gawain and the Green Knight: A New Verse Translation. New York:
    Knopf, 2002.
Collected Haiku of Yosa Buson. Translated with Lento Takako. Port
    Townsend: Copper Canyon Press, 2013.
Selected Translations: 1948–2011. Port Townsend: Copper Canyon Press,
    2013.

Contents

Introduction

At age eighty-eight, William Stanley Merwin is arguably the most venerated and distinguished living poet in the United States whose conversations have not yet been gathered in the renowned interview series published by the University Press of Mississippi. A major link between the period of literary modernism and its contemporary extensions—whatever label one wants to affix to them—this oversight is all the more surprising given the trajectory of a career that is already in its ninth decade. Beginning with short hymns to accompany his father's services as a Presbyterian minister, Merwin has been writing poetry since childhood, and he has been cultivating that craft to this very day, retreating each morning into his private writing space to contemplate and write. The result, by last count, is about twenty volumes of original poetry, each with the integrity of a French cathedral or, to speak with a metaphor even more in the spirit of Merwin, with the balance of a living ecosystem. Merwin writes *books* of poetry, not collections.

The Bollingen Prize for Poetry, the Maurice English Poetry Award, the National Book Award, the inaugural Tanning Prize from the Academy of American Poets, not one but two Pulitzer Prizes, and the appointment as the seventeenth United States poet laureate in 2010—these are only some of the major distinctions Merwin has earned for his poetry. Merwin, however, has accrued accolades not only for his poetry, but for his collections of essays and memoirs as well. A master of several genres, he has contributed essays, often on the early nuclear protest movement, to the *Nation*, and he has written several memoirs such as *The Miner's Pale Children*, his first book of prose reflecting on his upbringing in rural Pennsylvania, and *Summer Doorways*, for which he received the 2005 National Book Award. Similarly, as a lifelong Francophile residing for years in southwestern France, he has eloquently written about his appreciation for that region's natural beauty in *The Lost Upland* and in *Unframed Originals*, a collection of intertwining autobiographical narratives. His move to Hawaii in the late 1970s eventually occasioned, after years of incubation, *The Folding Cliffs*, a monumental prose-poetic history of the islands that combines the forms of the European elegy with those of vernacular Hawaiian chants. A singular genre-bender melding poetry and prose into a hybrid sui generis, the book received the Ruth Lilly Poetry Prize awarded by the Poetry Foundation.

Merwin's translations, too, suggest a master wordsmith at the height of his powers. While still at Princeton, he collaborated with a Spanish-born teacher on a translation of Federico García Lorca's *Romancero Gitano*, and following his degree in 1948 and intermittent graduate work in modern languages, extended sojourns in France, Spain, and Portugal helped him develop the linguistic expertise that prepared him for remunerative translation work. In the 1950s and 1960s, Merwin translated Spanish and French classics into radio scripts for the BBC, most prominently *The Poem of the Cid*, *The Satires of Persius*, and the medieval picaresque, *The Life of Lazarillo de Tormes*, which were later published. His reputation established, he received a PEN Translation Prize for *Selected Translations, 1948–1968* and, over the course of several decades, released major translations of such writers as Nicanor Parra, Antonia Porchia, Jean Follain, Pablo Neruda, and Lope de Rueda. In 2000, he published a new verse translation of Dante Aligheri's *Purgatorio*, the middle section of *The Divine Comedy*, followed by a new verse translation of *Sir Gawain and the Green Knight* in 2004. Interested in the cultures of the Far East, Merwin also tried his hand and ear at languages outside his realm of familiarity. Often working with an expert native speaker in a kind of linguistic triangulation, Merwin has been involved in, among others, the English renditions *A Thousand Years of Vietnamese Poetry* (with Burton Raffel and Nguyen Ngoc Bich), *Sanskrit Love Poetry* (with J. Moussaieff Masson), and, after more than a decade of collaboration, *Sun at Midnight: Poems and Sermons* (with Soiku Shigematsu), a collection of the works of medieval Japanese Zen master and garden designer, Musō Soseki.

Given this overwhelming productivity spanning seventy years and the generic spectrum of the literary arts—including, we should add, original plays and a script of *Huckleberry Finn* produced by British television—Merwin readers should be glad that his primary body of work has overshadowed the conversations he has been offering over the years. His poetry, essays, memoirs, and translations *should* take precedence over the interviews he has given, reflective as they are of his primary craft and the literary expression of the concerns that have been animating his writing since before World War II. At the same time, it is high time to give these conversations their due consideration as a self-standing category in Merwin's oeuvre. Often unrehearsed and less premeditated than the constraints of crafted poetry and prose, they show a Merwin as intellectually agile face to face as he is on the page; the footwork he does in conversation is fully analogous to the feet and cadences of his poetry. As well, more than offering casual observations on the occasional poem or relaying an occasional experience, they afford literary and cultural historians a view into the larger continuities of Merwin's thinking, especially when arranged chronologically. What is most apparent is that, like many poets aware of literary tradition and cultural ferment, Merwin sees his work in conversation with the larger cultural developments of his time(s) and with the writers that have preceded and parallel him. In the aggregate, these interviews allow for a reconstruction of his literary and cultural roots—stations in the making of a writer and thinker, activist and ecologist, and indeed *poète-philosophe*.

Chief among these formative influences is the early synergy of his teachers at Princeton, R. P. Blackmur and John Berryman. Berryman, as Merwin recalled in his interview with the *Paris Review*, taught him that "writing poetry is never a wholly deliberate act over which you have complete control," and hence admonished him to "pray to the Muse"—that old-fashioned agency of inspiration often dismissed by leading modernist poets.[1] Less romantic because more practical, as Merwin noted in the same interview, Blackmur was a self-taught intellectual gifted with "the most haunting literary intelligence," who became a father figure early on. Straddling the fence between ivory tower thinking and fierce individuality, Blackmur instilled a lifelong suspicion toward academia in his young protégé, who is one of very few poets of his generation never to have held a permanent university appointment. Foregoing institutional claustrophobia for creative flexibility, Merwin has preferred to subsist as a self-sufficient language worker beyond the pale of the academic establishment. As he put it to Bill Moyers, "after about a week in university, I begin to feel the oxygen's going out of the air very fast and I have to go somewhere else." Likewise, Merwin's well-known distaste for institutional creative writing programs connects to his early mentor's unease with curricular pigeon holes and streamlined education.

If Berryman and Blackmur were the primary academic influences of the fledgling poet, Ezra Pound and Robert Graves were the éminences grises to shape Merwin's work habits and early poetic sensibilities. Impressed by "the incredible ear that runs through much of the Cantos," and seemingly unaware of the political controversy surrounding Pound, Merwin in 1946 visited the godfather of modernism who had edited *The Waste Land* and launched the career of many a young poet (Folsom and Nelson). Sitting across from him in the psychiatric ward of St. Elizabeth's Hospital in Washington, DC, "with people wandering round, flushing imaginary toilets," Merwin remembers how Pound expounded on his poetic theories and dished out advice en masse (Hirsch). Not only is "there one thing that we all owe to him, the debt to his way of hearing" (Folsom and Nelson); Pound also impressed upon Merwin that poetry is the product of discipline and serendipity, and that working in a foreign language leads to a refined understanding of the poetic suppleness inherent in one's native tongue: "He said that it was important to regard writing as not a chance or romantic or inspired (in the occasional sense) thing, but rather a kind of spontaneity which arises out of discipline and continual devotion to something; and translation is a way of keeping one close to what one is doing, to the possibilities of one's own language" (Bourne). By way of daily practice, Pound urged Merwin to write "about seventy-five lines a day" and to "translate about seventy-five lines day," thus opening the path for Merwin's dual calling as poet and translator.[2] The synergy of translation is such that the skillful, ear-based rendering of poetry in English has the reciprocal effect of refining the original poetry of one's own.

Significantly, it is in the wake of this singular Poundian encounter that Merwin started translating seriously, eventually making a career out of it that paralleled the writing of his own poetry. Merwin became more self-consciously reflective about emerging new possibilities of form and syntax, as he crafted translations of his Spanish-language contemporaries into English. While not wanting to sound like the poets he worked on, especially Pablo Neruda or Federico García Lorca, he began to realize "that the possibilities were not just what they seemed to be at that time in English," eventually exploring new metric rhythms, stanza forms, and breaking out of the "little cultural pattern" that typified, and imprisoned, Anglo-American poetry of the postwar period. Shuttling back and forth between, especially, English, Spanish, and French—with the linguistic competence continually honed by a poetic ear—allowed Merwin to leave behind "the sort of belletristic sardine-can verse" other English-speaking poets, he felt, were stuck in.[3] Significantly as well, it is precisely at this moment, when he translates Spanish and French classics for the BBC, that the *Kenyon Review* accepts his first original poem, "The Ballad of John Cable and Three Gentlemen."

In Graves, Merwin found a prime example of Pound's poetic verities: an interest in foreign languages and cultures, and the literary use of ancient myth. *The Cantos* had of course already demonstrated the allusive texturing of modernism, and the ubiquity of Eliot's depersonalized, myth-based poetry was inescapable. As Merwin recalled to David Elliott, Eliot "seemed to be present the way Freud would be present if you were talking about psychology."[4] Merwin, however, was even more influenced by the author of

The White Goddess and the intellectual labor of his translations. Subtitled "A Historical Grammar of Myth," Graves's magnum opus—revised while Merwin was tutoring Graves's son in Mallorca—gave Merwin's first poems their mythological form as much as did his translation work. He began realizing "that mythology really informed everything, that mythology was not merely something you learned in school that the Greeks had to make statues to illustrate a couple of thousand years ago. It is everything that helps us to make sense of the world" (Elliott). A year later, this focus on myth ushered in Merwin's first book of poetry, *The Mask of Janus*, which was selected by W. H. Auden for the Yale Younger Poets' Prize, and which put him on the map.[5]

Paralleling this exposure to the poetic uses of myth, Merwin also observed and absorbed another of Pound's virtues exemplified in Graves: the discipline of writing. One of "the marvelous things about [the] experience" of working in Mallorca, as Merwin told John Amen, was "the way Robert worked all the time. Something would interrupt, or someone would come to the door, and Robert would deal with it and then go right back to work." Similarly, Merwin recalled that Graves refused for the longest time to have a telephone that might interrupt his work flow, and he likewise finds that the "telephone is a tremendous distraction. For years I didn't have one, and I don't think I've ever really gotten used to it." As well, just as Graves wrote everything in longhand, Merwin remarked to Bill Moyers that "I can't imagine ever writing anything of any kind on a machine. I never tried to write either poetry or prose on a typewriter," instead preferring scrap paper and pencil.[6] The craft-based, and fundamentally Protestant, work ethic Merwin brings to his writing, which easily synergized with the more Eastern writing practice he adopted in the late 1970s, goes back to Graves's early modeling, and it allowed him to produce a body of work unequalled in his generation.

Complementing the influence of his late-modernist predecessors on practice and procedure, Walt Whitman and Henry David Thoreau shaped the environmental and political sensibilities of Merwin's thinking. These had been slumbering in Merwin since childhood, but the writers of the American Renaissance gave these thoughts a specific literary frame of reference. One approach to Whitman came through Merwin's contemporaries on the American scene and, once more, his interest in foreign-language poetry. When Allen Ginsberg developed his long-lined idiom in the 1950s—much in contrast to Merwin's carefully constructed poetry—he did so through the conduit of William Carlos Williams, who offered "the only real tradition that was not basically rooted in England. . . . Williams was one of the ingredients of his background, and Whitman was the other."[7] Thus, in stylistic terms alone, Whitmanian circumlocutions were profoundly at odds with the concentrated sparseness of Merwin's own poetics. This contrast, however, was tempered by the way Pablo Neruda, Rubén Dario, and the poets of Latin America and Europe recuperated a quality in Whitman that "was not connected with the historical experience of the United States." In particular, these writers recognized "the democratic feeling of expansion, the optimism, that note of enthusiasm—of rather over-inflated enthusiasm—that's there in Whitman. And they manage to apply it to their situation—their feeling of claustrophobia, their feeling of being stuck in convention and so on—and it was a great liberation."[8]

Such a benevolent and fundamentally rejuvenating vision of Whitman, Merwin suggests, is understandable coming from writers working and living in countries with recent and ongoing fascist histories.[9] Divorcing Whitman's democratic vistas from the nineteenth-century American context of territorial expansion, however, Merwin further implies, without regard for the effects of such expansion on the natural world and on native cultures, is, especially as an American writer, irresponsible and naïve. What is more, embracing such an unquestioning approach also means turning a blind eye to the way literary writing shapes public consciousness, which is particularly the case with Whitman. As Merwin put it, "most of the time" Whitman "is making a speech. While acknowledging "passages of incredible power and beauty," Merwin is profoundly disturbed by Whitman's "rhetorical insistence on an optimistic stance." Such a stance "can be quite wonderful as a statement of momentary emotion, but as a world view and as a program for confronting existence it bothered me when I was eighteen and bothers me now. It makes me extremely uneasy when he talks about the American expansion and the feeling of manifest destiny in a voice of wonder." In particular, Merwin finds himself thinking "about the buffalo, about the Indians, and about the species that are being rendered extinct. Whitman's momentary, rather sentimental view just wipes these things out as though they were of no importance. There's a cultural and what you might call a specietal chauvinism involved" (Folsom and Nelson).

This second, profoundly resistant approach to the Bard sets Merwin apart from many of his predecessors and contemporaries, who see in Whitman one of the fountainheads of modern American poetry, indeed, of American poetry proper. For Merwin, this resistance is reflective not only of Whitman's good-natured, selective blindness toward the ideological—essentially capitalist—imperatives driving territorial exploration and exploitation; it also captures Merwin's own conflicted stance with regard to being an *American* poet. He has acknowledged that "the human institution that I feel is the context . . . is certainly not the nation of the United States; it's the English language," in the sense that his native idiom is his raw material of choice. Merwin pledges poetic allegiance to the American language, not to any sense of nationhood, in full awareness that English, and American English, is "an imperial language" carrying a heavy baggage of colonization, indoctrination, and silencing.[10] What is more, Merwin's ambivalence about Whitman also resonates with his mythological framing of history, whereby official narratives of celebration, such as the conquest of the American West, are inherently skewed and incomplete precisely because of their function of nation building and mythmaking. As he put it, "one can begin to see differently the great phony myth of the 'winning of the West'—it was the *destruction* of the West. It *was* heroic, but it was heroic in an incredibly cramped and vicious way." While settlers suffered extraordinary hardships, "they were also broken and cruel, and in the long run incredibly destructive, irreversibly destructive. What we've done to this continent is something *unbelievable*—to think that one species could have done this in a hundred years (Folsom and Nelson).

Thoreau, in Merwin's reading of the Concord Sage, has a more holistic vision of humans living in the world. He recognized, as Merwin put it, "that the human cannot exist independently in a natural void; whatever the alienation is that we feel from the natural world, we are not in fact alienated, so we cannot base our self-righteousness on that difference. We're part of that whole thing." Critical of even the presumption of human superiority, Thoreau is endowed with an ecological sensibility avant la lettre and understands the communion of humanity with its global habitat and with other forms of life. Similarly, unlike the static narrative of Whitman's poetry, with accumulations of detail filling an essentially given worldview, Thoreau, in Merwin's estimate, evolved a mode of seeing that is essentially processual and depth-perceptive. "[V]ery differently from Whitman," Thoreau "even in a paragraph takes his own perception and develops it into a deeper and deeper way of seeing something . . . I think that Thoreau saw in a way that nobody had quite seen before; it was American in that sense." Coming out of the American grain that is sensitive to ecological stewardship and responsibility, Merwin sees Thoreau's writing as more profoundly philosophical because of his transcendental mode of apprehension: "He realizes that the intensity with which he's able to see it *is* its significance. This is an immense gesture of wisdom in Thoreau that I miss in Whitman" (Folsom and Nelson).

The dialectic Merwin sees in these twin giants of the American Renaissance has fundamentally shaped his thinking about nature and the environment, and about the way literature can be meaningful in shaping the public discourse of these most complex of issues. Thinking and writing about Nature and the Other is, after all, the American Theme per se ever since Puritan settlers first set foot on the continent. If Whitman, for all his disarming embrace of Life, is a kind of negative pole whom to resist, Thoreau becomes the kindred spirit whose vision is close to Merwin's own, and this ecological conscience is a theme that runs throughout his life and career. Merwin's early years were marked by a sense of the presence of the earth in all things, beginning, perhaps, at three years of age, when a backyard apple tree was slated for removal. Merwin, as recounted here, angrily sought to prevent the wood cutters from completing their work. At that same age, he wanted to know what made the grass sprout through the gaps in the sidewalk, and when his mother replied that the earth was right under that stone, he "felt a great joy" (Crimmel). A few years later, observed Merwin, "What turned me into an environmentalist, on my eleventh birthday, was seeing the first strip mine. To treat the earth like that, to me, is like murder. Rape."[11] This early concern for the environment marks the beginning of a remarkable nine-decade interest in the nonhuman world, one that is perhaps unique among contemporary poets.

Indeed, the interviews in this volume (as well as the many that had to be excluded due to space limitations) make clear that on many fronts—from nuclear-related concerns, to deforestation, to extinction and climate change—Merwin, in the tradition of other great American writers, often foregrounds environmental issues, both in the United States and abroad. In 1958, as noted in the chronology included in this volume, Merwin published "Ecology, or the Art of Survival" in the *Nation*, his first major prose statement on the environment and the interdependence of life forms, and this theme would appear repeatedly in his work and in the interviews found here.[12]

An acute awareness of a growing ecological crisis characterizes many of these conversations. In David Ossman's 1961 interview Merwin reflects broadly on the notion of crisis, which is perhaps most evident during the periods of war subsequent to the Industrial Revolution. This movement set in motion a compounding series of ecological crises that have contributed to the notion that we now live in a new epoch—the Anthropocene—where the impacts of humans have significantly altered the planet.

This recurrent theme of environmental crisis found in the interviews does not, however, suggest that Merwin views his poetry or that of others as an effective vehicle for change. In a 1982 interview with Michael Pettit, Merwin stated, "I think that if our primary reason for making a piece of writing is to change other people, is to change events, probably what we want to do is not to write a poem anyway. We really want to do something effective. A poem is not going to be the most effective way of changing something."[13]

It's an interesting perspective from a poet who wishes not to be viewed as "political"—"Politics is the greatest bore in the world," claimed Merwin in his 1969 interview in the *English Record*, though politics did not seem inconsequential in his 1967 collection, *The Lice*. Poems such as "The Asians Dying,"[14] with lines containing reminders of how the Vietnam War destroyed forests and "poisoned farmlands," point to the poet's dedication to speaking out against injustice, yet Merwin is aware that poetry is rarely a match for entrenched political and corporate interests (Fitz Gerald and Heyen).

Merwin's cognizance of destruction certainly extends to the United States, both past and present. Extending his concerns about Whitman's environmental blind spots, Merwin has repeatedly stated that humans cannot exist independently of nature, and to somehow think that we can separate ecological destruction from historical triumph is folly. He has expressed grief at the treatment of his home region of western Pennsylvania, which by 1969 had become "abandoned industrial country, with slag heaps and empty blast furnaces" littering the landscape (Fitz Gerald and Heyen). By the time of his 2011 interview with Jordan Davis, the destruction of his childhood landscapes had gotten worse, due to mountaintop removal coal mining practices, which clear-cuts forests, then—to reach buried coal deposits—literally scrapes off the tops of mountains, pushing thousands of tons of rock into valleys, burying hundreds of miles of streams, and wrecking Appalachian ecosystems in the process. Indeed, Merwin's anger at the ongoing devastation wrought by industry has grown steadily over the years, especially after his 1976 purchase of agricultural land in Maui. Exhausted from decades of unsustainable industrial farming practices, the land began to recover as Merwin set about restoring native forest, vegetation, and soils; this restored tropical forest now contains over 4000 species of trees and is managed by the Merwin Conservancy.

His concern with the ecological assault on the Hawaiian islands first appears in his 1980 *American Poetry Review* interview with Michael Clifton, where Merwin condemns the "destruction of the natural world, the really insane exploitation of the whole environment, the pollution of the elements," and the impact of agricultural chemicals on the islands' plants and animals.[15] Clifton's interview is the first to note Merwin's concern with tropical forests, a concern that emerges from the poet's sense that Western civilization embraces the myth of human superiority in relation to all other living things. This "specietal chauvinism" has resulted in problems almost too massive in scale to comprehend: nuclear waste dumping, the Great Pacific Garbage Patch, climate change, endangered species, air and water pollution—all part of a process of "trying to destroy ourselves" and the "other forms of life around us." We see the earth as "an object of exploitation, rather than as something of which we are a part," Merwin continues, and when we "treat it with contempt and we exploit it, we are despising and exploiting ourselves" (Clifton).

Though specific places often trigger Merwin's sense of the injustices wrought on the environment, he ultimately views any destruction as a global issue: "Sometimes I feel more immediately concerned with what's happening to the elements, the sea, the animals, the language, than I do with any particular society. I don't make a distinction" (Bourne).[16] In this interview, Merwin also expresses the importance of land stewardship, which is in contrast to what he described more than a decade earlier as our "own bloated species-ego," suggesting that "our importance is not different from the importance of the rest of the universe" (Bourne).

Merwin echoes these concerns about systemic corrosion and contamination in his 1984 interview with David L. Elliott, where his distress over the environment seemed in no way diminished after nearly two decades: "If we're so stupid that we choose to destroy each other and ourselves, that's bad enough; but if we destroy the whole life on the planet! . . . I'm talking about something that is happening as we are sitting here talking about it—the destruction of the seas, the destruction of species after species, the destruction of the forests. These are not replaceable. . . . The feeling of awe—something that we seem to be losing—is essential for survival."

Survival is not just physical for Merwin—it's also psychological and, fundamentally, spiritual. Merwin has said that he "can't imagine being able to live without the natural world," and that "our destruction of other species is destructive to our own minds" (Elliott). He recounts that as a child he had a "secret dread—and a recurring nightmare—of the whole world becoming city, being covered with cement and buildings and streets." "There was something incomplete about the world of streets and sidewalks and cement," noted Merwin; these built environments deprive us "of something essential" (Hirsch). For Merwin, human life is incomplete without frequent and sustainable contact with nonhuman nature. And if the natural world can never be completely understood, its very mystery is the source of the poet's inspiration: "You don't move from what you know to something else you know. And it's the unknown that keeps rendering possibilities," as Merwin commented about the process of writing.[17] Perhaps for these reasons, Merwin rejects artifice, observing that our cultural "imagery continues to come out of the place that requires something beyond human fabrication, beyond the human origin of things" (Elliott), and beyond the burgeoning growth of urban and suburban areas globally and in the United States.[18]

Poetry can focus our attention on these losses, but action—above and beyond the act of writing poetry—is the best way "to do something effective."[19] His restoration of his land in Hawaii would seem to be an example of such productive engagement. As he observed in 2012, "the soil is back, the trees are on it, and the canopy is coming back" (Crimmel) in a very tangible example of how one can engage, one-on-one, in a hands-on method of reversing environmental mistakes of the past.

A mistake that troubles Merwin is humans' disregard for life broadly and at the level of individual species. In his 2010 interview with Ed Rampell, Merwin reminds us that "Every species is related to every other species. And they're built up like a pyramid. The simpler cell organisms, and then the more complicated ones, all the way up to the mammals and birds and so forth. The whole thing depends on every part of it. And we're taking out the stones from the pyramid." Here Merwin reiterates the pyramid metaphor used in his 1998 interview with J. Scott Bryson and Tony Brusate, where he lamented, "we have no conception of the extent to which we depend on simpler forms of life like insects, yet we're running on the assumption that we can exist without any dependence at all, that we can do it all ourselves, which is, to me, just nonsense. But we have a society and a set of assumptions and an economy which just go on as if that weren't even worth examining."[20]

Merwin's restoration project in Hawaii made him aware of how some of the stones have been removed from the pyramid, namely, the specific extinctions resulting from European settlement of the islands. In 1982, just a few years after his purchase of the Maui property, Merwin pointed out that

> Of the sixty-some species of endemic birds that were there [Hawaiian Islands] when Captain Cook arrived . . . half . . . are still alive. The rest are extinct. About two-thirds of the remainder are on the Endangered Species List, so that it's possible to grow up, even in rural surroundings, on the islands and never see a native bird. You see imported birds. (Pettit 18)

Extinction of native species is linked to the destruction of native Hawaiian cultures, and the linguistic imperialism pressuring the Hawaiian language is no different in Merwin's eyes than the ecological imperialism impacting the Hawaiian landscape, flora, and fauna.

Nearly thirty years ago Merwin told Edward Hirsch that "What is happening in the world is terrible and irreversible, and that history is probably a doomed enterprise. But in the meantime, it's important to live in the world as completely as we can." Whether measured by the number and quality of his publications and awards, by the restoration work on his Maui property, or by insisting on the value of the natural world, the interviews included in this collection—as well as those listed in the bibliography—should leave no question that W. S. Merwin has lived as completely in the world as any person could. Whether as poet, teacher, thinker, translator, activist, or gardener, Merwin has modeled what it means to live a life of responsible and responsive citizenship—both for his own generation and those of the future. We are very pleased to be able to present here this collection of interviews spanning Merwin's career.

Acknowledgments

This volume would not have been possible without the help of many individuals. We wish to thank Katie Keene at the University Press of Mississippi, who answered patiently and in a timely fashion our multiple questions over the course of the project. Research assistants Amanda Riter, Melody Navarro, and Zach Metcalfe, students in the Weber State University Master of Arts in English program, provided valuable assistance with this project. Nicole Beatty, the arts and humanities reference librarian at Weber State University, helped us with the initial search for interviews. Genevieve Bates in the Master of Arts in English program office assisted in numerous ways with this project. We also wish to thank the many interviewers, journal editors, and publishers who gave permission for us to use the interviews in this collection, as well as to those interviewers whose work we had to exclude for reasons of space. Photographer Mark Hanauer graciously provided the image of Merwin for the volume's cover. We also would like to thank our families for the patience they have shown as we worked weekends and evenings to complete this project.

MW
HC

Notes

1. Merwin acknowledged Berryman's teachings also in the touching poem "Berryman," first collected in *Flower & Hand: Poems, 1977–1983* (Copper Canyon Press, 1996), and he documented R. P. Blackmur's influence in the essay, "Affable Irregular: Recollections of R. P. Blackmur," in *Grand Street* 1.2 (1982): 151–64.

2. Michael Pettit, "W. S. Merwin: An Interview," *Black Warrior Review* 8 (Spring 1982): 8.

3. Jack Myers and Michael Simms, "Possibilities of the Unknown: Conversations with W. S. Merwin," *Southwest Review* 68.2 (1983): 174.

4. Merwin later met Eliot in London, who generously supplied him with fashionable French cigarettes which he himself no longer smoked. With few exceptions, the two men seemed not to have talked shop, but instead gave way to their patriotic yearnings: "We used to sit and reminisce about America. There was a side of Eliot that was very homesick for the States, and I was feeling homesick in London, too. We had several wonderful conversations—about the Ohio River and about his family out on the Mississippi in St. Louis and about the riverboats" (Hirsch).

5. In his foreword to *A Mask for Janus*, Auden explicitly refers to Merwin's "concern for the traditional conceptions of Western culture as expressed in its myths" (ix).

6. Elsewhere Merwin has acknowledged that "I use a computer like everybody else, but I'm not in love with it and I'm happy when I don't use it." He is profoundly concerned that, when people get up in the morning, "they go to the computer, and whatever else they've been doing, they go right back to the computer. I think that's a fixation" (Academy of Achievement, 2008). To this day, Merwin rarely communicates via email, preferring instead to have his arrangements being made through his literary agent.

7. Ken Weisner and Kevin Hearle, "Interview with W. S. Merwin," [on Merwin and Neruda], *Quarry West* 25 (1988): 76.

8. Ibid.

9. Distinguishing between Neruda and Whitman, Merwin notes that "I trust Neruda's optimism far more than I do Whitman's. . . . And it's a benevolence that is more aware of human suffering than that kind of deliberate drumbeating in Whitman" (Weisner and Hearle 80).

10. Weisner and Hearle 81.

Priorities shift. When Merwin was trying to be "an American poet" in the forties and fifties, he was eager to return from England back to the United States, in hopes of finding that voice. As he told Edward Hirsch, "I certainly knew that I was not an English poet. But what it is to be an American poet I still don't know. It's nice that we no longer have to think about that. We still seemed to have to worry about it in the forties."

11. Jordan Davis, "Talking with W. S. Merwin," *Nation*, May 16, 2011, 23.

12. This essay appeared about the time of the Aldermaston marches in the UK, and these antinuclear protests, as Merwin noted to *Brick*, "really started me off . . . and then I began to realize that the antinuclear ferment and poisoning the earth with agrabiz—the whole thing that really got going in World War II—that these were related, and I began to make these connections."

13. Pettit 19–20.

14. "The Lice" can be read in the 1968 Gregory Fitz Gerald and William Heyen interview contained in this volume.

15. One of these chemicals used in Hawaii is 2,4-D, an herbicide chemically similar to Agent Orange. As Merwin noted in his 2011 interview with Jordan Davis, the sugar industry is a significant user of this chemical.

16. Merwin told Roland Flint in 1994 that "the constant news of what's happening to the great forests of the world, I feel like an illness that I have to carry around with me" (n.p.).

17. Myers and Simms 168.

18. According to the U.S. Forest Service, "6000 acres of open space are converted to developed uses every day." See http://www.fs.fed.us/openspace/loss_space.html Accessed April 22, 2014. Six thousand acres per day totals 2,190,000 acres annually, an area about the size of Yellowstone National Park or slightly smaller than the state of Delaware. At current rates, the United States will lose farmland, forest, grasslands, and arid lands to development an area the size of the state of Ohio every twenty years.

19. Pettit 19–20.

20. Tony Brusate and J. Scott Bryson, "'This Absolutely Matters': An Interview with W. S. Merwin," *Limestone: A Literary Journal* 6.1 (1998): 3.

Chronology

1927   Born 30 September in New York City and raised in Union City, New Jersey, the son of a Presbyterian minister. Is named William after his father and Stanley after a clergyman from Western Seminary, Pennsylvania, where Merwin's father obtains his ecclesiastical training. Two years earlier, a first-born brother dies shortly after birth.

1929   Ruth, Merwin's sister, is born, his single living sibling.

1930   Grows up under a repressive, capricious, and punitive father, while mother, Ann, is a committed pacifist. Grows up in an atmosphere permeated by religious hymns and the King James version of the Bible. The mother reads children's stories and children's poetry, such as Robert Louis Stevenson's *A Child's Garden of Verses* and Tennyson's "The Brook," to William and Ruth.

1931   Associates his emerging ecological and environmental consciousness, at the age of around three, with several primal moments: he observes men felling a tree in his parents' backyard; his mother reassures him that earth is under the sidewalks of the city; and a watercolor book on Native Americans leads him to learn to read the captions and to a consequent fascination with native peoples. Growing up within sight of New York City, "the Indians represented to me a wider and more cohesive world than the one I saw around me that everyone took for granted."

1932   Recalls, about his beginnings as a writer, that "I started writing hymns for my father almost as soon as I could write at all, illustrating them. . . . But the first real writers that held me were not poets: Conrad first, and then Tolstoy."

1933–36   Parents become increasingly estranged and family moves to Scranton, Pennsylvania, a mining town that would provide the backdrop for *The Drunk in the Furnace* (1960) and his first volume of creative prose, *The Miner's Pale Children* (1970).

1936–40   Attends Wyoming Seminary, a Methodist preparatory school, in Kingston, Pennsylvania, where he suffers under a strict regime.

His language teacher Lawrence Sampson cultivates a sensibility for Spanish, French, and German in the young student.

1940–44   During World War II, the father takes a leave of absence from church and family to serve as an overseas troop chaplain, and the adolescent Merwin comes into his own. Enlists in the United States Navy, later asks to be put into the psychiatric ward of Chelsea Navy Hospital, Massachusetts, for declaring himself a conscientious objector.

1944–46   Attends Princeton University on a scholarship where he collaborates with a Spanish-born teacher on his first translation, *Romancero Gitano* by Federico García Lorca. Meets fellow poet Galway Kinnell, who later describes Merwin "as a kind of prodigy . . . , writing poetry that was so incredibly resonant." Merwin spends time working the neglected polo ponies and the horses of the Reserve Officer Training Corps in the university's stables.

1946   Over Easter, makes a formative "pilgrimage" to visit Ezra Pound at St. Elizabeth's Hospital, Washington, DC. Pound encourages him to exercise craft through translation and by writing "seventy-five lines" a day. Pound presents Merwin with copies of *The Unwobbling Pivot* (1945) and *The Draft of Cantos XXX* (1930).

1946–47   Studies with R. P. Blackmur and John Berryman. An autodidact gifted with "the most haunting literary intelligence," a paternal Blackmur encourages Merwin to pursue his own ambitions, leading to a lifelong suspicion of academic institutions. Also protects Merwin from being thrown out of Princeton for failing to do assigned classwork. Berryman teaches Merwin to take poetry "very seriously" and to "pray to the Muse."

1947   Marries his first wife, Dorothy Jeanne Ferry, a secretary to a physicist at Princeton.

1948–49   Following graduation with a BA, returns to Princeton to pursue a course of graduate study in modern languages, which he eventually aborts. Also spends a summer at McGill University in Montreal studying Old French. Publishes his first translations and creative and critical prose in *Perspective* magazine and the *Hudson Review*. Takes first tutoring job with the Stuyvesant family in New Jersey.

1949–50   Moves to Spain, where he studies Romance languages and begins translations of medieval poetry. Takes a tutoring job in the household of the Portuguese royal family, the Princess of Braganza, and travels on milk trains across Spain to meet Robert Graves on the northwest coast of Mallorca. Eventually, tutors Graves's son for one year, while continuing to write poetry. At Graves's house, meets Dido Milroy, who is fifteen years his senior and with whom he collaborates on a verse play. She arranges for him to translate *The Poem of the Cid* into a radio script for the BBC *Third Programme*, and they eventually marry and live in London.

1951   Lives mostly in London, from 1951 to 1956, supporting himself largely by doing further translations of Spanish and French classics for the BBC. Has his first original poem, "The Ballad of John Cable and Three Gentlemen," accepted for publication in the *Kenyon Review*. Meets T. S. Eliot, whom he remembers as a kind and nostalgic man, sharing French cigarettes and reminiscences about America. Later, the critic Helen Vendler describes Merwin as "a lesser Eliot" and his poems as "elusive pallors."

1952   W. H. Auden selects Merwin's first book, *A Mask for Janus*, for the Yale Younger Poets' Prize. The book reflects the influence of Graves and Eliot, the formality of postwar poetry, and the medieval poetry Merwin had been translating at the time.

1953   Amidst further translation work, Merwin publishes several original plays, among them the children's play *Huckleberry Finn*, which is produced by British television.

1954   Purchases a dilapidated farmhouse in Lot, in the *Causse* region of southwest France, with money inherited from his mother's sister, Aunt Margie. The region resonates with the tradition of medieval troubadours and Provençal poetry and becomes a fixpoint for Merwin for the next quarter century. Receives *Kenyon Review* Fellowship in Poetry and publishes *The Dancing Bears* with Yale University Press, the first of several collections to center on allegorized creatures of the animal world. Marries Dido Milroy.

1956   Receives Rockefeller Fellowship and works as a playwright for Poets' Theater in Cambridge, Massachusetts, which eventually produces his play *Favor Island*. Is glad to be back in the United States, where he can hear American speech. With Knopf publishes *Green with Beasts*. Meets poets Robert Lowell, James Merrill, Adrienne Rich, Donald Hall, Ted Hughes, and others, who seek to break free from the poetic conventions of the 1940s and '50s. A competitive Lowell one day says to Merwin, "You'll always be a good poet, but not a great poet."

1957   Receives National Institute of Arts and Letters grant and works at the Playwriting Bursary, Arts Council of Great Britain. Abandons ambition to become a playwright after writing five plays (some in verse), which he deems unsuccessful but which lead to changes in the way he writes new poetry.

1958   Publishes "Ecology, or the Art of Survival" in the *Nation*, his first major prose statement on the environment and the interdependence of life forms.

1959   Publishes his first of several major translations, originally commissioned by the BBC, *The Poem of the Cid* (Dent), to be followed by *The Satires of Persius* (Indiana, 1960), *Some Spanish Ballads* (Abelard, 1961), and the medieval Spanish picaresque, *The Life of Lazarillo de Tormes* (Doubleday, 1962).

1960   Publishes *The Drunk in the Furnace* with Macmillan, in which American themes—its promises and values—are first fully visible, prompting critics to see Merwin as a twentieth-century counterpoint to Whitman's effusive vision of America. *Furnace* leads to a breakthrough in style and tone and a greater openness toward irregular forms.

1961–62   Lives mostly in a small apartment in New York's Greenwich Village. Receives Rabinowitz Foundation Grant and the Bess Hokin Prize from *Poetry* magazine. Writes occasional pieces on the emerging peace movement for the *Nation*, and is, for a short time, appointed poetry editor of the magazine. Turns increasingly bitter and hopeless after the Cuban Missile Crisis and returns to France. Merwin and his wife also live for periods in London, where they reconnect with Plath and Hughes and where Plath (according to Dido's memoir) becomes infatuated with Merwin, who does not return her affections. After a period of creative dormancy, lasting about eighteen months, writes the first half of *The Moving Target* in six weeks.

1963   Publishes *The Moving Target* (Atheneum) and a joint translation of *Medieval Epics*, with Helen M. Mustard and William Alfred, for Modern Library. That same year, after studying the work of several Spanish poets, Merwin is credited with forging the Deep Imagist movement—poetry free from punctuation and notable for its austere simplicity and political edge.

1964–65   Returns to France and associates with Roger Planchon's Théâtre de la Cité, Lyon, for about ten months. Receives Ford Foundation Grant.

1966   Chapelbrook Foundation Fellowship. *Collected Poems* appears from Atheneum.

1967   Receives the Harriett Monroe Memorial Prize from *Poetry* magazine. At the height of the Vietnam War, publishes *The Lice* (Atheneum), which remains one of his most critically acclaimed and influential volumes to date. The book is recognized as an environmentalist manifesto and characterized by indirect, unpunctuated narration. Involved in the first major translation of Chilean poet, mathematician, and physicist Nicanor Parra's *Poems and Antipoems* (New Directions).

1968   Spends significant amounts of time at home in France. The region's natural beauty, in danger of despoliation, reappears in *Unframed Originals* (1982) and *The Vixen* (1996). Separates from Dido and begins living part of the year in New York City with new partner, Moira Hodgson, an English writer twenty years his junior.

1969   Lives much of the year in New Mexico and Arizona and receives a PEN Translation Prize for *Selected Translations 1948–1968* (Atheneum) and a Rockefeller Foundation Grant. *The Lice* is nominated for the 1968 National Book Award. Explains his experiments in metrical irregularity and indirect narration in an essay entitled "On Open Form." Is often associated with Vietnam War–era poets Robert Bly, Adrienne Rich, Denise Levertov, Robert Lowell, Allen Ginsberg, and Yusef Komunyakaa. Publishes *Animae* (Kayak), with illustrations by Lynn Schroeder, which continues his totemic use of animals. Publishes translations of four major books: *Products of the Perfected Civilization: Selected Writings of Chamfort*, including an introduction (Macmillan); *Voices: Selected Writings of Antonio Porchia* (Follett); Jean Follain, *Transparence of the World* (Atheneum); Pablo Neruda, *Twenty Poems and a Song of Despair* (Cape).

1970   Publishes *The Miner's Pale Children* (Atheneum), his first book of creative prose, and *The Carrier of Ladders* (Atheneum), which continues his preoccupation with ecological concerns and other-than-human nature. Often fuses legend and myth—the feature of his early work—with personal and biographical themes.

Publishes *Signs* (Stone Wall), with A. D. Moore, and a translation of Pablo Neruda's *Selected Poems*, with others (Dell).

1971   Wins the Pulitzer Prize for Poetry for *The Carrier of Ladders*. Merwin donates the prize money to the draft resistance movement and outlines his objections to the Vietnam War in an essay for the *New York Review of Books*, "On Being Awarded the Pulitzer Prize," which elicits an angry public reaction from W. H. Auden.

1972   In "The New Transcendentalism: The Visionary Strain in W. S. Merwin," critic Harold Bloom first describes Merwin as the successor to the writers of the American Renaissance and "indubitably" as the "representative poet of his generation." The translation of Neruda's *Twenty Poems and a Song of Despair* is released as a musical score by Samuel Barber entitled *The Lovers; for baritone, mixed chorus and orchestra [op. 43]* (Schirmer).

1973   Becomes a counterculture phenomenon and fixture on college and university campuses and in coffee houses. Publishes his eighth collection of poetry, *Writings to an Unfinished Accompaniment* (Atheneum), in which he reflects on his own complicity in the destruction of nature. Also publishes two major translations, *Asian Figures* (Atheneum), and Osip Mandelstam's *Selected Poems*, with Clarence Brown (Oxford).

1974   Receives the Academy of American Poets Fellowship and the Shelley Memorial Award.

1975   Meets his new partner, young aspiring poet Dana Naone while on a reading trip to Hawaii. Their interest in Buddhism leads to an invitation to the Naropa Institute in Boulder, Colorado, where Allen Ginsberg teaches. The couple has disagreements with guru Chögyam Trungpa, who eventually orders his bodyguards to force the couple to undress on Halloween. This incident becomes mythologized as "The Great Naropa Poetry Wars," distinguishing between Ginsberg's declamatory and long-lined poetics and Merwin's more formal, unpunctuated restraint. Merwin releases *The First Four Books of Poems* (Atheneum) and, with Burton Raffel, is involved in the translation *A Thousand Years of Vietnamese Poetry*, edited by Nguyen Ngoc Bich (Knopf).

1976   Relocates to Maui, Hawaii, and with an inheritance from his mother builds his house on a former pineapple plantation. Begins to study Buddhism seriously and starts restoring native forest and vegetation on his property. Later purchases additional land with money left to him by George Kirstein, former publisher of the *Nation*. Appropriately, for a poet, their community is named Ha–ikū, for an ancient land section meaning "talk abruptly" or "sharp break." Buddhism and the tropical landscape of Hawaii have a lasting effect on Merwin's formal and thematic vision. His writings become more autobiographical and anchored in a personal self.

1977   Publishes his ninth volume of poetry, *The Compass Flower* (Atheneum) and his second book of prose poems, *Houses and Travellers* (Atheneum). Releases the translation *Sanskrit Love Poetry*, with J. Moussaieff Masson, as part of UNESCO's collection of representative works—Indian series (Columbia).

1978   Publishes *Feathers from the Hill* (Windhover), a collection of haiku-like poems and the translation of Euripides, *Iphigenia at Aulius*, with George E. Dimock Jr. (Oxford).

1979   Receives the Bollingen Prize for Poetry, Yale University Library. Releases *Selected Translations, 1968–1978* (Atheneum).

1981   Publishes the translation *Robert the Devil* (Windhover) and rereleases *Sanskrit Love Poetry* under the title *The Peacock's Egg: Love Poems from Ancient India* (North Point).

1982–83   Accepts, for the first time, an academic appointment, at Cooper Union in New York City. Marries his third wife, children's books editor Paula Schwartz, in a Buddhist ceremony in Maui. Publishes the poetry volumes *Finding the Islands* (North Point) and *Opening the Hand* (Atheneum), as well as *Unframed Originals* (Atheneum), a collection of six intertwining autobiographical narratives.

1984   Publishes translations *Four French Plays* (Atheneum) and Lope de Rueda's *From the Spanish Morning* (Atheneum).

1987   Receives Governor's Award for Literature of the state of Hawaii for his poetry and writings about the islands.

1988   Attends symposium, "Pablo Neruda and U.S. Contemporary Poetry," at the University of California, Santa Cruz, which includes fellow poets Robert Bly, Philip Levine, Charles Simic, and Bruce Weigl. Merwin rejects the label "surrealist" for some of his early poetry on grounds that surrealist imagery tends to be one of artifice and human fabrication divorced from the natural world. He similarly takes issue with the Language poets for reasons of poetic gamesmanship, overt self-reflexivity, and lack of political commitment. Publishes *The Rain in the Trees: Poems* (Knopf) and releases *Selected Poems* (Atheneum).

1989   Publishes translation of the works of medieval Japanese Zen master and garden designer, Musō Soseki, as *Sun at Midnight: Poems and Sermons* (North Point), with Soiku Shigematsu, after more than a decade of collaboration.

1990   Receives Maurice English Poetry Award.

1992   Partly inspired by Thoreau's *Walden*, publishes *The Lost Upland* (Knopf), a book-length tribute in prose to the ancient farming country above the Dordogne in the South of France.

1993   Receives the inaugural Tanning Prize for mastery in the art of poetry from the Academy of American Poets, over the initial objections of poet and co-judge, Carolyn Kizer, who wanted to award the prize to African American poet Gwendolyn Brooks.

1994   For *Travels* (Knopf), his fourteenth book of poems, receives the Lenore Marshall Poetry Prize, co-administered by the *Nation* and the Academy of American Poets and awarded annually for the best volume of poetry written by a living US citizen and published the previous year in the United States. Also receives Lila Wallace–Reader's Digest Writers' Award. Releases a reprint of his second book of prose poems *Houses and Travellers* (Holt), and a translation of Federico García Lorca's plays, *Blood Wedding and Yerma*, the first of which is a translation by Langston Hughes unpublished during his lifetime (TCG Translations #5).

1996   Compiles and contributes to *Lament for the Makers: A Memorial Anthology* (Counterpoint), a tribute to the poets who had become his friends and mentors. Publishes *Flower & Hand: Poems, 1977–1983* (Copper Canyon) and *The Vixen* (Knopf), a poetic tribute to his early years in France.

1998   After years of incubation and note-taking, publishes *The Folding Cliffs* (Knopf), a prose-poetic history of Hawaii in a verse form reflecting the elegiac tradition of Europe and the vernacular forms of Hawaiian chants. Receives the Ruth Lilly Poetry Prize ($100,000) awarded by the Poetry Foundation for *The Folding Cliffs*.

1999   Appointed poetry consultant to the Library of Congress, a jointly held position with Rita Dove and Louise Glück. Publishes his sixteenth volume of poetry, *The River Sound* (Knopf), including the long autobiographical poem, "Testimony," and poems about the loss of the tip of one of his fingers through chainsaw use during planting season. Publishes *East Window: The Asian Translations* (Copper Canyon).

2000 Publishes verse translation of Dante Aligheri's *Purgatorio* (Knopf), the middle section of *The Divine Comedy* and one of Merwin's favorite books.

2001 Publishes *The Pupil* (Knopf), a volume of poems self-reflectively subjecting his earlier work to critical analysis and correction.

2002 Publishes *The Mays of Ventadorn*, his sixth volume of prose (National Geographic).

2003 In the lead-up to the Iraq War, Merwin joins Poets Against the War and issues the statement, "Mr. Bush and his plans are a greater danger to the United States than is Saddam Hussein." Dedicates his reading in Washington to Laura Bush, who had invited poets and scholars to discuss Walt Whitman, Emily Dickinson, and Langston Hughes as part of the White House symposium, "Poetry and the American Voice," which was eventually cancelled.

2004 Receives the Golden Wreath Award of the Struga Poetry Evenings Festival in Macedonia and the Lannan Lifetime Achievement Award. Publishes the essay collection *The Ends of the Earth* (Shoemaker & Hoard) and *Sir Gawain and the Green Knight, a New Verse Translation* (Knopf). The translation of Neruda's *Twenty Poems and a Song of Despair* (1969) is reprinted with an introduction by Christina García and illustrations by Pablo Picasso (Penguin). The translation of Osip Mandelstam's *Selected Poems* (1973) is reprinted as *The Selected Poems of Osip Mandelstam* (New York Review Books Classics).

2005 Publishes *Migration: New and Selected Poems* (Copper Canyon). Receives National Book Award for Poetry for *Migration*, declared by the *New York Times* as one of the "100 Notable Books of the Year."

2006 Union City, New Jersey, renames Merwin's childhood neighborhood—the corner of Fourth Street and New York Avenue— "W. S. Merwin Way" in his honor.

2007 Publishes *Present Company* (Copper Canyon). Writes an elegy for his lifelong friend, James Wright, which appears in *From the Other World: Poems in Memory of James Wright*.

2008   Publishes *The Shadow of Sirius* (Copper Canyon).

2009   Receives his second Pulitzer Prize for Poetry for *The Shadow of Sirius*, followed by reading and speaking tours throughout the United States.

2010   Receives the *Kenyon Review* Award for Literary Achievement. Appointed as seventeenth United States poet laureate. Decides, after some hesitation, to assume this public role to declare what "I don't hear anybody else saying clearly. . . . I think the imagination is *the* talent we have as a species. Not the intelligence." With his own means and philanthropic support, founds the Merwin Conservancy to preserve "the living legacy of W. S. Merwin, his home and palm forest on Maui, for future study and retreat for botanists and writers" (http://www.merwinconservancy.org/).

2013   Receives the inaugural Zbigniew Herbert International Literary Award for "outstanding artistic and intellectual literary achievements on the world stage." Publishes *Selected Translations: 1948–2011* (Copper Canyon).

2014   Publishes *The Moon before Morning* (Copper Canyon).

Conversations with W. S. Merwin

A Conversation with W. S. Merwin

Audience / 1956

From *Audience* (Cambridge, MA) 4.3&4 (1956), 4–6.

Audience: Auden, in discussing your first book of poems, wrote that your themes were "universal and impersonal," frequently myths, in which the personal experience of the poet *is* implied rather than stated. Would your new book alter this judgment?
Merwin: Maybe the critics will tell you. The blurb says "more range." I hope myself that means "more directness."

Audience: Does this increase in directness have any effect on your verse patterns? They seem to be often formal and exacting, bizarre, or archaic, at least in your first two books.
Merwin: You can't help being pragmatic about it. When it comes to patterns, a poet is a practical person. I try to make forms, or make a control over them, if I seem to need them. I try to develop them as they seem to work. Yet they never really quite work. That's the exciting thing about them. The only trouble comes when you start making patterns for their own sake, and don't need them. That's why the experimentalists aren't of much use to us—because in inventing more patterns than they needed, they often had to exaggerate what they were up to. You might say they made a habit of it.

Audience: Would you say that you belonged to a current movement in poetry?
Merwin: I don't know what movements there are. I'm not tempted to subscribe to any movement. They never seem quite real. The experimental movement was struck with feeling that it had to go on making new patterns and new theories to go with the patterns. One of these was that if something wasn't original, it wasn't worth anything. I don't agree with that. Like all

3

theories, if you adopt it and expect it to work one way, it may very well work another. In fact you're lucky if it works at all more than once. Theories are like friends—cozy—but the dangerous thing is how much they may protect you from doing. If a work is real, it will be original, because if it's real, it will be unique. The hard thing about getting older is keeping your mind open to all the ways a thing can happen. I find that you've got to discover what will work as you go along.

Audience: What would you say about poetry in general? What good, if any, is there in it?

Merwin: I hate to generalize, talking about poetry. But if I must, I'd say that man needs some sort of image to live by, and that he creates patterns in the arts to give shape to this image. I don't like to theorize though about this sort of thing. Balzac, in the *Chef d'Oeuvre Inconnu*, makes someone say that a painter should never think about painting except when he has a brush in his hand. That's one of the dangers of universities.

Audience: And of interviews?

Merwin: No. They're fun—you just avoid the questions.

Audience: What effect has your working with drama had on your poetry?

Merwin: Dramatic verse tends to stress clarity, and in doing so, it occasions a certain immediacy and directness.

Audience: Has it had much effect on the form of your poetry—form, say, as opposed to content?

Merwin: I don't think you can oppose them. I have to assume that you can't. . . . Yesterday I might have had no use for complicated verse forms; tomorrow, I may need them. It depends on the poem. The form grows out of the poem.

Audience: What kind of poem, for instance, would a sestina grow out of?

Merwin: I don't think it happens that way. But your asking the question makes me wonder—the immediate reaction is that a sestina is usually rather elegiac. I wonder what it would be like for a satire.

Audience: What would you consider a satire?

Merwin: Hard to say. If too heavy, or not particular enough, it gets called tragedy, if too light, comedy.

Audience: Are you writing plays now?
Merwin: I'm working at plays for the Arts Theatre, London, and the Poets' Theatre here.

Audience: The Poets' Theatre recently scheduled your translation of Marivaux's *Les Fausses Confidences*. When did you write that?
Merwin: A year ago, I think. It's a good, wicked, play.

Audience: Any prose?
Merwin: A little, recently. A couple of stories, travel stuff. There's been the odd review, mostly when I was broke, as mostly I was.

Audience: What do you do when not writing?
Merwin: Avoid questions. Indulge my own curiosity.

Audience: Where?
Merwin: Not around people who read my books mostly. Or anybody's. Too many educated people around all the time—not bad. I'm not recommending this, only describing it. Education is a fine thing.

Audience: Then you don't want any affiliations with a university?
Merwin: No. I don't personally like universities. Constitutionally incompatible. You start feeling that the end of the world is a block beyond the edge of the campus. People go around patting each other on the back, and you start to think you're a lot better than you really are.

Audience: But aren't most of your readers, or anyone else's for that matter, from the universities?
Merwin: I suppose so. But then, you just write hoping that everybody is going to read—you don't have to stop and remember their addresses.

Audience: How about money—making a living?
Merwin: I don't think that a poet should be ashamed of wanting money, as long as he's dead sure of what he's prepared to give for it. That's one of the reasons why I like England. The English put my plays on and pay me for them.

Audience: Do you intend to stay in America after your fellowship expires?
Merwin: I want to go back to Pennsylvania and write about it. Pennsylva-

nia's where I come from, you know. Then I have to go back to Europe too. I have commitments there.

Audience: Do you want to visit Princeton again?
Merwin: I don't know if I want to go back.

Audience: Would you take a position there?
Merwin: If they just paid me, and didn't ask me to do anything.

Audience: Did you like Princeton when you were a student?
Merwin: It affected me, I suppose. I slept through classes most of the time. We parted without regrets.

Audience: How long have you been writing?
Merwin: I started writing hymns for my father—he was a clergyman—when I was five years old. I found some of them a few weeks ago. Very stern they were. They had little pictures on the sides. I had thought of becoming a painter, but I didn't have much talent that way. I don't know if I'm a writer, I'm just pretty sure I'm not anything else.

Audience: Noticing your fondness for complicated verse forms, some critics have said that you write "the hard way." What do you think of that?
Merwin: I remember. Louise Bogan said it. It seems to me to be the only way, the way dictated by the poem. And it is hard.

Audience: Most of your reviews have been favorable, haven't they?
Merwin: Oh, I've had lots of unfavorable ones. You know that stinker in the *New York Times* on my first book—and a rough one in the *Spectator.* Then my play, *Darkling Child*, was praised some on one hand, and got panned angrily on the other.

Audience: Did you learn anything from the reviews?
Merwin: Don't think so. Not to take them too seriously. But you probably knew that beforehand. Critics have to make a position for themselves to work from.

W. S. Merwin

David Ossman / 1961

From David Ossman, *The Sullen Art* (*New York: Corinth Books*, 1963), 65–72. The interview was conducted in January 1961, just after Merwin began as poetry editor of the *Nation*. Reprinted by permission.

David Ossman: You have written several plays; is playwriting incidental with you?

W. S. Merwin: I think it's not only incidental, but past. I think I'm working my way out the other side of that. I thought for several years that I was a playwright, but I was probably fooling myself.

Ossman: You had a Rockefeller Fellowship and a play produced here in 1956 . . .

Merwin: Those things don't make you a playwright. I wrote four plays, each of them quite different from the others and none of them satisfied me. I ended up after the fourth without any great desire to write any more. I think that answers it for the time being anyway.

Ossman: What was the impulse to write plays in the first place?

Merwin: Great fascination with the theater, which I no longer have, and a fascination with simply writing plays—with that way of writing—which I don't have any more either. The first play was a verse play, and that made me feel that I didn't want to write any more verse plays, for a number of reasons. I don't feel terribly identified with those plays, least of all the verse play. I wrote that very young, I don't think it was a very good subject and the development was melodramatic.

Ossman: What about verse plays in the style of Beckett and Ionesco?

Merwin: Well, that's something quite different. I mean, if you call that a

7

verse play, that's still interesting. But that's the only kind of playwriting that I'd be remotely interested in.

Ossman: Your last book was published by Macmillan and the one previous was imported by Knopf. Could you tell me what the feeling on the part of such major book publishers is about the publication of poetry?

Merwin: This is pure hunch on my part, because whenever something of mine was published, I seem not to have been around. It can't be based on any knowledge of the publishing field, but I've a feeling the publishers are welcoming poetry more than they were fifteen years ago. Why they should be, I don't know; perhaps they've felt that, after all, they may not make much money on poetry, but they aren't going to lose much either—which is a reasonable position.

Five years ago, everybody wanted autobiographies. Every time you had anything to do with a publisher, he said, "What about writing an autobiography?" and I could never understand this, because publishers are always losing their shirts on autobiographies. They never lose their shirts over a book of poems. I think it's probably that more people are interested in poetry than were interested in it ten years ago.

Ossman: Why do you think there is a resurgence of interest in poetry?

Merwin: That's a hell of a big question. I think the penny's dropping, that's why. Or I think that's one reason—the feeling that there's not much time and it can't last the way it is. If a feeling of crisis goes on long enough, I suppose, one of two things happens—either a person or a society becomes numbed or they get interested in poetry. This has happened in practically all the wars you can think of since the time of the Industrial Revolution. The great periods when people were interested in poetry, though not necessarily the great periods for writing it, were times when something critical was, at least, in the wind. Having said this I immediately think of a whole barrage of exceptions.

Ossman: It seems to me that you, among others, represent a kind of "middle ground" in contemporary poetry—neither "Academic" nor "New American." Would you agree with that?

Merwin: I suppose so. I don't know what either "school" is supposed to consist of, but I don't think I've ever been a part of either. I don't quite see that that necessarily lands me in the "middle" of anything though. Whatever you want to call it, my position, insofar as I have one, wasn't sort of worked out in advance; I was living a great part of the time away from literary doings, not seeing many other writers or literary people, and it worked out that way. And there's another thing—I had the luck to start publishing when I was really pretty young and it's sometimes just assumed that what I'm doing now or trying to do now must be just about the same as what I was doing as much as ten years ago. Or more.

Ossman: T. S. Eliot recently caused a stir by saying that poetry should not be taught. What's your reaction to that?
Merwin: Right. I think it ultimately obscures what the whole thing is about and I've had deliberately little to do with it, because I feel quite strongly that it's not for me. Most of my friends have either taught "creative writing," or had something to do with the teaching of it at some time or another, but I think it's quite wrong for me, and so I've never had anything to do with it. The time at which students are being taught these things is when they should be finding out a number of things for themselves, and the worst people to teach them is the older generation—unless they themselves seek out the older generation. Even that's suspicious.

Writing should be a completely unorganized, uninstitutionalized thing; it shouldn't be a matter of generalizations, such as I'm making now. One of the things I think potential writers, particularly poets, should be finding out is the fact that they have to learn to confront their own experience in their own way. And to be told about relations with traditions and with writing and with "making an honest attitude" by somebody older—however wise and however well-meaning and liberal—is pretty dangerous. These things can only be learned by risks—risking learning nothing at all and getting into trouble and making a fool of yourself. I've a rather romantic feeling that if you reach an age somewhere in the twenties without making a big fool of yourself in some way, it's unlikely that you're going to be much of a writer. If too much gentle wisdom and rightness come too early—it's impossible to be right or to be taught to be right at that age.

What you can be taught is that the present is not separate from the tradition, but it's not the same, either. You can be taught that people have been in danger before and the way they behaved, then you can figure out what all that has to do with you. Between the ages of sixteen and twenty, if you aren't finding out any of this yourself, you're going to find it hard to find out for yourself later—you're going to go on taking other people's advice. I suppose that this is far too intimate and too personal a thing to be taught.

Ossman: One reason that so many writers end up teaching is simply to support themselves and their family. Where else can they go?

Merwin: This *is* a problem every poet has to figure out for himself. I think this is a problem for which there shouldn't be an answer. However, I think that the "creative writing" thing is excellent for somebody who isn't going to be a writer. It's a way of teaching him things about writing which he wouldn't otherwise know. He'll know how to read things better—as long as he doesn't become too presumptuous and figure he knows the whole thing better than the people who wrote it. That's another fault of this thing—people come out having had some sort of reading of Melville and figure they know more about *Moby Dick* than Melville himself knew. Nobody who taught them creative writing had any lessons to teach Melville, I don't think.

Ossman: My experience has been that the first two years of college are spent largely in teaching the student to be a critic . . .

Merwin: Well, I think that one of the troubles with criticism in America in particular is the same thing that's the matter with a lot of the other writing: the technical end of it has not become so proficient. In the first place, I'm slightly prejudiced against this form of writing—in general, it bores me. The other thing is that the sense of urgency isn't there—the reason for writing it was probably that some joker had to write another paper in order to keep his next year's tenure at you-name-it college. I don't feel that this is a reason for writing anything. I don't want to ever read another dissertation on "The Middle Years of Henry James."

Ossman: How do you feel now that you're an editor?

Merwin: I've been an editor for three afternoons now. It's a very sort of strange experience for me—I've never done it before. I feel very keenly that I'm not an editor, not a teacher, because I pick up an occasional poem and I think, "This is very interesting, but on the other hand, isn't that an awful line or word or phrase and if only this bit were cut here." And then what do you do? I'm aware that, insofar as I'm anything I'm more a writer than I am an editor, if I start monkeying with this, I'll be monkeying it toward the way I would do it—and this isn't fair—this is quite dangerous and highly presumptuous on my part, because if there is any virtue in the poem, it's for the writer himself to find it and not for me to tell him.

So what do I do? Instead of saying, "Why don't you cut your poem and do this," in general, I simply send it back and say, "This was very interesting and

I hope you'll try again." If you write to all these people and say to fix it "this way" and then send it back again, then you're practically obliged to publish it and it may not be any better than it was in the first place. This would be old hat to anyone who's edited—but I'm just finding these things out. There's a distressing amount of stuff that smells of "creative writing," you know—and an awful lot of poems about poetry and poems about writing poems. I should be more interested in poems on this subject than I am, I suppose.

I think a writer taking up editing as a pinch-hitting job for a short period comes to it with all his prejudices—at least I do—and I'm trying for them not to be operative, though I haven't got anything else to work with. I haven't got a "critical system." I don't think I could swing one.

Ossman: One can't put the *Nation* into the little magazine category. Why does it publish poetry?
Merwin: I think they always have published poetry, for one thing. This was a tradition—after all, the *Nation* is a very old periodical. It goes back into the nineteenth century, and liberal magazines of opinion in the nineteenth century automatically published poetry. I think such magazines were rather important in American poetry at one time, and I think this is a good thing. I mean, I like the idea of poetry being published in nonliterary, ungentlemanly periodicals.

Ossman: Do you get a lot of submissions?
Merwin: An awful lot. In ten days there've been three large cardboard boxes filled to the top with papers. I'm amazed there's as much written as there is.

Ossman: What's your impression of all this? Is it good?
Merwin: Most of it is not very good—that goes without saying. That's an enormous understatement too, because most of it's just terrible. And it's pretty depressing, because it's depressing to read bad stuff all the time and besides, these are the poets' pigeons—they've brought them up and they're fond of them, and there's absolutely nothing good you can say about most of them.

Ossman: Why is this?
Merwin: I don't see how it can be otherwise. I don't see the theory that there are ever going to be hundreds of thousands of people who can write exciting poems, however much "creative writing" they've learned for however many

years. The most that can be taught is skill and there's even a limited number of people who can learn any skill in something as devious and strange and odd in the way it works as poetry.

Ossman: Do you see any uniform characteristic in the bad poetry?
Merwin: Yes, there's a certain tendency toward great vagueness and diffuseness. A poem in which there may be imbedded a marvelous poem will run three times its length; or you'll get a poem which sort of tails out into imagery which is absolutely so vague and abstract that nothing can either be understood or seen—a sort of cloud. These are the two main characteristics. Another is the great characteristic of a lot of bad writing—you just can't see any connection between that piece of writing and any conceivable kind of experience. That is simply literary writing.

Ossman: In other words, you would like to see a specific and a specifically oriented kind of poetry?
Merwin: Yes, I would. I don't see that I can change this simply by walking into the *Nation* office and taking up a box of poems. But I think this is one reason I was asked to do it—because I did have very definite ideas as to what I wanted to do. All that I can do is to try not to let the prejudices be totally subjective and personal, though some of them amount to principles, I suppose. I think that diffuseness, unless there's a very good reason for it, is a bad thing. I think that concision and sharpness and impact and directness and relation to recognizable experience, however peculiar and remote, are good things.

I like to feel that a poem was about something to the writer—that he wasn't just writing the poem because he had a rainy afternoon or that he felt he'd like to have a poem published. I want to be acutely aware of an experience which the poet has been trying to remake or give sense to as directly as possible. I know there are other kinds of poetry, with their own virtues. What I hate is poetry so-called which is just literature. It's always around—I've written some myself; it seems almost everybody has. I'm looking for exceptions. Among other things, for surprise.

"Tireless Quest": A Conversation with W. S. Merwin

Gregory Fitz Gerald and William Heyen / 1968

From *English Record* (New York State English Council) 19.3 (February 1969), 9–18. The interview was conducted and videotaped in February 1968 in Brockport, New York, and was edited by Philip L. Gerber and Robert J. Gemmett. Reprinted by permission.

Mr. Merwin, in February 1968, accepted an invitation from the English Department on the Brockport campus of the State University of New York to read from his own works and to lecture on the art of poetry. During this visit a television conversation was recorded by the campus Television Center, and from the resulting videotape the present dialogue has been edited. In the studio with Mr. Merwin are Gregory Fitz Gerald and William Heyen, both discussants being members of the English Department at Brockport.

The conversation opens with Mr. Merwin's reading of his poem, "For the Anniversary of My Death."

Every year without knowing it I have passed the day
When the last fires will wave to me
And the silence will set out
Tireless traveller
Like the beam of a lightless star

Then I will no longer
Find myself in life as in a strange garment
Surprised at the earth
And the love of one woman
And the shamelessness of men
As today writing after three days of rain

Hearing the wren sing and the falling cease
And bowing not knowing to what

Heyen: I'm impressed with the conversational, quiet, subdued quality of that poem. It seems to me that your work has changed quite a bit since your earlier volumes. I'd like for you during this time to read us at least one of your early poems. I especially like "Leviathan" from *Green with Beasts* [1956], your third volume. Would you read that for us for the sense of contrast?
Merwin: Yes, I would. There's a big contrast in the "noise" of it. I should begin by saying the first part of the poem is a deliberate echo of an Anglo-Saxon poem about a whale.[1] And Leviathan is, of course, the name of a whale.

This is the black sea-brute bulling through wave-wrack,
Ancient as ocean's shifting hills, who in sea-toils
Travelling, who furrowing the salt acres
Heavily, his wake hoary behind him,
Shoulders spouting, the fist of his forehead
Over wastes gray-green crashing, among horses unbroken
From bellowing fields, past bone-wreck of vessels,
Tide-ruin, wash of lost bodies bobbing
No longer sought for, and islands of ice gleaming,
Who ravening the rank flood, wave-marshalling,
Overmastering the dark sea-marches, finds home
And harvest. Frightening to foolhardiest
Mariners, his size were difficult to describe:
The hulk of him is like hills heaving,
Dark, yet as crags of drift-ice, crowns cracking in thunder,
Like land's self by night black-looming, surf churning and trailing
Along his shores' rushing, shoal-water boding
About the dark of his jaws; and who should moor at his edge
And fare on afoot would find gates of no gardens,
But the hill of dark underfoot diving,
Closing overhead, the cold deep, and drowning.
He is called Leviathan, and named for rolling,
First created he was of all creatures,
He has held Jonah three days and nights,
He is that curling serpent that in ocean is.

Sea-fright he is, and the shadow under the earth.
Days there are, nonetheless, when he lies
Like an angel, although a lost angel
On the waste's unease, no eye of man moving,
Bird hovering, fish flashing, creature whatever
Who after him came to herit earth's emptiness.
Froth at flanks seething soothes to stillness,
Waits; with one eye he watches
Dark of night sinking last, with one eye dayrise
As at first over foaming pastures. He makes no cry
Though that light is a breath. The sea curling,
Star-climbed, wind-combed, cumbered with itself still
As at first it was, is the hand not yet contented
Of the Creator. And he waits for the world to begin.

Heyen: Mr. Merwin, Stephen Stephanchev is one of the critics who have lately been attracted to your work, and he says this: "There is a point in the career of a poet when he is no longer excited by his own manner; he must change for the sake of his survival as a poet . . . This seems to have happened to Merwin. At any rate, the style of *The Moving Target* (1963) could not have been predicted on the basis of the four earlier books."[2] Would you comment on this change in your style?
Merwin: I feel very "split" over that. I don't like Mr. Stephanchev's language; I mean, I don't think that the poet has a career, for one thing. He may have a career as something else, but he doesn't have a career as a poet. You know that passage where Thoreau quotes a Chinese text about an emperor who had inscribed on his bathtub: "Make it new, make it every day new and every day new"?[3] I don't think a poet ever really gets excited by his own manner for more than thirty seconds at a time, or if he does, there's something very dangerous going on. But yes, there certainly was a deliberate change in my style. In 1958 when I completed *The Drunk in the Furnace* I thought that if I were ever going to write again, it would have to be in a very different way.

Fitz Gerald: Exactly how do you explain the changes, and what are they?
Merwin: I wanted something that was more direct and in which the experience, the thing that was trying to make the poem (which was a private experience), would have a relationship with the language that was completely different. In other words, the poem would be something which con-

sidered the language as existing apart from itself. It would be something in which the experience was really trying to get into the words and come right through them if it could.

As for the result, I kept thinking I was writing things that were clearer all the time. I found that some people thought the poems were clear, but other people thought they were absolutely incomprehensible!

Fitz Gerald: The rhythms have certainly changed, as well as the diction. For instance, the kind of rhythm apparent in "Leviathan" is no longer present in *The Lice* [1967].
Merwin: No, and "Leviathan" was not really even typical at the time it was written.

Heyen: But as far as these changes are concerned, "you feel by going," don't you, rather than setting up a form or a manner for yourself? I mean, isn't the approach to a poem, rather than being rational, something like Roethke's statement in "The Waking": "I learn by going where I have to go"?
Merwin: Oh yes, yes.

Heyen: And I'm sure you'd rather leave it to critics to define your changes in style.
Merwin: You know, there are two lines in *The Tao* about going forth where there is no road and rolling up a sleeve where there is no arm.

Fitz Gerald: You have an image like that in one of your poems: the sleeve-less arm.[4]
Merwin: Yes, but I didn't know that line from *The Tao* when I wrote it.

Heyen: Would you read for us now a poem in a different voice? Perhaps the title poem of *The Drunk in the Furnace* [1960]?
Merwin: Yes, it was the last poem that was written in that book, too.

> For a good decade
> The furnace stood in the naked gully, fireless
> And vacant as any hat. Then when it was
> No more to them than a hulking black fossil
> To erode unnoticed with the rest of the junk-hill
> By the poisonous creek, and rapidly to be added
>   To their ignorance,
>   They were afterwards astonished

To confirm, one morning, a twist of smoke like a pale Resurrection, staggering
out of its chewed hole,
And to remark then other tokens that someone,
Cosily bolted behind the eye-holed iron
Door of the drafty burner, had there established
      His bad castle.

      Where he gets his spirits
It's a mystery. But the stuff keeps him musical:
Hammer-and-anvilling with poker and bottle
To his jugged bellowings, till the last groaning clang
As he collapses onto the rioting
Springs of a litter of car-seats ranged on the grates,
      To sleep like an iron pig.

      In their tar-paper church
On a text about stoke-holes that are sated never
Their Reverend lingers. They nod and hate trespassers.
When the furnace wakes, though, all afternoon
Their witless offspring flock like piped rats to its siren
Crescendo, and agape on the crumbling ridge
      Stand in a row and learn.

Heyen: The townspeople in that poem don't quite know what to make of the drunk who has taken up abode in their town and caused their children to flock to him.

Merwin: There is a sort of an "umbilical connection" here: My father's family comes from a very tiny town on the Allegheny River. It is a very rough community, but only part of it misbehaves and the other part is teetotaler. It has always been that way.

Fitz Gerald: Would you mind if I asked you a question quite distant from this subject? I wondered what your comment would be about the role of the poet in politics? I mean, does the poet have any business in politics at all?

Merwin: I have to do some qualifying here. I wouldn't presume to prescribe as to what the poet should do. I mean I have no idea. I don't know who "the poet" is. I find it hard enough to try to ponder what *I* should do. For me, politics is the greatest bore in the world. But in our time I think it morally damaging to anyone to close his eyes to what's going on. I don't see how one can. While we're sitting here talking, people are being burned to death who probably never carried arms in their lives. This goes on around the clock. Others are starving to death. This isn't politics. This is simply something that, if one doesn't shut one's mind to it, one feels desperately helpless to do something about it. And that feeling of helplessness, that feeling of everything from anger to bewilderment, to bitterness, is a direct and inescapable part of one's daily experience at the moment. And one writes out of one's experience, that's all—and one acts out of it, too.

Fitz Gerald: You have written a poem about this. I wonder if you would read it for us.

Merwin: There are a couple of them. Maybe I could read them both. "When the War Is Over" is a short one and it alludes, of course, to a song with a rather rude part to it.[5]

> When the war is over
> We will be proud of course the air will be
> Good for breathing at last
> The water will have been improved the salmon
> And the silence of heaven will migrate more perfectly
> The dead will think the living are worth it we will know
> Who we are
> And we will all enlist again

Fitz Gerald: That has a rather ironic ending to it.

Merwin: I hope it does.

Fitz Gerald: What's the title of the other poem you wanted to read for us?

Merwin: The other poem is called "The Asians Dying." I would like to think that if such a book were opened years from now its readers wouldn't even know what it referred to. That's a strange thing to say without qualifying it. I mean the fact that this kind of war was ever possible would be something unimaginable, far in the past, not that those people's deaths were simply forgotten.

> When the forests have been destroyed their darkness remains
> The ash the great walker follows the possessors
> Forever
> Nothing they will come to is real

Nor for long
Over the watercourses
Like ducks in the time of the ducks
The ghosts of the villages trail in the sky
Making a new twilight

Rain falls into the open eyes of the dead
Again again with its pointless sound
When the moon finds them they are the color of everything

The nights disappear like bruises but nothing is healed
The dead go away like bruises
The blood vanishes into the poisoned farmlands
Pain the horizon
Remains
Overhead the seasons rock
They are paper bells
Calling to nothing living

The possessors move everywhere under Death their star
Like columns of smoke they advance into the shadows
Like thin flames with no light
They with no past
And fire their only future

Heyen: Mr. Merwin, the artist today can't help feeling intensely the things that are happening. We are bombarded by television and the newspapers and other forms of mass media, but how does one handle a topical issue in a poem so that it becomes art rather than propaganda?

Merwin: I think this is a question that really is never solved for very long, and one always tries to get around it. One really doesn't, actually. Every issue is topical and in the sense that you mean it, there's a genuine mutual revulsion between art and topical things. On the other hand, poets in every age have tried to make art of topical events with more or less success. It's always, I think, in terms of making the topical into something larger that it works as a poem. If you keep it simply to the topical, it ceases to be a poem and moves toward propaganda.

Heyen: Someone has said of Robert Frost that we can read through his collected poems and not even be aware that the two world wars through which he lived even grazed his consciousness, but I think that this won't be said of you.

Merwin: I don't know whether it is true of Frost. I have heard it said it can be argued that *Ulysses* is one of the great books about World War I. But there is a poem that was an attempt to do what you are asking about—to make a myth out of the topical thing, which is, I think, the way one proceeds. It is called "Presidents." It might be worth reading at this distance from the election. I suppose we'll have another one. Much good it may do us.

> The president of shame has his own flag
> the president of lies quotes the voice
> of God
> at last counted
> the president of loyalty recommends
> blindness to the blind
> oh oh
> applause like the heels of the hanged
> he walks on eyes
> until they break
> then he rides
> there is no president of grief
> it is a kingdom
> ancient absolute with no colors
> its ruler is never seen
> prayers look for him
> also empty flags like skins
> silence the messenger runs through the vast lands
> vast lands
> with a black mouth
> open
> silence the climber falls from the cliffs
> with black mouth like
> a call
> there is only one subject
> but he is repeated
> tirelessly

Fitz Gerald: Mr. Merwin, you have said on occasion, I believe, that you would not enter the Academy because you felt that somehow this would change your art, or in an adverse way affect what you are doing. Would you care to elaborate on that somewhat? What would happen, for instance, if some large university made you a substantial offer? Would you be willing to accept it?

Merwin: Not at the moment I wouldn't.

Fitz Gerald: I see. What are your objections to the Academy, if you have any, or am I loading the question?

Merwin: A little bit. But they are my *own* objections. I have general suspicions about the role of the poet in the university in general. I mean, every man knows whether he is doing the right thing—that is not for me to say.

Fitz Gerald: But in your case?

Merwin: I don't think I'm a teacher, in the first place. I think this is something that one really ought to be able to know about oneself. I don't have that kind of patience. What I'm interested in is never regular and formal so far as imparting things goes; and as a matter of principle I find it difficult, finally depressing and oppressing, to have to talk about poetry regularly and indiscriminately.

Fitz Gerald: Do you feel that teaching would diminish your creativity?

Merwin: I have no idea. I mean I've avoided it.

Fitz Gerald: Your comment is interesting in view of the large number of academic poets that we have in America today. It's a real issue, and I wanted to get your responses to it.

Heyen: Certainly, poets in the university are mushrooming, and may I jump to one of your poems, the last poem in *The Lice*, called "Looking for Mushrooms at Sunrise"?

Merwin: Yes, I'd rather talk about mushrooms!

> When it is not yet day
> I am walking on centuries of dead chestnut leaves
> In a place without grief
> Though the oriole
> Out of another life warns me
> That I am awake
> In the dark while the rain fell

The gold chanterelles pushed through a sleep that was not mine
Waking me
So that I came up the mountain to find them

Where they appear it seems I have been before
I recognize their haunts as though remembering
Another life

Where else am I walking even now
Looking for me

Heyen: I suppose that this is one of the tireless quests of the poet, isn't it—looking for self?
Merwin: I think, yes.

Fitz Gerald: May I ask you a technical question? Anyone who picks *up The Lice* notices immediately that there is a lack of punctuation in all but one poem.
Merwin: *Is* there a punctuated poem?

Fitz Gerald: I was thinking of "The Last One."[6]
Merwin: Oh, I guess that poem is punctuated, yes, but it is not a conventional punctuation. It is a deliberate marking of the ends of the lines, which I could just as well have done with a dash or some other mark.

Fitz Gerald: Except for that, *The Lice* is free of punctuation. I wonder if you could tell us why?
Merwin: I didn't choose to do it that way rationally or deliberately. I came to it gradually. It seemed better; it seemed right to do with less and less punctuation and finally with none. Having done it, there seems all kinds of reasons for it. For example, if you don't punctuate, you throw much greater weight on the actual motion of the poem, on the motion of the grammar and sentences, on the way everything is put together. When you can't rely on actual punctuation, you have to rely entirely on other movements in the actual language, and I think this also "pulls the poem off the page." If the poem exists at all, this makes it simply "lift up."

But finally, one of the simplest effects of the unpunctuated style is to draw an absolute line between poetry and prose. Prose *has* to be punctuated.

Language in poetry has an irreversible finality: if you were going to make a definition, this would be one of the essentials. The language can't be changed without changing the whole thing that the poem *is*. This isn't true of prose. Prose punctuation doesn't work in the same way in poetry. I moved toward the omission of punctuation by recognizing that there was a real difference between using a comma in a poem and using it in a paragraph in prose.

Fitz Gerald: Is this largely visual, or is it both visual and aural?
Merwin: Well, of course, it wouldn't work if you didn't have a printing press.

Fitz Gerald: True. I think now we have time for just one more poem.
Merwin: I'd like to conclude with a poem which is a very deliberate attempt to make myth out of personal, private, and local material. It is called "Grandfather in the Old Men's Home." The part of the world from which the material, if you want to call it by that terrible name, comes is western Pennsylvania. The same country from which "The Drunk in the Furnace" came. It's mining and industrial country with the remains of beautiful agricultural country around it. My grandmother's generation was very fundamentalist Methodist and didn't believe in alcohol—I mean, there are those who believed that buttermilk was sinful because sometimes it had as much as two degrees in it. But much of it is abandoned industrial country, with slag heaps and empty blast furnaces, because the big iron and steel companies have pushed the little ones out of business a long time ago. About "Grandfather in the Old Men's Home," I should say that my grandfather was a pilot, so I'm told, on the Allegheny River and a legendary local drunk. And he was put into the old men's home by his sons. I think the rest of the poem explains itself.

Gentle at last, and as clean as ever,
He did not even need drink any more,
And his good sons unbent and brought him
Tobacco to chew, both times when they came
To be satisfied he was well cared for.
And he smiled all the time to remember
Grandmother, his wife, wearing the true faith
Like an iron night gown, yet brought to birth
Seven times and raising the family
Through her needle's eye while he got away
Down the green river, finding directions

For boats. And himself coming home sometimes
Well-heeled but blind drunk, to hide all the bread
And shoot holes in the bucket while he made
His daughters pump. Still smiled as kindly in
His sleep beside the other clean old men
To see Grandmother, every night the same
Huge in her age, with her thumbed-down mouth, come
Hating the river, filling with her stare
His gliding dream, while he turned to water,
While the children they both had begotten,
With old faces now, but themselves shrunken
To child-size again, stood ranged at her side,
Beating their little Bibles till he died.

Notes

1. The reader should consult "The Whale's Nature" in *The Bestiary*, a thirteenth-century rendering from a Latin source. Mr. Merwin in "Leviathan" blends the rhythm and alliterative technique of earlier Anglo-Saxon verse

The great whale is a fish,

The greatest that in the water is:

with the subject matter of his poem.

2. *American Poetry Since 1945* (New York: Harper & Row. p.118).

3. From Thoreau's *Walden*: "They say that characters were engraven on the bathing tub of King Tehing-thang to this effect: 'Renew thyself completely each day; do it again, and again, and forever again.'"

4. The last line of "When You Go Away," in *The Lice*: "Like the tucked sleeve of a one-armed boy."

5. An aberrant version of "The Battle Hymn of the Republic."

6. Each of the fifty-six lines in this poem ends with a period.

W. S. Merwin: An Interview

Michael Clifton / 1980

From *American Poetry Review* 12.4 (July/August 1983), 17–22. The interview took place in September 1980, in Merwin's just-completed home on Maui. Reprinted by permission.

M.C.: You were writing for the *Nation* from '58 to '62 . . .

Merwin: No, I wrote some things that were published in the *Nation*, that's true, but I was never actually writing for them. I did a lot of pieces for them. Most were things to do with the embryonic peace movement, you know, which became something much larger later but was really small at the time, in the early sixties.

M.C.: And you were poetry editor for a while.

Merwin: For a very short time in '61.

M.C.: What was it like to be living and writing at that time here in the United States?

Merwin: Part of the time, of course, I wasn't; part of the time I was in France, but the beginning of the sixties was a very exciting time. I was back in New York where I wanted to be—I don't altogether understand my relationship with that place, which is fine—but I'd been away from it for a long time, and I was very happy to be back there and excited to be living at that point in my life. I was very much aware that it was a time of great transition, but everyone's aware of that all the time—it's part of the twentieth century. But for me it was largely a matter of relation to the place. In fact, a lot of *The Moving Target* is about New York, especially the latter part of it about "The Crossroads of the World," and so on. It was bound to be New York: New York for me is the archetypal city. So if you want to write a poem about the archetypal city it's just a way of summarizing it. I think it's very important for a poet to have a strong sense of place in most poems. Of course, the place that's evoked is not going to be the place that the reader sees, even if it's a place that's named.

M.C.: That sense of transition we were talking about that you say is familiar to this part of the twentieth century—would you want to hazard a guess about when that started?

Merwin: I expect we all grow up with that kind of feeling. I don't know what it's like for children growing up now, whether there's any real sense of continuity and security left. They must have something in order to maintain a kind of coherence in their lives. They do, but it's hard to see what the consistency, what the sense of continuity would come from. Kids, for example, on this island, that grow up in Kahului—for them the center of the world is the supermarket, the shopping mall. Everything relates to that—what's over in Kraft Drugs. Their mythology comes from that and bears very little relation to the island the shopping mall is on.

M.C.: What kind of mythology was emerging when you were back in New York?

Merwin: How do you mean?

M.C.: Well, there were strands, trends—you said the peace movement was just beginning. That would be one, I suppose. I'm just wondering what sorts of things contributed to the sense of transition.

Merwin: A strong, deep feeling of historical pessimism. I don't feel any less pessimistic now, but my relation to the pessimism, I think, has changed. I don't feel as floored by it, and that's really something unusual, because the things that made me feel pessimistic then are certainly still with us and more so: the destruction of the natural world, the really insane exploitation of the whole environment, the pollution of the elements, and an economy that's really based on war and greed—we just seem to be heading straight for complete physical destruction. These things were already there in the sixties. We were a little bit more simple-minded about what could be done about them. It wasn't so far, for example, from the publication in the *New Yorker* of the things that became Rachel Carson's *Silent Spring*. I understand that the immediate reaction to that in the agricultural chemical industry was simply to decide how much more they were going to have to pay in public relations the following year to offset the truth—not what could be *done* about this situation, but what could be done to prevent this situation from damaging their sales. And that's still pretty much what's going on. You can see it on this island—what the agricultural chemicals are doing to the plants and animals in places. Certainly, the international scene hasn't gotten any less dreadful—or more hopeful—in twenty years.

M.C.: Had anyone you knew been expecting a change with Kennedy's election?
Merwin: Oh yes. There were a lot of my contemporaries who I think had a lot of high hope for what was going to happen with Jack Kennedy as president. I must say I didn't share it. I didn't feel swept up by Kennedy's charm. I didn't feel attracted by him. There was something really fishy about Kennedy. I think maybe, *maybe* I would have felt differently about Bobby. He'd really gone through some changes in his life. He was quite capable of doing something utterly surprising.

I've never been very politically astute or aware, I suppose, but I can remember the disbelief and shock the day the news came of the dropping of the Bomb. And I was at a university where the physics department had had a good deal to do with the development of the atomic bomb. You know, it took a long time figuring out what this meant to us, although you could sort of feel what it meant in your bones almost immediately.

M.C.: Was it the same sort of thing with the concentration camps, or did that go as deep?
Merwin: I think that was a generation older. The news of the concentration camps was coming out when I was a child, and of course it came out after the war, but the whole thing of Hitler and Stalin and all of that was a generation just before mine. The people who were much more alive to that were people like the Jarrells, the Berrymans—the *Partisan Review*. What really woke us up was the Bomb.

M.C.: It's interesting that you pick the two different crises for the two generations. We were saying last night that Roethke had his problems at times, and Berryman and Lowell had theirs, certainly. They seem to have reached a despair in the system and—if I can go this far—in reason. That's what the concentration camps were; a reasonable means toward an insane end. But in spite of Roethke's efforts, they couldn't find their way through the despair, whereas your generation could and did. You say you stopped writing for a month and a half . . .
Merwin: A year.

M.C.: . . . a year and a half before you found what you were looking for with *The Moving Target*. Do you have any idea why your generation managed to find a way of exploring the despair?

Merwin: I don't know, and I doubt that any of us that you're talking about is typical. There's something similar that we all went through—this change in the way of writing—but I certainly think that none of us is typical of anything in particular. And I don't know that my life fits into any recognizable pattern. I grew up in the shadow of the New Critics, as I suppose Robert and James did, but I realized early that I was going to have to get out of the academic world, or I was going to have to stop living my own life. I didn't want to see the world on those terms—didn't want to feel that if I got to the edge of the campus I was going to fall off and I *would*, but I could feel that happening in college and realized that a great many of my contemporaries felt that. Somehow, the world was not quite real if you got away from the university.

I think this is probably less true at the moment. There are more undergraduates who feel the option of just dropping out and doing something else. On the other hand, academic standards are lower, and they seem to me to be stiffer too, and not in a good sense. The people who do go through with an academic career get traumatized by it, so that they may feel that the options are fairly rigid: you either do this, or it's the outer dark for you, too, boy. I feel that that's come back in again in the last ten years, just as the age of criticism has resumed, and it probably has to do with economics, too. In the sixties, people were much more happy-go-lucky about what they could do, what they had to do—all of that with *The Greening of America* and the subculture. The subculture's pretty sunk.

You know, I just sort of subsisted for years, and it wasn't in the States. I got out of graduate school and had a job that took me to Europe. I lived for a number of years on tutoring jobs that paid nothing at all, but they gave me a roof and meals. The thing that seemed most important was not to have a job, not to be responsible to somebody's schedule, or to have to go to meetings, not to teach freshman English. I don't know what's right and wrong in these things, and I may have been quite wrong, but I simply felt that I would avoid this as long as I possibly could. I'd try to get past a certain age, after which I could decide.

M.C.: Do you think you were more aware of this country, and of New York, because of your absence?

Merwin: Yes, I think so. I was away the first time for seven years, because

I knew if I came back I would have to give up my independence. I'd been living on very little money, but I'd been living on my own time, working on translations and poems. I could do that in Europe, but I knew I couldn't do it in the States. There was no way I could afford it. On the other hand, I got very homesick. It wasn't a matter of approving of what was happening at home, it was just a matter of hearing your own language. Lowell has a line in one of his poems, when *he* was living in England those last years, about one of his trips back to New York. He said, "At least I don't have the feeling that I'm growing deaf," which is something I felt for several years. You're listening to your own language. But if this is your own language, you know that it's not the source of your poetry.

M.C.: So you were looking for a way to live your life without being bound up in the academy, which would have happened if you'd stayed here and written: you would have ended up with a university job. And you gradually came to feel that way about the forms, the poetic forms, you'd been working in up to *The Moving Target.* Can you be specific at all about how that happened?
Merwin: It's hard to, because, for one thing, it's hard to remember. I think that having come to feel dissatisfied with a way of writing, you don't simply say, "I'm going to give up A, because I would prefer B." At the point when you're making this decision, B doesn't exist, or at least you don't know what B is. So in a sense, you simply say, "I have to stop writing this way, it's finished. The energy, or my relation to the energy, somehow has reached an end. If I go on writing poems like this, I'm imitating something. These aren't really poems, these are confections about writing poems. I know too much about this, and I'm just doing." This may or may not be true, and I must say I don't have any theory about that either. I don't think this is something that everybody must necessarily do, that every poet must always do this. I just don't believe that, and I'm very suspicious of people who have theories and say every poet must do such and such—all poems must be such and such. I suspect immediately there's something wrong there. For example, Andrew Marvell all his life wrote pretty much, basically, in the same mode. It was recognizably Andrew Marvell, and he's a very good poet. If Andrew Marvell should somehow have felt that he had to try writing like William Carlos Williams, then there's something very wrong.
    One of the things that I'm suspicious about in the whole wave of creative writing, and the way poetry is regarded in some places in the academic world, is these inexhaustible quests for formulae. Everywhere, you see this tendency to have a formula that clusters around a teacher, or a theory that if

it's a particular kind of poem, then, ipso facto, it's better than another kind of poem. Not necessarily so. But I think it's quite possible when the relation with the tradition has gone the way it's gone in our lifetime, nobody knows quite where the energy in the tradition is. If you listen to Allen Ginsberg, and some of the school of William Carlos Williams, and so forth, art is supposed to be that way. That's one way, but even Whitman and Williams didn't automatically write good poems.

M.C.: No, some of Williams's stuff is awfully flat.
Merwin: Yes, and there are all sorts of ways of being influenced by it. Williams's great influence on Denise Levertov, Ed Dorn, Creeley, Allen himself, and Archie Amnions—those are all poets with works that are very different from each other. Their individual ears survived the influence. But there are lots and lots of kids trying to write like Williams, and it comes out like nothing at all. But it probably would come out like nothing at all, anyway.

M.C.: So you reached this nonexistent point B . . .
Merwin: Well, what I'm saying is that when I reached that point we were talking about, I didn't know *what* I was going to write. If I had, it would have been very clear, I would have sat down and started writing. I wouldn't have sat for a year and a half not knowing what I was going to do. I remember that I wrote some poems I didn't keep that were more formal than what I'd been writing before *The Moving Target.*

M.C.: They were even tighter.
Merwin: Um hm. Just exploratory things that I happened to write on those occasions, and I realized that I was using what I knew rather than writing what I felt I wanted to. But I think any poem that's a real one is going to come out of some balance between what you know and what you don't know. One trouble about writing courses is that you tend to always put a great deal of emphasis on what you do know, even when you're calling what you do know "using the subconscious." Playing it a little bit safe. There's always that temptation. Everybody does it, to some degree. You never stop doing it, and you can't really stop doing it. Otherwise, you'd be writing automatic writing. I've never been enthralled by random theories. If people want to write at random, that's fine; I don't see why other people should be expected to read it.

M.C.: What do you think about the wholesale influence that you and some others—Bly and Wright, for example—have had?

Merwin: I don't know. I've seen different manifestations of it as it regards me. One sees it in literary magazines, and I've seen it in manuscripts that have been sent to me. There's an awful lot of it that I just abhor, because it seems to me awfully easy. I suspect that there's a certain kind of student-writing that imitates people because it's easy to imitate them. I don't know that that's fair to lots of other students. I've got some wonderful letters from people who have written about the effect of a poem bringing embryonic ripples of their subsequent development who've sent me things that were not obviously, just imitations. But the imitations in which they take a few obvious images that have recurred out of poems of mine, or ways of saying things, and they just tack them into theirs and call that influence. I just think, "It's really too bad that I ever wrote any of those things, because it's done them more harm than good."

There's a kind of reading of an older poet—probably not one of the immediate generation before yours, I would think—but Pound used to say you should try to get influenced by people from other ages, and from other languages, and I think that's true. They're more remote from you and that's just safer. But there's no such thing as a good or bad influence; it depends on how it's used. And if you're just trying to use the earlier poet to do your own work, you're going to find it's damaging. Your own relation to your own work has suffered. What influences you should really open some doors for you, and then what you should walk into are your own rooms. How can anybody be interested in reading poems which are imitations of themselves? They're like reading phony poems of your own.

There's another big difference—less so for Robert—which is that both James and I had a real love for the formal tradition of England. James did as long as he lived, and I do, too. I don't feel that just because one writes in open forms, as they're now called, that automatically makes one superior to someone who writes in heroic couplets. I think it's unlikely that people are going to be able to write in heroic couplets, in formal verse, right at the moment with full conviction and at full capacity, and with full integrity. I don't think many people are going to be able to do that but James Merrill does, and he does fine in formal verse.

M.C.: But most people can't.
Merwin: No, and partly because they're not brought up to it. I think that people read Alexander Pope and figure he's totally irrelevant to what they're doing; he's not—he's one of the great poets of the English language, and it's the fact that they don't know how to listen. He had one of the subtlest ears

of any poet. I remember James—James Wright—and me sitting up reciting Pope back and forth to each other, and James with tears running down his face.

M.C.: Do you think there are any other reasons besides lack of education and lack of preparation that the poem that carries the culture won't work for us now?
Merwin: The poem that what?

M.C.: The poem that carries the culture—the literary tradition.
Merwin: I'm not sure that it won't. We just have to find someone who knows how to write it. The poems of Merrill seem to me to be perfectly authentic; I don't doubt them at all. They're very special and very specialized; the audience is going to be limited. I think some of that's deliberately so, and it's deliberately elitist. That's bad and good—there's no such thing as totally popular poetry. There's no such thing as poetry which does not demand a certain recognizable, consequently limited, frame of reference. The generation ten years ago that was listening to the lyrics of Bob Dylan—some of the kids growing up now don't know what those lyrics mean, so that what seemed to be totally popular poetry was limited very much by its time and circumstances.

M.C.: Would you go so far as to say that there was a whole new frame of reference starting in the early sixties? In the late fifties and early sixties?
Merwin: Well, there must have been, but I don't think anyone thought of it in those terms. We were interested in getting poems written, not in solving the cultural dilemma of the latter half of the twentieth century. I suppose we were all interested in that, too, but not with any notion of being seriously affected.

M.C.: Yes, there's always the more immediate problem of finding out you're one stamp short.
Merwin: Um hm. I don't know I've ever talked with Robert about it before—whether he feels that there was this marked transition in his work as there was in James's and mine. I don't think there is between his first and his second books, do you?

M.C.: No. He has, he said, a first collection, a formal collection, that he did *not* publish, whereas other people went ahead and did publish. He hung on to his until after he discovered Neruda and Trakl and the others.

Merwin: Well, that was very refreshing, too. I think that one of the great contributions of Robert has come out of his enthusiasms—the people who he's taken up with and been very carried away by. Those have opened up people's oddest intentions to ways of writing.

M.C.: How did you happen to find Neruda in 1949?
Merwin: I was in college and reading Spanish, working on translations of Lorca, and so forth, and there it was. I couldn't read it very well; it seemed to me kind of wild and wooly. It was there in the Princeton bookstore against some odds and ends. I'd never read anything like it. There *isn't* anything like it.

M.C.: No. I wonder—well, we won't talk about influence. I refuse to ask that question.
Merwin: Well, there are such odd coincidences, or odd things that seem like accident. There was a guy who lived upstairs whom I admired very much, who was quite a few years older than me, and who killed himself a few years later playing Russian roulette. He was the son of an admiral and had a whole, brief career as a journalist in South America before coming back to get his degree. And he either recommended Neruda or was very enthusiastic about Neruda when he saw that I had him. That made me pay a little more attention to him, too, although I was trying to write surrealist poetry when I was an undergraduate, heavily influenced by Lorca, by *The Poet in New York.* I must say that Breton and all of the surrealist period in poetry made a great impression on me at eighteen. You wouldn't have known it a few years later, hmm? So maybe this was a surfacing of some kind twelve years later in my life.

M.C.: The thing that's struck me, though, in my reading is that throughout the formal poems—very naturally—the same kinds of startling images are tucked very neatly into the poems. Would it be fair to say that it's the context that's changed? That's made the image more prominent?
Merwin: Or maybe more of a reliance on the image itself, rather than on the image as part of the texture. The poet—I guess what would now be called the modernist poet—to whom I paid most attention when I was an undergraduate, and in the first years of Europe, was Pound, and through Pound, medieval poetry, which cut through a lot of the things Robert's concerned with, including a great deal of the English tradition. It was quite possible to live with that without feeling totally hemmed in by it. And then when I went abroad I lived outside the English-speaking countries for several years.

I lived in Spain and France and Portugal, and read the medieval poetry of those places, too. So the formality that appealed to me then—and still does, indeed—was the formality of medieval poetry—the formality of the troubadours, the English of Chaucer—much more than the formality of the nineteenth century.

M.C.: You said that there was a kind of clarity to the poetry, that the form didn't get in the way of the medieval or troubadour poetry. Could you explain that a little more?

Merwin: Well, in medieval poetry, during the great period of the High Middle Ages, from let's say, the late troubadours—well, it runs all the way through the troubadours and gets into Chrétien de Troyes and Chaucer, and I suggest it's even down in Spanish in Jorge Manrique, and certainly in Chaucer—one has a feeling of great transparency, as though the form, the natural and final, definitive way of putting this, has simply floated together. It was a real way of presenting it.

M.C.: And the form didn't get in their way at all.

Merwin: Clearly, it must have. When I was nineteen, I thought that Villon—how great it must have been for him, because it must have been so *easy* for him to write. He must have had the same kind of trouble writing that everybody had and always did. Of course, their relation with their tradition was utterly different. It never occurred to them to suddenly start writing in open forms, nor was there any reason why it should. Those poems that seem to be so devastatingly original to *The Divine Comedy* and both *The Grand* and *Le Petit Testament* of Villon had plenty of precursors. There's probably no single main element of Villon that wasn't current at the time. There were lots of people writing poems about wills and testaments, and so forth; he just happened to write the one that was so incomparably the most alive and painfully illuminating, and there were other poems about journeys to the underworld and the other worlds that Dante had to draw on, too. They didn't feel the tradition as an impediment, and I doubt that the tradition is ever wholly that. Through the whole modernist period of the early twentieth century I think a lot of the energy of the original free verse comes from the fact that it's being played off against an ear which is very well-acquainted with iambic pentameter. Consequently, there's a tension set up. And that supplies some of the energy to the other form of writing. Eliot's hearing blank verse all the time, whether he's writing it or not. So's Pound, although he's railing against it. Pound wrote the most Chaucerian lines of the century.

I don't think that there's anything good or bad about any of these conventions. The good thing is to have a convention that channels and excites and electrifies—adds to the available energy at a given point—and the bad thing is to have one which puts it to sleep, tangles it up and makes it fall on its face, or makes people just pay lip service towards it, which was happening in the early years of this century. But just the fact that you're writing or not writing in iambic pentameter, or writing or not writing in free verse—one formula is no better and no worse than any other. There must always be, I think, a tension between the form and the limits of the form, and it's from that tension, the harmonizing of that tension, that you get the energy that makes the poems that are worth keeping, and that are different and a new phase of the tradition. It'll *be* a tradition if it's any good, and it won't simply come out of the void, either. It'll be linked with what's happening before it, and not simply in terms of rejection. You talk about Roethke revolting against the *Quartets* of Eliot, but he was deriving a great deal of what he was revolting against even as he wrote it—inevitably.

M.C.: How conscious were you of being under the shadow of the New Criticism?

Merwin: Oh, conscious in different ways. I was very lucky because the person whom I revered most—I was in awe of—was someone who had not got a degree, and who, although he played academic politics, and so on, was never wholly caught up and never wholly swallowed by the academic system. That was Blackmur, and he was very definite. He said, "You don't want to get a doctorate, you don't want to teach, you don't want to get stuck in this." It was my own voice I could hear coming back, telling me he was right, he was absolutely right. He was saying it doesn't do you any harm to get a good education, but don't get stuck here. But he also said—I did a year, not a very reputable one, I didn't do very well—in graduate school, and he told me I really should get out. I shouldn't play around anymore.

M.C.: Was that the year you were exercising all the horses in the Reserve Officer Training Corp stables?

Merwin: Oh, that was earlier. Where'd you hear about that?

M.C.: It was in *Contemporary Authors.*

Merwin: Oh yeah? I didn't know it was in there. . . . And he also said when it was clear that I was going, "I don't think you should read any more criticism for a long time." I didn't, either. I thought he was a very wise man. Whether he was or not, he was one of the keenest literary intelligences that I've ever been near. He was a kind, generous man.

M.C.: There was a lot of energy in American poetry in the sixties and not much criticism. Now that there's more criticism, would it be fair to say that that might indicate a slacking off of energy in the poetry, or not?

Merwin: I don't know, and I'm beginning to think I'm getting too old to judge in matters like that, because it would involve pronouncing on people who are quite a few years younger than I am now. And I don't altogether know where they're coming from. It's really hard to make sweeping statements like that about what's happening in a country the size of the States, with that many people writing. I seem to see signs of real energy coming from different places. There seems to be an enormous amount of talent. I keep reading first manuscripts or first books put together by people—I don't mean hundreds, but every year there are two or three that really seem to me remarkable at the time. They're really very good—something that I want to read two or three times. Then, very often. I'll read their second manuscripts and think, "Oh, that's not so good; the first one was better."

It seems to me that, partly because of this break with the tradition, and consequently, a break with the kind of energy they're either fighting with or drawing on, it's so very hard for young talents to continue to grow and develop. So whether the actual energy of a whole generation is dying out, I don't know. Survival in the twentieth century for an artist in any of the arts seems to me to be particularly hard, and this is partly because of the fact that the relation with the tradition is so attenuated, and is so vexed and strange and unknown, and partly because of the demand for originality in the most crass senses in sophisticated places like literary magazines and creative writing programs—this idea of originality, as though this were something that could be judged from outside. Originality is a matter of where something comes from. It's not a matter of what form it takes when it comes. If something is authentic, it's original. I think it's as simple as that. So what you're looking for is authenticity.

M.C.: But it does seem that young writers reach a problematic stage a little earlier.

Merwin: It seems to me that they reach a very high level of sophistication very early, much earlier than they used to. And consequently, they get the feeling that they know how to do this without ever having had to call certain things about it in question to see what their relation to it is.

M.C.: And then, suddenly, that relationship *is* questioned.

Merwin: Inevitably. Because there aren't any formulae, and there aren't any real answers. And in a way, I think that something—I don't know whether this is a fair generalization, but it's an impression—I have the feeling that, as the relation with the tradition has become more groping, and has been called into doubt, and has been given a bad name, the reliance on the institution has taken its place, and I think that's what counts.

M.C.: The institution instead of the tradition.

Merwin: Yes. You look for answers from the organized intellectual community around you, and that's deadly.

M.C.: That's a whole transference of the way you write poetry.

Merwin: Yes, and I think that one of the symptoms of this is being able to get an MFA for writing a book of poems. I'm very old-fashioned; I find this rather shocking. I think it's fine that you should get all sorts of rewards for writing poetry, on the one hand; on the other hand, I think you should always be aware that there *are* no rewards for writing poetry.

M.C.: It means, too, that the poetry moves from being an absolutely private struggle to a public, more structured struggle.

Merwin: Yes. And then the different conventions of our time of writing poetry become institutions themselves—there's the school of Ginsberg and the Beats, the Olsonites; and I see students who are just absolutely locked into these. They can't hear anything without following these patterns. I don't think that's any better than trying to write like John Masefield: it may work fine for a year or two, but . . .

M.C.: You're going to have to come back up against that private struggle.

Merwin: Well, you're not only going to have to come back up against it, you are *in* that private struggle all the time whether you know it or not, and anything that diverts your attention somewhere else is not doing you a service, it's pretending to you that things are easier than they are.

You know, you're talking about Robert Lowell, and James Wright, and me, and I think that one of the things I'm saying is that the assumption has been made—I've read it in print—that both James Wright and I completely rejected the whole tradition of poetry in the English language, and I don't think that's true. I'm not happy seeing great reams of the modern blank verse poetry, but I'm very fond of a great deal of traditional lyrics and traditional work in English. There are plenty of tilings in blank verse that I do love very much, too. I used to love Milton very much when I was in college.

M.C.: No one does . . .
Merwin: No one does anymore.

M.C.: You said earlier that you've come to a different way of dealing with the despair. I think you said that you weren't so "floored" by it anymore, that you've simply come to live with it.
Merwin: I mean I don't feel that we're going to suddenly come to the end of that. I don't see that there is any secular way out. But on the other hand, I don't see that this is more than an intensification of something which has been there for a very long time. I think that history is a record of despair. It's not a very happy story when you start reading it in high school. And the only thing that will give us any hope at all is something which is not there in history; it's something which is *not* part of the temporal pattern, and it's not something which is born and dies. If one is simply caught in the material patterns, there is no way one can have anything but despair, or distraction. Consequently, that's where we are. If you pick up the newspapers, that's what you have: despair and distraction in many forms. It's savage. Turn on the radio, that's what you get. The advertisements assume your despair and they provide you with distraction.

M.C.: So you wouldn't pick a spot and say, "Somewhere in this period"—the industrialization of England, for example—"is where things started to get rocky"?
Merwin: No, although you could certainly pick spots where the gear changed and it got a lot worse, and I think that's one of them. But the thing that makes me feel particularly bleak about now is—I don't know, have you ever looked at the *Greenpeace Examiner*, for example? And what's happening to the seas, and the seals, and the whales, and the forests? The Black Hills? It's happening so fast, and it's not just us. We're rather better than some places. In Thailand, apparently, the destruction of forests is happening faster than anywhere else in the world. When I was living in Mexico, in Chiapas, the destruction of the forest there was simply terrible, and the erosion of topsoil from a cut forest took three years—it was all gone. And since I was there they've introduced chainsaws.

M.C.: Three years?

Merwin: Yes. If you cut, slash, and burn some of these mountain rainforests, within three years its topsoil is washed off and the forest won't grow back: it just starts turning into desert. Now, you can fly over great areas of Chiapas which, not many decades ago, were covered with virgin forest, and you have desert. But this is such a terrible topic that we could pick it up anywhere and come out with total despair.

M.C.: So you'd say that, as a species, we've had an attitude of exploitation all along?
Merwin: Um hm. I think this is part of our myth about ourselves, the new Western myth which has to do with the superiority of this race and of this species to all the other species. A superiority which is so great that you can simply eliminate other species if they become inconvenient to you. This is perfectly okay; we have a right to do it. You talk about "male chauvinism": this is specietal chauvinism. They're just the same. The species has got some kind of absolute right to anything it wants for its own convenience. Anything it wants or chooses to have is encouraged. The result is that one of the species that we're certain to get rid of is our own. I don't figure that we can carry this nonsense on, and I think the point is approaching fairly rapidly. We have some friends who just sailed a boat from San Francisco to here. It took them weeks to sail across the Pacific to here, and they said they saw garbage floating every single day. A lot of it.

M.C.: Every day?
Merwin: Um hm. Plastic bottles, and so on. Well, you know the story without me giving the details: the destruction of the wolves in Alaska, the actual changing of the climate, the wrecking of the water table. What's happening to the atmosphere, the things that we put in it that go round and round the planet, changing the atmosphere itself, including nuclear waste. Things that we don't even know about until long afterwards. It just turned out a year or so ago that the Navy had been dumping nuclear waste in Honolulu Harbor. Years! Nobody protested; they didn't pay any attention. They were finally caught. Now we don't know where they dump it. They don't dump it there. And the airport is within easy rifle fire of huge nuclear storage caves.

M.C.: I didn't know that. It doesn't give me an easy feeling.
Merwin: No, except that there are big storage things all over the country. Plutonium in Colorado, and bacteriological and chemical warfare stockpiles in Maryland, and in other parts of the West. Of course, nobody knows what

the effect would be if they dropped a nuclear bomb on the nuclear storage thing here. This is probably a prime target, the Hawaiian Islands, because they could send a threatening message and fire one missile in here, and it would give the United States a sharp lesson, if it didn't start the whole thing off. But even if a nuclear blast on Oahu didn't pulverize the rest of the Islands—which is probably what it would do—it might set the whole chain off with an eruption. These are pretty big volcanoes, some of them. We're sitting right on top of one.

M.C.: That's true. A good, deep crack would cause a lot of trouble. Can you remember vividly what you were doing when you heard the news about the first atom blast?
Merwin: Um hm. I was waiting on tables in the Common Room, working my way through college. I came in for the evening meal, and we sat down to eat before supper. And somebody said, "We set off an atom bomb. Dropped it on Japan." I thought he'd been reading too many comic books. I couldn't believe it. I looked around and realized that people were totally serious. Everyone was shocked, incredibly. It was a very silent table—first there were bursts of chatter trying to figure out what it was and then people just started falling silent, totally.

M.C: The whole room.
Merwin: The whole room—a big Common Room. Several hundred people. And, of course, people saying, "Well, this means there'll be no more wars. That's something, anyway." I didn't know what it meant. (Laughs.) It doesn't mean that, though.

But we were talking about the early sixties, and I know that there was some hope then that somehow one could alter things. I think some of the hope in my case came from having lived in England, and had to do with what was then the CND and the Committee of a Hundred. The CND meant the "Committee of Nuclear Disarmament" and the Committee of a Hundred was a hundred people who got together to try to do something about nuclear weapons. There was a great phrase about us being "the last men to start a revolution." And it really did seem to some of us then that by some kind of show of good faith, and by limiting the arms race unilaterally, we could actually reduce the arms race considerably and perhaps even stop it. Then I came back and was involved with the analogous thing in the United States. The demonstrations were very small in those days.

But the thing that abruptly brought that to an end for me, and I think for a lot of other people, was the Cuban Missile Crisis. Khrushchev or Kennedy, or what the personal blame there, I really, at this point, don't know; it seemed to me much clearer then than it does now. But they really were very close to bringing the world to nuclear catastrophe by just taking their chances. If you read the accounts, poor Kennedy had no choice and was being pushed around by the CIA. But I know that its effect on me was one of great bitterness, and feeling that the peace movement had just been ended like that, that the country really was more interested in some kind of paranoid self-justification, and in the destruction of whatever gave it the jitters, than in finding a decent and good way of living. And I thought, "Well, I better find a better way of living, myself," and retired to a farm in France.

M.C.: And wrote *A New Right Arm.*
Merwin: Yes, I wrote that in New York before I left. But really, the thing that followed, that came out of it, was the very end of *The Moving Target* and then a good bit of *The Lice.* I suppose that's a part of the darkness of *The Lice.* The feeling that as a nation and a species we were involved—and one is never involved completely unconsciously, some of this is deliberate and conscious—possibly helplessly involved in a kind of lemming race. We're just trying to destroy ourselves. And one of the forms it took was trying to destroy the other forms of life around us.

M.C.: Almost in a form of projection. I was looking at your books on the shelf over there. I had no idea you were so interested in American history, in particular.
Merwin: Especially the 1890s.

M.C.: Why?
Merwin: It seems to me one of the real turning points in American history, and one that's not been given as much attention as some of the others.

M.C.: What kind of turning point?
Merwin: Well, did you know that in the same year as the Chicago Exposition the first industrial army marched on Washington, or the first protest army—Coxey's Army? The whole great dream of the frontier had come to an end.

M.C.: And that's how the protests began?
Merwin: Um hm. There was no longer any West for a man to go to, not in

the old sense. It ended. The buffalo had been killed off, the Indians had been rounded up, mostly—none of this destructive afflatus was going to work anymore; it wasn't the answer. Doing such things was an anachronism. And so we had the first petitioning groups walk on the White House lawn. This wasn't treated as anything of great importance, but I think it was a crucial moment.

M.C.: It would be a clear call to the lemmings, an indication that that particular process is starting.

Merwin: The protest marches make the image of it, I suppose you could say, but it's like a counter-lemming rush—to make a march and *not* do anything self-destructive, to try to wake the whole place up.

M.C.: You called your translation of Chamfort *Products of the Finished Civilization* . . .

Merwin: He called it that. It wasn't used for many, many years, but that was his title for the book which he never published. This was his title for his manuscript.

M.C.: . . . and you said in, I think, the preface that you wouldn't labor the parallels between his age, the Enlightenment, and ours. Would you go ahead and labor them now?

Merwin: Oh, only the very obvious ones. His was the great revolutionary age before ours, and consequently it was full of all of the things that we can recognize very well. The thing of being in one set of circumstances and describing another set of circumstances as a panacea which one finds. If you're living in a capitalist system's situation, all you have to do is go to Maoist China and everything is just great. It's a new earthly paradise. Privately, I don't think that this ever happens, but this is a wonderful formula for all kinds of intellectual dishonesty, which allows for great cruelty, because if it's going to be a real Utopia, then it's quite easy to say that the end justifies the means. Both ages have this thing in common: they were both in the shadow of a revolution which then came to stay. It was very cruel and involved great deception, self-deception, destruction, made some real changes for the good, and just wiped out a whole lot of things that were also pretty good. I think there are lots of parallels. It's just easier to see in Chamfort's time, because society was smaller and less intricate. They didn't have these immense bureaucratic institutions which manage to cover things up just with proliferation; you can tell the truth, but if you do it in a fourteen-hundred-page report, nobody's going to read it anyway, so you can get away with it.

M.C.: Can we talk about *The Compass Flower* for a minute?
Merwin: You can ask the questions.

M.C.: O.K. It seems to me that the book is a lot happier . . .
Merwin: Well, I met Dana. But before that, going back to the earlier change, when I did that move from New York after the Cuban Missile Crisis, I felt, "I'm waking up every morning and I know what I disapprove of and what I hate, and if someone said, 'How would you live if you had a chance?' I really wouldn't be able to give a good answer, and I suppose I ought to find out if I can't find other things that I can feel differently about." And I felt at that point, that staying on the Lower East Side of Manhattan was not the place to do that. I would go into bars and hear people say, "We should have dropped the Bomb on them long before this," and so on. And I thought, "I don't know, this is just giving me toxin at both ends of the day and all through the middle, and I can't handle this very well. It's not getting me anywhere." So I suppose what you're saying is that a lot more of *The Compass Flower*, by contrast with earlier ones, is that it has to do with places and people and ways of existence that I respect and love, which doesn't abolish the context of the star of pessimism, of not much hope for our material prospects at all. But that's not simple; it's not a matter of simple condemnation, and when I say "pessimism" I'm not talking about judgment or condemnation. I think that New York is an incredibly destructive place, but I love it in some strange way. I've never quite been able to figure it out. If I could figure it out, I probably would never bother to go back again. I'm not really interested in going to the moon. The earth is still a very beautiful place; it's seldom enough that it's seen. It's seen as an object of exploitation, rather than as something of which we are a part. We are neither superior nor inferior, we are a part of it. It is not different from us. So when we treat it with contempt and we exploit it, we are despising and exploiting ourselves.

M.C.: That sounds like a nice place to stop the tape.
Merwin: Um hm.

"Fact Has Two Faces": An Interview with W. S. Merwin

Ed Folsom and Cary Nelson / 1981

From *Iowa Review* (University of Iowa) 13.1 (Winter 1982), 30–66. This interview took place on October 11, 1981, at Cary Nelson's home in Champaign, Illinois. Reprinted by permission.

Ed Folsom: You have rarely done interviews. Why?

W. S. Merwin: I gave one in Los Angeles about six years ago, with a couple of students who wanted to do one, but they hadn't prepared anything. I think that's one of the reasons for distrusting it. If the interviewers are unprepared or the questions are remote, you have to give a monologue to save the occasion. Then the risk is self-indulgence. The interviews we know well, I suppose, started with those in *Paris Review*, about twenty-five years ago. Then it became a very popular form, and I think it's been a happy hunting ground for all sorts of self-indulgence, both in the making and in the reading. It's often a substitute for really thinking about a problem and trying to say something coherent. It can be spontaneous, but sometimes it's just louder, given more seriousness and attention than it probably deserves.

Cary Nelson: I think the last detailed interviews I've seen with you are the 1961 interview published in *The Sullen Art* and the interview with Frank MacShane published in *Shenandoah* in 1970.

Merwin: Both were a long time ago—ten and twenty years, but I assume we're doing something different.

Folsom: You were telling us recently that you have been reading *Leaves of Grass* again. I'm curious about what you find there now.

Merwin: I've always had mixed feelings about Whitman. They go back to reading him in my teens, having him thrust at me as the Great American

44

Poet. At the time, coming from my own provincial and utterly unliterary background, I was overly impressed with Culture (with a capital C) so the barbaric yawp didn't particularly appeal to me when I was eighteen, which is an age when it is supposed to, nor did I feel that this was *the* great book written by an American. I've tried over the years to come to terms with Whitman, but I don't think I've ever really succeeded. I've had again and again the experience of starting to read him, reading for a page or two, then shutting the book. I find passages of incredible power and beauty. . . . Yet the positivism and the American optimism disturb me. I can respond to the romantic side of Whitman, when he presents himself as the voice of feeling, but even then it's not a poetry that develops in a musical or intellectual sense. It doesn't move on and take a growing form—it repeats and finds more and more detail. That bothers me, but in particular it's his rhetorical insistence on an optimistic stance, which can be quite wonderful as a statement of momentary emotion, but as a world view and as a program for confronting existence it bothered me when I was eighteen and bothers me now. It makes me extremely uneasy when he talks about the American expansion and the feeling of manifest destiny in a voice of wonder. I keep thinking about the buffalo, about the Indians, and about the species that are being rendered extinct. Whitman's momentary, rather sentimental view just wipes these things out as though they were of no importance. There's a cultural and what you might call a specietal chauvinism involved. The Whitmanite enthusiasm troubles me for the same reasons; it seems to partake of the very things that bother me in Whitman. I don't know how to say it better than this, which is one reason I didn't write to you about it. I'm not sure I'm very clear about it.

Folsom: I think you're very clear about it. We were talking this morning about the problems inherent in putting together a *Collected Poems*, especially for you, since you have developed individual books so clearly and with such integrity. People who follow your writing closely, I think, conceive of your career in terms of the various books, more so perhaps than in terms of individual poems. The books are each organic wholes, and each is a separate and clear step in your development, with growth and change in evidence. Each marks an important evolutionary shift. Whitman, on the other hand, is a poet who insisted on writing one book over a lifetime, and that's part of the reason for the uncomfortable positivism that pervades his work, isn't it? He starts out with this incredible positivism which is rampant in the mid-century, in the 1850s, which grows out of his sense of exhilaration about manifest destiny, about America as a ceaselessly growing field of unified contrarieties. As his career developed, though, the two major historical events of his adult life—the Civil War and the closing of the frontier—destroyed the persona that he had taken on with such burgeoning enthusiasm. Consequently the book—his one growing book—became a burden to him in a way. He could not contradict the book because he was not writing new ones; he was adding on to and readjusting the old one. I'm wondering if some of that positivism in Whitman is there because he refused ever to set his past aside and begin again?

Merwin: Several times Whitman sees something essential about the American situation. F. O. Matthiessen describes it too: in a democracy one of the danger points is rhetoric, public rhetoric. I think now, looking back, that he is also describing his own weakness. Both Whitman's strength and his weakness is that he is basically a rhetorical poet. And he's rhetorical not only in the obvious sense that all poetry is rhetorical, but in the sense of rhetoric as public speech: you decide on a stance and then you bring in material to flesh out that stance, to give details to your position. This is one of the things that makes me uneasy about Whitman. The stance is basically *there*; and much of the poetry simply adds detail to it. So many of the moments in Whitman that I really love are exceptions to this. Yet to my mind, these exceptions occur far too infrequently. Most of the time he's making a speech. The whole *Leaves of Grass* in a sense is a speech. It's a piece of emotional propaganda about an emotional approach to a historical moment. It's almost set up in a way which makes it impossible for it to develop, to deepen, or to reflect on itself and come out with sudden new perspectives.

Folsom: What about some of the poems of the "Drum Taps" period like the "Wound Dresser"?

Merwin: They're some of my favorite passages, you know, because his theory won't support him there. He's simply paying attention to what he sees in front of him. I find those poems both sharper and more moving than many other things in Whitman.

Folsom: But they tend to get lost in that vast programmed structure *of Leaves of Grass . . .*

Merwin: He allows himself to get lost in it, insisting on inciting the bird of freedom to soar . . .

Nelson: Even in those poems in which he is depressed by what he sees and admits his difficulty in dealing with it—rather than announcing it yet again as an appropriate occasion for his enthusiasm—some of the same role as the representative speaker for the country, the role of the speaker voicing the collective condition of America, continues to be foregrounded, though perhaps with less mere rhetoric, less oracular theatricality.

Merwin: I'm very anxious not to be unfair to him. I'm not altogether convinced, as you must guess, by the deliberate stance, but there's obviously a wonderful and generous human being behind it, and a quite incredible and original gift, equally incredible power. But those misgivings have been quite consistent now for all these years, so I guess I'm going to have to live with them.

Folsom: Do you conceive of your own writing, your own career, as the creation of one large book?

Merwin: Well, your whole work is one large book, because there is a more or less audible voice running through everything. At least I would like to think that one's work becomes a coherent project eventually, that poems are not merely disparate pieces with no place in the whole. But I don't conceive of deliberately trying to construct a single book the way Whitman was trying to do with *Leaves of Grass*. I don't think of that even in terms of the separate books. I never set out to write *The Lice*, or to write *The Carrier of Ladders*, but wrote until at a particular point something seemed to be complete. On what terms, or on the basis of what assumptions, I wouldn't be able to say, any more than I would with a single poem be able to say, "Ah, that poem is finished."

Folsom: You have said that when you go back to nineteenth-century American writers for a sustaining influence, it's not Whitman you turn to, but Thoreau. I think a lot of people throw Whitman and Thoreau together as part of the American Transcendental and Romantic tradition. What draws you to Thoreau that doesn't draw you to Whitman?

Merwin: I suppose the way in which he meant "In wildness is the preservation of the world" for one thing. Or the recognition that the human cannot exist independently in a natural void; whatever the alienation is that we feel from the natural world, we are *not* in fact alienated, so we cannot base our self-righteousness on that difference. We're part of that whole thing. And the way Thoreau, very differently from Whitman, even in a paragraph takes his own perception and develops it into a deeper and deeper way of seeing something—the actual seeing in Thoreau is one of the things that draws me to him. I think that Thoreau saw in a way that nobody had quite seen before; it was American in that sense. I don't know if Williams talks about Thoreau, but I would have liked to hear what Williams had to say about Thoreau's capacity to see, even though Williams's great sympathy is more toward Whitman. Indeed I've suspected for a long time that an American poet's sympathy would tend to go either toward Whitman or toward Thoreau, not toward both. Gary Snyder at this point is rather snippy about Thoreau, says he's very uptight, WASP, and so forth. That's a way of describing Thoreau's weaknesses all right—such as his lack of any automatic spontaneous sympathy for his fellow human beings. Thoreau is not all-embracing. The kind of hawky thing in Thoreau puts off the enthusiasts of enthusiasm itself, the great Whitmanite hugs of feeling, the lovers, "I love my fellow man." Perhaps if you really are there you don't have to say it so often and so loudly. Dana recently has been reading Henry James and Thoreau and getting very impatient with James and reading a passage of Thoreau and saying, "You know, for James the natural world is scenery outside the window." There's never anything alive out there. And for Thoreau, when he sees it, it's alive, completely alive, not a detail in a piece of rhetoric. And he leaves open what its significance is. He realizes that the intensity with which he's able to see it *is* its significance. This is an immense gesture of wisdom in Thoreau that I miss in Whitman. Whitman's wonderful expansive enthusiasm isn't there in Thoreau, though he has things of equal beauty and power. The last page of *Walden* is certainly one of the most beautiful things ever written, and of a kind of elevation that Whitman himself was trying to reach all the time.

Folsom: Yes, Whitman does tend to dwell a bit too long on "cameraderie," as if it's something he's trying to *invoke* rather than to *describe*. I think in that sense there's a real loneliness at the heart of Whitman.
Merwin: There is at the heart of both of those writers, but it's quite obvious in Thoreau, he makes no bones about it. There's that wonderful passage where he says, I don't pay enough attention to my fellow human beings, I don't feel strongly enough about them, I don't take enough interest in them, and I'm going to do something about that: these people down here working on the bridge, I'm going to walk closer to them and see if I can't think of them as though they were groundhogs.

Folsom: Do you read Thoreau often?
Merwin: Well, I keep him in the john. He's been there for years. So I go back and read things over again. I think *Walden* is an incredible book. I feel

grateful to Thoreau in a way. He's been a companion. Yet I see Thoreau's limitations, too, including whatever it is that makes him write by tacking one sentence onto another sentence out of notebooks, and putting them together. It's a strange way of writing, though he's not the first person in history to write that way, after all.

Folsom: Your myriad translations suggest all kinds of affinities for you from outside America, but are there other American writers besides Thoreau that you find yourself returning to, that you would call sustaining influences?
Merwin: Thoreau is really the main one that I go back to. There's nobody really before Thoreau. There was a time when I used to read Mark Twain for fun, but apart from *Huckleberry Finn*, which I love, I find that he doesn't last very well. I don't even find him very funny anymore. And then I read an early book, his book about Hawaii. It's amazing how much racism and John Wayne-ism there was in that generation.

Nelson: Has Thoreau been behind some of the prose that you've written recently? You're writing about your family and your past, which are very different topics from his, but there's a certain humility about phenomenal existence that I see both in Thoreau and in these pieces from your new prose book, *Unframed Originals*.
Merwin: I hadn't thought of that, Cary; that's interesting. Maybe so, who knows?

Folsom: Certainly that position you put yourself in when you buy the old abandoned house in France at the end of that one autobiographical essay, called "Hotel"—the position of moving into that house only so far, not wanting to clear the floor and put panes in the windows and paint the walls, but rather only lie there on a simple cot—is a very Thoreau-like position. It's like his bean-field: half-cultivated and half-wild.
Merwin: Yes. I guess that's part of what I was talking about a minute ago. That's a wonderful way of putting it, too—his humility before the phenomenal world. If you don't accept the genuine chairness of the chair, if it's all just background, as it is for a great many people in the contemporary world—first the separation from the natural world, then from the phenomenal world—things tend to be seen only in terms of their uses, or in terms of what abstraction they can serve. If the reality of the unreal objects cannot be accepted as an infinite thing in them, you can't see anything. You only see counters in a game that is of very doubtful value.

Nelson: I feel in your recent pieces a real wariness about rhetorical over-statement, a wish to write in a very delicate and lucid way and not to fall into what might be a Whitmanesque mode of thinking about your own past, but to speak in simple and direct terms about it if possible.

Merwin: Well, of course I don't have to tell you that you're always writing in a rhetoric of one kind or another, but I am working to avoid as much as possible a kind of rhetoric which is an emotional screen that keeps you from seeing what you're trying to look at. That's something I did want to do. And I also realized, part way through, since one of the main themes of the book is what I was not able to know, what I couldn't ever find out, the people I couldn't meet, that reticence was one of the main things I was writing about. Indeed it was a very reticent family. But I felt if I could take any detail, any moment, anything I could clearly see, and pay enough attention to it, it would act like a kind of hologram. I'd be able to see the whole story in that single detail—just the way, if you could really pay attention to a dream, the dream would probably tell you everything you needed to know for that time and place. But obviously any exaggerated rhetoric you were using at that point, in the sense of waving an emotional flag in front of the thing itself, would prevent that from happening.

Nelson: I have been trying to distinguish between the way your poetry of the last twenty years makes me think about language and the rather differ-ent view of language that I detect in *Unframed Originals.* At least from *The Moving Target* on, it seems you felt it necessary—if you were to write as the present conditions of the world required you to write—to let language *do* to you what it would, to let language in effect have its way with you. In these recent prose pieces I sense a new wariness about that, a desire *not* to let language have its way. I'm wondering whether that rings true at all, or even whether you have some sense that the recent prose pieces are written in a significantly different mode, that they show a real change in your relation-ship to words?

Merwin: It must be, but I wasn't aware of it when it was happening. And to connect that with what we were just saying, when you're trying to avoid that one kind of rhetoric, of course you're developing a different kind of rhetoric. I had a feeling of trying to write in what years ago I suppose I would have de-scribed as a kind of classical way, in which the form of the prose, the form of the writing, was in the service of but not swallowed up by the subject, so you were really deliberately formed through the language. The language ordered what you were seeing, unlike, to choose a very different alternative, a stream of consciousness style. Yet I'm unaware of some of the other differences. I certainly don't want to keep doing what I've done before, and if it feels as though I'm just doing something I've done before, then obviously I don't want to be doing it. But I don't very often have some deliberate, conscious notion of what direction I want to move in; when I started off to write those pieces, I knew that I wanted to handle that material, to put it down, to give it what would be the clearest and sharpest possible form, but I didn't know how to go about it, and having finished the book, I would still feel I didn't know how to go about it, and don't know now. I don't think I *know* how to write anything, but particularly I don't know how to write prose.

Folsom: Certainly there is a dramatic shift in the way your prose *feels* from *The Miner's Pale Children* to *Unframed Originals.*
Merwin: How do you see the difference?

Folsom: I see the difference corresponding to the difference between the poems from that period and your most recent poems. The change of voice in your most recent poems is surprising, and moves further in the direction of the more colloquial language of *The Compass Flower.* Your recent poems are allowing a much more colloquial language into themselves than I've heard before. They're allowing a kind of clear narrative development that they have not had before—one of the ones you read the other night, as I told you, reminded me of Williams's "Plot of Ground." It seems to me a movement that is first evident in many of the poems of *Compass Flower.* The language seemed to grow less gnomic in tone, much more inviting. The voice became more relaxed, and I sense the same thing in the recent prose. As I'm describing this, I realize I'm not saying the same thing Cary is—Cary senses something almost opposite to this in the recent prose, a reticence and a tightening. . . . But we would both agree that *The Miner's Pale Children* is a book which goes much more with the period of *The Lice* and *The Carrier of Ladders* than these recent pieces. Do you feel that?
Merwin: But I don't think there's a contradiction. You're saying different things, but I think it's possible for both of these things to be happening at the same time. I certainly wanted the prose to handle material that it never had before, and to do it as plainly and directly as possible. Plainness is the thing you are both saying is involved here.

Nelson: It seems that it would have been immensely dissatisfying for you to write about this subject matter in the style of *The Miner's Pale Children* or *Houses and Travellers.*
Merwin: But I also think there's been an impulse in the direction of plain-

ness for a long time. It's been growing, and it goes back quite far. I've seen some critical commentary confusing plainness and what's been called the *quietness* of the poems. I don't know if they really are quiet or not. They don't seem quiet to *me* obviously. But there are not so many decibels as there are in Whitman, though Whitman has moments of another kind of power. A line like "A woman waits for me" seems to me to have at least as much emotional power as "I hear America singing"—you know, I don't care if he hears America singing; I *do* care when he says "A woman waits for me."

Nelson: But there are moments, at least in *The Lice* and *The Carrier of Ladders*, when one might say you hear America dying. There is something of that role of speaking in a representative way for the culture, obviously not with Whitman's enthusiasm, but with virtually the same energy in reverse. Were there times in working, say, on the American sequence in *The Carrier of Ladders* and on some of the poems of real horror in *The Lice*, when you felt yourself in Whitman's position but with a very different message, with a very different tone?

Merwin: Very much, yes. One of the things that I found happening, not deliberately, as I tried to write those American poems at different times, again and again—I don't think it's possible for me to see or to approach that subject—it never has been—without the feeling that Ed was describing as we drove across the country yesterday, this feeling of inhabiting a palimpsest. However long the culture may have left, we are *not* just sitting here on a Sunday afternoon. Insofar as there is any historical or temporal continuity at all, that continuity involves these many layers, many of them invisible, and they are not different at all from the repressed, pressed, and forgotten layers of our own experience. And if we really are so dishonest and so mutilated that we can't make any sense of the world, or come to any terms with them, then our lives are maimed and truncated accordingly—our imaginative lives and probably our physical lives too. You know I've felt various things about that over the years and very often the rage that you, Ed, said that your father felt when he saw what was happening to the soil of this country—I can imagine feeling it about the soil, too. For a while I used to think of it in terms of two myths, two Western myths, one of them the myth of Orpheus obviously—the important thing there is that Orpheus is singing with the animals all around him listening—and one can take that as a myth of arrogation or as a myth of harmony. It's both, you know, it is homocentric but it's also inclusive, and everything is there in the act of singing. And the other is the myth of Phaethon, who says "Daddy, I want to drive those horses," and ends up with a holocaust . . . and the beginning of racism. It's probably not as simple as that, but at one point I kept seeing it in terms of those two myths. But the American poems. Let me approach them in another way.

F. O. Matthiessen, as I remember, years ago was talking about the attempt of a number of American writers to find an American myth of history; Richard Howard quotes that wonderful passage at the beginning of his book, from which his title comes, *Alone with America.* You know, one can begin to see differently the great phony myth of the "winning of the West"—it was the *destruction* of the West. It *was* heroic, but it was heroic in an incredibly cramped and vicious way. People did suffer and were magnificent, but they were also broken and cruel, and in the long run incredibly destructive, irreversibly destructive. What we've done to this continent is something *unbelievable*—to think that one species could have done this in a hundred years. Right where we're sitting. And this is our lives. This is not something to have an opinion about, this is what we live with, this is our bodies and our minds, this is what our words come out of, and we should know.

Folsom: Cary was suggesting that in *The Lice* and *The Carrier of Ladders* you sometimes take on the voice of the culture in a kind of negative way. I'm wondering if sometimes too the voice in those books is not that of the other animals, if your desire throughout your work is not in part to accomplish what is both impossible and absolutely necessary, that is, to give voice to the voiceless beings, to those creatures that cannot speak their rage. Do you at times feel your voice coming not from the human culture but instead from the silent herds being destroyed by that human culture?
Merwin: It would be very presumptuous to agree to that, but insofar as I dare to suggest a formula for myself or anyone else, I think it's very important to remain open to that possibility, to welcome it, and to evoke it if possible. Otherwise, what else is there? Otherwise, one is there in an ego-bound, historical, culturally brainwashed, incredibly limited moment. One can't perceive anything because one has no perspective at all. The opposite—the nearest thing I can imagine to what I would think of as a sound or even healthy approach and attitude toward existence as a whole (as distinct from the endless separation of the human species from the rest of existence that leads to evaluating the one at the expense of the other)—would be Blake's "How do you know but ev'ry Bird that cuts the airy way, / Is an immense world of delight, clos'd to your senses five?" It works both ways, one both can be and can never be the bird.

Folsom: I think of "For a Coming Extinction," where the voice shifts a great deal, trying to speak to the gray whale while being aware of the fiction that the gray whale can hear us anyway, and then at the end of the poem becoming the voice of the culture: "Tell him / that it is we who are important." The most ironic lines in your poems occur when your voice shifts into that mode of speaking for the culture.

Merwin: I hadn't thought of that.

Folsom: And when the voice seems least ironic and the most enraged, it seems to be speaking from somewhere that one cannot name, that is not within our culture. It is not a voice speaking from within, but a voice that has to dismiss itself from the culture for a time in order to speak the rage.

Merwin: Like "Avoiding News by the River."

Folsom: Yes.

Nelson: It's more difficult, it seems to me, to decide what voice is speaking in the passage right before that in "For a Coming Extinction": "Consider what you will find in the black garden / And its court / The sea cows the Great Auks the gorillas / The irreplaceable hosts ranged countless / And fore-ordaining as stars / Our sacrifices." At first in that passage there's an extraordinary and, I think, powerfully unresolvable sense of anger . . .

Merwin: I was going to say, even when you read it, that all I hear is the anger with which it was written. It overrides these other distinctions.

Folsom: But there's a clear double-voice there: "Our sacrifices" carries all of the pride of the destructive culture.

Merwin: Yes.

Folsom: And yet it comes out sounding incredibly angry because we know that the voice that is really speaking this poem and mouthing those words is not emerging from the source that would speak those words with pride.

Nelson: One also hears a certain contempt even, earned.

Merwin: Yes, and you know, driving in the West, I've thought and remembered afterwards, and see it in Hawaii watching these things: you drive along and you see some pile of ditched cars, or a little place where they serve trash—deep fried food, or something like that, and you think, in order to bring this about dozens of young men were sent off to die of leprosy in the leper colonies, or hundreds of Indians and thousands of buffalo were killed and the whole place has been poisoned for years in order to bring about this little pile of shit. And it's described in terms of the triumph of civilization. What kind of impossible lie is this that we're all subscribing to?

Nelson: I have a poster version of "For a Coming Extinction" upstairs that I see each time I walk in that room. It's a more immediate and continuing relationship than one can easily have with a poem in a book. Every time I read the poem I enter into a cluster of remarkably divided emotions. Each stanza seems simultaneously fractured and sustained by contradiction. "The End / That great god" suggests at first our lust for extinction, for a kind of demonically hieratic narrative conclusion. Yet a sense of transcendence also enters into the reference to "The End" as a "great god." To the extent that the poem confers a static immortality on the gray whale, it too participates in that act of "sending." There is a certain beauty in these animal "hosts ranged countless," a beauty not cancelled either by a sense of loss or by their status as a collective indictment of human history. If we are appalled at the numerical accumulation of slaughtered animals, we are also in awe of the "irreplaceable hosts" now ranged before us. These two impulses are inextricably linked by the poem; it becomes fascinated with that miraculously awful achievement and thus puts forward a far more radically compromised voice than anger alone would permit.

Merwin: It would be very difficult and very rare to make a poem out of pure anger, or out of pure anything. Even love poems are seldom made out of pure love. Actually, they're made out of words, so all of the paradoxes that are built into any phrase come into it. Pure anger would just be a scream.

Folsom: And there can't help but be a fascination with those people who at the end of the poem say, "It is we who are important." You can despise those people, but there's a fascination with them, and you have to come to terms with them because they've constructed the layer of the world we're living on and dying on right now.

Merwin: Yes, you *have* to come to terms with them; that doesn't mean that you have to say it's okay.

Nelson: No, but there are texts of more unqualified anger about this kind of subject matter, not necessarily in your work but elsewhere in contemporary poetry. I think yours is a poem that forces you, if you want to read the poem carefully, to think through your own motivations. It doesn't let you away easily. It doesn't let you off being convinced that you won't continue in this pattern. You may already be part of it.

Merwin: That aspect of it is even more apparent probably—from what people have told me, whether they've responded to it with pleasure or with annoyance—in that pineapple poem that was published last year. People obviously find that they're being got at in different points in the poem, and don't like the attack.

Folsom: That reminds me of another poem from *The Lice*, "A Scale in May," where this issue of a double-voice is central. The "I" in this poem seems to be able to identify the problem of human arrogance while simultaneously recognizing his own participation in that arrogance.

A Scale in May

Now all my teachers are dead except silence
I am trying to read what the five poplars are writing
On the void

————————

Of all the beasts to man alone death brings justice
But I desire
To kneel in a doorway empty except for the song

————————

Who made time provided also its fools
Strapped in watches and with ballots for their choices
Crossing the frontiers of invisible kingdoms

————————

To succeed consider what is as though it were past
Deem yourself inevitable and take credit for it
If you find you no longer believe enlarge the temple

————————

Through the day the nameless stars keep passing the door
That have come all that way out of death
Without questions

————————

The walls of light shudder and an owl wakes in the heart
I cannot call upon words
The sun goes away to set elsewhere

————————

Before nightfall colorless petals blow under the door
And the shadows
Recall their ancestors in the house beyond death

At the end of its procession through the stone
Falling
The water remembers to laugh

Looking back on it now, what can you tell us about the voice in this poem?
Merwin: I'm trying to remember exactly when the poem was written, and I can't. Obviously it was written sometime in the sixties, in the spring. I'm not a theorist and in any case I don't want to embed it in a theory that implies it was written with the whole thing worked out intellectually in advance. But in hindsight I think I see that certain things I've been trying to say for years seem to have been converging all the way along. I see quite a number of them in that poem. But I'd better say something first about the progression; the middle part—the second, third, and fourth sections—are set up in ways which can be taken either straight or ironically, and I would like them to be taken both ways. They've been written about, in criticism, from both points of view, as though each excluded the other, and that wasn't the intention. And, as Ed has pointed out, the use of language in a particular way to possess the world is part of what *I felt*, much of my life, to be a very dangerous human arrogance, one which no one is exempt from—we're sitting here as part of that arrogance. We arrogate to ourselves things that do not belong to us, that don't belong to anybody. I don't want to develop that as a kind of ethical matter and say how I think we should solve the ecological problems, pollution, and so on. As I suggested the other night, I think that the first hope of mankind begins in simply caring about those things.

The thing that I *do* want to try to say something about, as a basis for talking about the poems of that time, and probably all of the poems I've written since, is that—to put it personally first—I used to feel that it was a terrible fault of character not to be able to come to clear resolutions and decisions about things, that I would always be seeing two sides of something, and saying, "Yes, but." Of course that *is* a fault of character, but at the same time the character *does* use a left and right hand, the heart does beat both ways. And I've come to believe that existence—and by that I don't mean just human existence, I mean existence as a whole— has always got, basically, these two aspects to it, one which is relative, and the other which is not relative at all. The second, of course, is the teacher who is not dead, the world of silence. But that's also the world in which you can't call upon words. The arrogance comes from saying that that world doesn't exist or is of no importance, when of course in my view it's that world that gives words their real life. It also allows them to be luminous, transparent, and to illuminate the world, which in itself is transparent and luminous. Arrogance and an attempt to possess that world as something which is absolutely solid and can belong to somebody, completely nullifies that whole dimension of existence, and deprives existence of any kind of sense, and it deprives it of its senses. It deprives us of our own senses. The sense of smell is the first, most obvious one; we've almost lost it; it's going away from us. If you take that as a basic note to the poem, I think it will help make the poem ring clear. And I don't think that idea is a very difficult one, though it's probably a difficult *feeling* to come to terms with. And very little of our public, social, and historical experience, our experience in the time that we live in, fits us for coming to terms with it; we're being shunted away from it all the time, and it is very uncomfortable, until we accept it. Then I think it is the only comforting thing there is. That's why the water remembers to laugh.

Folsom: I'm curious about what you might have to say about the form that you used in this particular poem—a three-line stanza which becomes a form you return to quite often: in *Asian Figures*, in *Feathers from the Hill.* In this poem these varying perceptions are all captured in those three-line moments. What attracts you to that form?

Merwin: Well, it goes farther back than that. There are poems in *The Moving Target* which are in that form, and I wrote a number of poems in the form at that time, but I didn't publish most of them. A little later I tried to develop and figure out what I was doing. One of the things I wanted to find . . . you know, when people say, "I don't understand modern poetry" or "I don't understand any poet," sometimes they mean they have difficulty in apprehending intention and subject and so on, but I think that sometimes it's a temporary inability to grasp an unfamiliar sense of completeness, a new recognition of how things can be complete. And at one point I wanted to see what it was that made a poem complete as a small, if not the smallest, unit; it was a way of discovering what was the single thing that would stand by itself. Why I gravitated to a three-line form I don't know, but that seemed to me the ideal small form. And in *Asian Figures* I really was trying to see just what was the *smallest* form, not that I wanted to stay there, but I wanted to explore this idea of completeness. And then when you start putting these complete things together, do you see them as separate or in relation to each other? It's a question, I think, that art is always suggesting: this is complete, yet at the same time, what is its relation to everything?

Folsom: Returning for a moment to the irony, the double-voice, in this

poem—to what extent does the "I" separate itself from the world of fools?
Merwin: Well, you're asking a question that has a double answer: how much
do I remember about my intention of the poem, and what do I feel now,
which is the only place I can answer it from. I think that was deliberately
left up in the air because the "I" is *not* separate from the fools; on the other
hand, the "I" is judging a kind of human action, a human gesture, it wants
to be separate from. Of course we're all fools; I have a watch in my pocket
(I don't have it strapped on). The foolish thing is to take that world which
we have made as the real, total, absolute final world, and say we have it—it's
ours. You know, I doubt whether one can come to anything that resembles
a moral judgment without seeming to be outside it. On the other hand,
you can't altogether make one without identifying yourself with the person
you're judging, whether you know it or not. You don't see it if you're totally
separate from it. But deploring an action doesn't necessarily mean that one
is saying, "It's them"—it's us. If you see someone beating a dog, and there's
nothing you can do about stopping it, you feel angry, but part of your anger
probably is bound up with the fact that somewhere inside you, you're capable of beating a dog. But you may not stop to think, "Is it me? Am I being
self-righteous?" You want to stop the beating of the dog. I want "them" to
stop destroying the Northwest, killing the salmon, killing them both in the
sense of thinking that they're unimportant, and in the physical sense of pol-
luting the rivers; both of them are really the same thing.

But I can't really remember with any close or absolute accuracy what I
was trying to do in this poem. And, you know, it would not be an authentic
poem if the *intellectual* intention were the real, final guiding force in the
poem. This is another way of recognizing that other dimension; I think a real
poem comes out of what you don't know. You write it with what you know,
but finally its source is what you don't know. There's a passage where Thoreau says, "How can someone find his ignorance if he has to use his knowledge all the time?" The arrogance would be the assumption that what you
know has some kind of final value and you can depend upon it, and it will
get rid of a whole world which you will never know, which really informs it.
Both of these worlds, in my view, are without meaning; there is absolutely
no meaning in either, but the *sense* of the world of relation comes from them
nonetheless.

Folsom: When we get to *The Compass Flower*, the ecological rage and
ironies and devastations that I feel everywhere in *The Lice* seem to have
changed dramatically. The ecological poems in *The Compass Flower* tend to

have a tone like that of "The Trees"—a sadness at what's about to be gone and a recollection of what it is that the trees have offered. It's a very different tone from that in *The Lice.* Obviously you could not remain at the point you had arrived at in *The Lice,* where it seems to me that you were on the verge of not writing poems at all . . .

Merwin: Absolutely right. In fact most of the time that I was writing *The Lice* I thought I had pretty well given up writing, because there was really no point in it. For different reasons—much the same way that I think some writers of continental Europe felt late in the Second World War and after, that there was really no point in going on writing; what they had experienced was just terrible beyond anything that language could deal with, and there was no point in even trying, and there was probably no one to write it for either, for very long. That can easily be described as despair, but I think it may not be just despair—it may be a kind of searing vision: a dumb vision, and I don't think you can stay there if you're going to go on living.

Folsom: Your books since *The Lice* form a clear and eloquent record of how you have come to grips with that despair, and moved beyond it. But I'm interested in your own personal version of how you came to terms with going on to write after *The Lice.* What happened to the rage and the anger and the despair?

Merwin: Oh, I think they're all still there, but I suppose some lucky recognition that the anger itself could destroy the thing that one was angry in defense of, and that the important thing was to try to keep what Cary described as humility before phenomenal things: the fact that that chair may be destroyed tomorrow is no reason not to pay attention to it this afternoon, you know. The world *is* still around us, and there is that aspect of other human beings which has *not* been solely destructive, and to which one is constantly in debt, and which involves simply the pleasure of existing together, being able to look and see the trees, the cat walking in and out of the room. The answer to even one's anger is in the way one can see those things, the way that one can live with them. Not very often, perhaps for no more than a few seconds at a time. Even so, one lives second by second.

Nelson: I have been reading *The Compass Flower* the past few days and thinking about its relationship to the four books preceding it. From *The Moving Target* through *Writings to an Unfinished Accompaniment,* your special vocabulary—including words like silence, darkness, emptiness— is taken up by historical circumstances, permeated by a particular feeling about our culture's destiny. During that time it seemed to many of us that our culture's destiny was being played out in very visible and unarguable ways. In *The Compass Flower* you are often trying to write very different poetry, including love poetry, yet this vocabulary in a way returns to haunt you. In writing the poetry of *The Compass Flower* was it a struggle to deal again with words that were colored by a different sense of history, or at least words that seemed decisively to belong to the public world and its power to enter into and transform our private lives?

Merwin: I think so. They are words that I used with increasing caution, because they can become habitual, they can become counters. They can have an emptiness which obscures their real emptiness; they can become sentimental indeed in that way. They can simply become one's own signatures that are habitual. That's really self-defeating.

Nelson: I would say that some of those same words become habitual in Kinnell. Indeed it's a risk for many poets—a vocabulary like that becomes so much a part of the way they write that it's merely instinctive.

Merwin: Yes. Well, obviously I'm not going to try to never, never use those words, but I use them with increasing, deliberate self-consciousness. If I use them now, it's with a kind of self-consciousness I wouldn't have had using them fifteen or twenty years ago.

Nelson: In the period of *The Lice* the self-consciousness would have gotten in the way.

Merwin: That's right. The funny thing is now, when you're both talking about that, I realize that there is a small group of poems from the beginning of this year—new ones—in which the kind of magma that produced *The Lice* suddenly insisted on writing, bringing out the same vein again, just before the inauguration of Reagan.

Nelson: Well, we're going to have more occasions like that. The history that wrote *The Lice* or that's there in *The Lice* has hardly left us.

Merwin: I think so. I didn't set out to write those poems. Several poems suddenly came out with more of that quality than I knew was going to be there. Just the beginning of this year particularly, I felt a great deal of that: the British presence in Ireland, what Reagan was up to, and Watt, my return to Pennsylvania and seeing what the result of the new policies was there—total devastation.

Folsom: Those most recent poems surprise me somewhat. I feel in them the same anger that was in *The Lice*, the same rage, but what is different is that the historical allusions are direct and clear. The allusions are not defamiliarized for the reader, as often happens in *The Lice*. In *The Lice*, you may be talking about an assassination, but the name of who was assassinated does not appear, and in fact there would not be a direct or clear allusion to any of the actual events of the assassination.

Merwin: Actually both of the assassination poems in *The Lice* were written before the assassinations.

Folsom: So they really were not historical poems . . .

Merwin: The one was written very shortly before the Kennedy assassination; the other one very shortly—about three days—before Martin Luther King was killed. I better not write any more of them.

Nelson: I think it's difficult to say the poems in *The Lice* are not historical poems. The process at work for a reader is one in which a core of precise historical referentiality becomes uncertain and unstable, even blurred, in the poem. Yet in a way the poem's historicity becomes more representative as a result. The poem presents a history potentially more possessive of us and where we are in time. The specificity begins to erode as the poem proceeds.

Merwin: I have a recent poem with a reference to the IRA hunger strike, but I'm uncertain about that passage, and I'm thinking of taking the extremely specific reference out of the poem. Although I very much wanted it to be in there when I wrote the poem, I'm not sure it belongs there. I don't think it strengthens the poem, or even serves the reasons for having that specific passage there in the first place.

Folsom: This talk of referentiality ties in with your description of how you came to deal with writing poetry after arriving at the wordless position you were in upon completing *The Lice*. There seems to be a gradual realization that the world is still here, that you could still be attentive to the things that were around you—that's certainly the feeling that I sense growing book by book after *The Lice*. A striking example of this new feeling is "St. Vincent's" in *The Compass Flower*. This is a poem that to me marks a new kind of attentiveness, a new kind of use of language, that I find more and more, as I've said, in your autobiographical prose pieces. We have that same concern with wanting to keep the senses open—there seems to be a feeling in this poem that there's been a place there for a long time that has been part of your common experience; you see it every day, and yet you've never seen it. You've never paid attention to it, never really looked at it. "I consider that I have lived daily and with / eyes open and ears to hear / these years across from St. Vincent's Hospital." And what happens in the poem, then, is a kind of opening of the eyes and ears to the sights and sounds one has learned to dull one's senses to, so that "long / ago I learned not to hear them / even when the sirens stop / they turn to back in / few passers-by stay to look / and neither do I." So there's a sense now of *staying* to look, staying to record, staying to imagine what might be going on beyond the things that one can see and hear if one is attentive enough. And then the poem ends with a question, "who was St. Vincent": the name given to the thing that one has lived across from all the time—I take it that the question *does* ask for an answer, who *was* St. Vincent, and I think of St. Vincent who defined his life by paying attention to those elements in society that no one else paid attention to. So, too, this is a poem about learning to pay attention, it seems to me, to things that one has learned not to pay attention to, by custom, by habit, and then learning to overcome that.

Nelson: Before you read "The Last One" the other night, you said that you wished that the poem would become so untopical that no one would know what it was about, a comment that I found appealingly subversive. "St. Vincent's" is a poem whose referentiality is more or less inescapable: I wonder if you are comfortable with that, or do you sometimes wish that it, too, had a quality of undecidable plurality, making it impossible merely to link it with that building and that structure.

Merwin: No, I don't feel that; I'm very fond of that building. The poem was written in January, I think it was 1975. I've had an apartment for many years across the street from St. Vincent's Hospital, so that's the time and place of it. And it was, I suppose, a particular attempt to do that thing we were talking about, to honor the very specific historic immediate circumstance, to make the poem directly out of that. The poem was a deliberate attempt to practice something closer to the tradition of Williams and Whitman. One of the things that I envy about that tradition sometimes is the ease of address, the immediacy of the use of historical circumstance, which sometimes I would very much like to have been able to use more familiarly myself. But obviously I can't believe that I'm ever going to be in the center of that tradition; I don't share any of the original assumptions. It has seemed to me that *fact* has two faces, too. Fact is in the world of relation—one is always looking at the outside of facts. One sees all the facts from the outside. One is never going to be on the inside until one is caught up *in* the *relation*, then of course you don't *see* the inside; there is no separation between the inside of you and the inside of what you're looking at. They're the same thing. "Who was St. Vincent" remains a question, and it's a question that one goes on asking; it's the question that asks what the relation *is* between the world of history and the world that's shared. And between them and oneself.

There's a moment in St. Vincent's biography when he gave up the life that he'd been living and went to live with the poor whom he'd been serving, because he felt that what he'd been doing was inadequate . . . and after the first night of introduction to this terrible squalor, with people beating each other and misery and hunger and the lives falling apart, he woke up in the middle of the night in tears, saying, "Forgive me, God, I did not *know* that this was going on. I didn't know that suffering went this far. I didn't realize that this was in the world."

Folsom: In "St. Vincent's" the referentiality is very clear; it's all there—we're given the name of the hospital, we're given the context—in the book of poems to let us know we're in New York, we know exactly what the building looks like. Is the original St. Vincent's still extant, by the way?

Merwin: It's still there, but, you know, like everything else, it's changing. They're tearing the inside out of part of it now, and keeping the facade, which is quite beautiful, the old part of it. But they're expanding. I had a surprise when the poem was published. I met somebody who said that they'd been over there to St. Vincent's for medical reasons, and they'd found the poem pasted on the walls of the elevators. I got a letter from the nun in charge of public relations who said, "There are a lot of questions in that poem, and if you'd really like them answered, please come by and I'll take you through the hospital," and I did, and had a whole afternoon going around St. Vincent's. . . . The questions are still unanswered.

Folsom: But the unanswered questions are very different from those in your earlier New York poems. I think, for example, of "Before That" from *The Moving Target*, where you have an image of "Cemeteries sifting on / the city's windows." Do you anticipate that your reader will see the referentiality that you described at your reading the other night, about the crosses being the white X's on the windows of condemned buildings, or is that something that you *remove* from the realm of referentiality in the poem, and only restore at the reading?

Merwin: Well, assuming there is going to be a historic future, which is an assumption that we make but we have no real reason to, one can't double-

guess which of our historic circumstances are going to be known or matter to people a hundred, two hundred years, hence. I'm unsettled to realize
that as the natural world recedes, and as generations of students grow up
without having had any contact with it, an enormous number of really very
basically simple images are becoming remote, increasingly inaccessible, in
traditional poetry and in our own. There's an image in a poem of mine about
flies in the middle of the room going around a statue of nothing, and a poet
came to visit me one day and was talking about my poetry being surrealist
and used this image as an example; I said, "Come on," and I took him to a
room and opened the door and said, "Look." There's a whole lot of simple
sensual experience related to the natural world which is becoming a thing of
the past; I don't think this *can* continue indefinitely. I don't see how we can
exist in such an attenuated and deprived context.

Nelson: When you introduce a poem like "Before That," a poem that seems
very open and in some ways gnomic and unstably suggestive, and you gloss
certain lines by identifying their object or their occasion, seeming thereby to
grant the poem a source and the writing process a moment of origin, what
do you feel you've done to the text?
Merwin: I feel that I've obscured it. Because I think that I probably provided
you and anyone who reads the poem with a distraction. The important thing
is to arrive at that insight not through referentiality but through response.
Now of course there would be no response without some kind of reference.
But obviously I didn't feel that the poem should have more reference than
it had when I wrote it. And in a sense putting more "chat" around it than it
had then betrays it. Not that I want for it to be a kind of mystification, or
anything like that. I want it to present a kind of experience in terms which
are not those of the habitual and customary referentiality which is dulled
and blunted and exterior. It *is* a cemetery, you know; it's not *like* a cemetery,
it's not a lot of white things painted on a window. And its sense is the sense
of cemeteries on windows. Just that.

Nelson: Is it just the pressure of a reading, then, wanting to break the
rhythm and make things, at least for a moment, accessible?
Merwin: It's a moment of weakness and friendliness.

Folsom: This whole matter of referentiality, historical allusion, is tricky
business. Specific references in your poetry can be quite explicit when they
are personal or derive from a personal experience. References like that never

become "topical" in the way that references to current events do. Topical things fade in a way that personal references don't.

Merwin: It has to do with a consistent feeling about poetry, and probably about all of the arts, but certainly about my own poetry, which is that no deliberate program for writing a poem works. A poem begins to be a poem when a sequence of words starts giving off what you might describe as a kind of electric charge, when it begins to have a life of its own that I sense the way I would if I suddenly picked up a shorted electric wire. If it doesn't have that, even if it's got what I would very much like it to have, then it's not working as a poem. I suppose all poets work that way in one way or another, but I notice in many of my contemporaries a more deliberate approach to what they want to put in their poems, though they do it differently and in ways that I have never been able to do it. There are many things I would like to write about or to include in poems, but I've never been able to work that way. The life of the language doesn't happen when it's done that way, so I have to wait . . .

I had a conversation with Allen Ginsberg eleven years ago, in New Orleans, when Allen said, "Okay, how would you write a poem about this room?" And I said, "Well, Allen, the difference is that you assume, I guess, that you could write a poem about this room just because you chose to, and I can't make any such assumption. I'm not sure I could write about this room. Perhaps at some point I might be able to, though I wouldn't start necessarily by just jotting down details." It would start with the room, obviously, but we might not agree about what "the room" was. It's a different way of approaching the whole idea of how you write a poem. I'm not sure that I can write a poem just by deliberately setting out to write a poem about, you know, the sofa, or . . . It's a nice idea, but basically there's a part of me that would think, well, you could always do it as an exercise, but if a certain extra dimension isn't there, the brilliance of the exercise won't disguise the fact for very long. This seems to me so obvious that I almost take it for a doctrine, but I realize that there are many poets who don't see it that way at all. I feel that way when I'm reading poems, too. If I can't eventually find that quality there, the poetry bores me.

I think I'm probably often deluded about what I'm doing in my own writing because I keep thinking that I'm getting nearer and nearer to an immediacy of historical detail, and yet when people talk about the poems I realize that may not be their impression. But then for years I thought that I was writing more and more simply and directly, and people kept saying the poems were getting more and more difficult, opaque, harder to read.

Folsom: We've discussed your relationship with Whitman and other American writers, but what poets do you feel the most natural affinity with?

Merwin: My favorite poets, the two that I live with as talismans, are very remote in time and didn't write in English. I would feel even rather diffident about naming them, both out of superstition and awe: François Villon and Dante—not very far apart from each other in time, both medieval poets. And when I began I was fascinated with medieval poetry. I think some of that was due to Pound's influence; I had great admiration for Pound when I was in college. That was partly it; a rebellious stage, because almost no one else admired Pound, and I used to walk around with a beard which I grew just like Pound's. There's one thing that we all owe him, the debt to his way of hearing. That incredible ear runs through much of the *Cantos*. I find them hard to read, not because of intellectual references, which are reason enough, but I keep getting irritated with what the man is saying, the stance, and that cornball American lingo that he keeps lapsing into. But my debt to him began very early.

Whether the affinity with the medieval poets is as close as it was I don't know. I have a debt, as I think everyone does whether they know it or not, to Anonymous; to oral literature as the best one can work toward it. That's the real matrix of possibilities that's always there. I keep saying I'm going to stop translating, and then I find someone else I want to translate. There's still so much possibility that one hasn't touched, found, heard.

Folsom: I'm curious about how your translation work teaches and forms voices for your own poetry, or how much your own poetic voice predetermines the voice of your translations. When you read "The Last One" the other night, you mentioned that you had in mind a creation myth—is that the "Creation of the Moon," which you translated from the Amazon native original? A part of that translation reads, "So the head started to think what it would turn into / If it turned into water they would drink it . . ." and so on. It moves on with that repetitive line structure, and the feel of the poem is very much like "The Last One." Do your translations modify your own voice, or vice-versa? I guess it can't help but work both ways . . .

Merwin: Yes, I think it works both ways. I'm very anxious not ever to do that—and I don't mean this as a pejorative comment on Cal Lowell's work at all—but I never wanted to do what he did; I never wanted to take the work of someone else and use it simply as a springboard for providing poems of my own. And I persuaded myself, for the sake of practice, until the late sixties, and that first book of selected translations, that I did keep them separate. There were various ways of keeping them separate. On the other hand, something that you become involved with as intimately as translation, if you're working at it over a period of time, and something in which you use words as deliberately as you do in translation, is bound to affect your own writing. And besides, what you want to translate is already an indication of an affinity that you had before you found that poem to translate. So I was not ever deliberately looking around in translation for something that I could use as the starting point for poems of mine. Yet that particular kind of movement—the repetitive line structure—that you're describing is an example of something that provided a suggestion, something I wanted to echo, a deliberate allusion.

A great deal of anonymous oral literature seems to me endlessly suggestive, not as something to be imitated, crudely and directly, but as a reminder that the possibilities open to us at any moment are not as limited as we might suppose. The world is not as simple and as codified and conventional as you thought it was. There is even a convention that recurs in oral literature in which the consideration of possibilities becomes itself a kind of form. In one Spanish ballad a girl has had her dead lover for seven years in the room, and she says, "If I tell my father, this will happen; if I tell my mother, this will happen; if I tell my brother, this will happen," and so on. And you can think of many fairy tales in which that happens. I think that's something that you find much less often in written literature than you do in oral literature. Eliot talked about tradition in that way, at least once as I remember it, in a lecture on Dr. Johnson. He was comparing Marlowe and Tennyson, saying as the verse form developed, and as literature developed, in a way it refined itself at the expense of possibility. In the earlier, apparently cruder way of doing it, you have not only a different kind of energy, but you have a different sense of possibility. I think this is one of the things that happen in English—the metrical verse form that was most traditional in English begins at the time of Chaucer with an importation of the romance form of iambic pentameter into a language which is already a mixture. And of course the new meter replaced a basic parallelism in Middle English, which Middle English shared with Hebrew poetry and with a great deal of oral poetry, with a great deal of the poetry of the Americas. I think that parallelism is probably one of the deep basic forms of poetry, perhaps the basic structure of verse, and is never really lost . . .

Nelson: "The Last One" is a poem that's always troubled me a bit, because I've heard you read it before and, with its energy and parallelism and repetition, it's a poem that often generates a murmur of approval and satisfaction from an audience. I tend to suspect that positive reaction, though, because my guess is that people feel the poem gives them a secure moral or ethical vantage point. It's a poem that may seem to be simply in the mode of the conventional science fiction "revenge of the despoiled earth on those who despoiled it." Yet I don't think that's what the poem does. The poem begins "Well they made up their minds to be everywhere because why not," and in a sense the poem in the end makes up *its* mind to be everywhere because why not; or at least the poem, in the voice and manner of the shadow, proceeds to carry out a rhetorical appropriation of the same totalizing, universalizing, covering motion that the possessors begin with as the poem opens. And in that sense—although I think the sense of pain and despair at the kind of ecological tragedy that the poem communicates is not undercut—what *is* undercut, it seems to me, is any secure moral position that we feel we can take in the midst of that catastrophe. Somewhat the same exaltation in power occurs again in "Now It Is Clear" from *The Carrier of Ladders*, which includes the lines "As though I were a great wind / which is what I pray for." The speaker in the poem, and the poem itself in a way, becomes the great wind, as the second half of the poem moves forward. These formal and rhetorical co-optations should force people to call their own moral certainty into question, though at the same time the poems leave that moral certainty as something that is immensely desirable to us.

Merwin: I'm so glad you said that, because my chief doubt about the poem is precisely what you have suggested, that it might be understood as simply saying, from a secure moral vantage point, that *those* people are doing such dreadful things. That's not the poem, as I see it, and I think the index of what I mean is in the last line—with its suggestion that the relation with what the shadow is in the poem has been ignored, despised, thrown away; that's quite as important to me as the science fiction aspect of the narrative. I'm reminded of the line in the psalm, "Yea they despised the pleasant land." The pleasant land was themselves.

Nelson: There are a number of irreducible ironies in that last line, "The lucky ones with their shadows." Are their personal shadows uniquely their own, as they (or we) might like to believe; i.e., are their shadows unlike the consuming, generalizing shadow of the rest of the poem? Or do they each already carry within themselves the semblance, the vestige, of that covering shadow they hope they have escaped?

Merwin: Both. When two people stand together and their shadows run together, whose shadow is whose? Who owns the shadow?

Nelson: We've talked about how translations can help initiate your own poems, but more generally how do your poems *start?* What are the first things that happen as you begin to write? Is it that sense of a certain sequence of words coming alive? Does a line or two come to mind as a first step?

Merwin: There's that sort of excitement coming from somewhere. Sometimes it's not even in words yet; it's just somewhere around. But I never got very far away from that more or less spooky feeling about poetry, you know, that it does have something to do with the muse's presence, as Berryman used to describe it—some really very ancient presence that is referred to and alluded to and invoked again and again in all talk about poetry up until very recently. It's talked about very foolishly very often, and very embarrassingly, but without that presence what the hell are we paying attention to. Without it we're playing an intellectual game and there are some very brilliant intellectual games going on in the world at the moment, but among games it's a matter of taste, not a matter of importance.

Folsom: You mentioned the other day something Berryman said to you when you were nineteen . . .

Merwin: He said, "At this point I think you should get down in a corner on your knees and pray to the muse, and I mean it literally."

Nelson: Once the muse has departed, do you revise a lot?

Merwin: Well, I don't know quite how to answer that, Cary; in a sense, a lot—if I look over a draft of a poem, I see that things have been scratched out and scratched out and scratched out, but actually what I really do is write very slowly, and change it a lot as I'm going on. Although very often getting quite close to the final thing right at the beginning, then making minute verbal adjustments until it seems to come out right. But once it reaches a certain point I very seldom go back to it, except maybe either to throw it out or cut hunks out of it, see if I can do with less, see if I've overwritten it.

Nelson: Do you save chunks that didn't fit in and use them other places?

Merwin: I keep thinking I'm going to, but as a matter of fact I very seldom look at them again.

Folsom: Do you have this same "spooky" feeling when you're about to write a piece of prose? Or is writing prose a very different kind of act for you than writing poetry?

Merwin: It's not a *very* different kind of act. There's something of the same thing there. I can't write anything without that, because I don't know what else holds imaginative language together. And writing anything else, I find it rather boring, wearisome, and a rather depressing process. That doesn't mean that there's not a great deal of labor involved in writing. I find writing very hard, and I find writing prose in particular very hard. It takes a long time before this mass of writing begins to generate an energy of its own that sustains it, keeps it going. But I don't mean a kind of baroque energy either—sometimes the plainer it can be the stronger it is.

Folsom: At what point do you sense when an experience or a feeling will become a poem instead of a piece of prose? I'm curious about what draws certain experiences into prose for you and others into poetry.

Merwin: I'm not sure about that at all. Eleven or twelve years ago when I was starting to write *The Miner's Pale Children* I wondered about that quite a lot, and sometimes I would start to write something as the one and I'd realize it was the other. The differences I still don't know, yet I've come to the conclusion, thinking about this, that the more passion or intensity there is in a piece of writing, whether it is prose or poetry, the more it calls into question the writing's generic allegiance. In other words, the more charged a piece of prose is, the more it tends toward the condition of poetry. Then you begin to describe it as poetic, or you begin to ask what it was that separated it from poetry. And oddly, I think that this happens with poetry too. The more charged poetry is, then the more it's driven to the point where it does some of the things that prose does. I suppose I believe that because to me the ideal poet is Dante, and some of the most powerful passages in Dante are, as Eliot said, rather flat. At least they look rather flat, though you realize they are anything but flat, but the *plainness* of Dante leads you to think it's just like prose, except it's utterly unlike prose.

Nelson: Earlier in your career you were writing poems about your family and about your past, some of them never collected in books. Now you're writing prose pieces about the same things.

Merwin: New poems about them, too.

Folsom: That's what led me to think about that corresponding nature of the prose and poetry, because some of the new poems sound very much as if they are the corollary in poetry of these new prose pieces.

Merwin: Those connections I don't know, of course, because they're not deliberate. As you notice them, or I notice them, then I can guess at what the connections are, but I don't really *know*. One doesn't really know what the connections are between so closely related but obviously distinct things. You don't in your own writing or in your own life.

Nelson: Is there a sense of return, circularity, completion, in coming back to those topics after so many years?

Merwin: There's a sense of it happening, but it's not utterly deliberate, except it was deliberate in that I wanted to deal with that family material in that book of prose, *Unframed Originals*. I've been waiting for two or three years to get circumstances together where I could do it. My notes were in a warehouse and I had no desk to work on, and so forth. A lot of it was done in the house that we were trying to build, before the carpenters would show up in the morning. I'd go down when it got light and work until they arrived about ten o'clock, then stop and start hammering pieces of wood the rest of the day. I never know how to answer those questions about the connections of different writings of the past, because so few of the connections are plotted beforehand. It's like saying, what's the connection in your mind between different parts of a poem—well, you can describe them in terms of the poem, and maybe you set it out beforehand, but maybe it developed as you went along and then you saw what the connection was both as you wrote it and as you look back on it. But a great deal of it is bound to be very subjective, and finally it's not something you can articulate or describe yourself.

Folsom: You've mentioned your fondness for Williams. As you talk about the differences between prose and poetry, Williams is certainly one figure in American literature who has worked with that distinction—or lack of it—quite a bit.

Merwin: Who calls it constantly into question. I think that's a measure of imaginative richness, calling it into question. You don't wonder about it when you're reading Sidney Lanier, but you wonder about it when you're reading Melville. You wonder about it when you're reading Thoreau, whose verse isn't very interesting, but the power of the wonderful passages in *Walden* is the power of poetry. The energy of the language is as intense as anything in nineteenth-century poetry. You have to think of Keats or Hopkins for something comparable.

Folsom: Do you go back to Williams?

Merwin: Yes. But not as a cult figure, as some people do. I go back to him with great affection and reverence. I really do love Williams, and I read him over and over when I was about twenty; I still read him. I go back to him, how shall I say it, as an engraver. It's the visual quality of individual moments in Williams: not the magnificence of the long poem in *Paterson*, but passages in *Paterson* which I see as separate poems, or the early collected poems, *Spring and All* and that period. Or some of the very late poems.

Folsom: *Pictures from Brueghel*?
Merwin: Yes. He's come back to that vein with a wonderful serenity by that point. And such purity of language. The element of Williams which some of his admirers like so much, the "experimental" element, sometimes seems to be just fooling around. Nothing the matter with fooling around, but I don't find myself returning to it irresistibly. But I imagine I will continue to reread parts of Williams with fondness and gratitude.

Folsom: Do you go back to the prose of *Spring and All*, or only the poems?
Merwin: Less to the prose. I don't like his prose so much as the poems that I'm fondest of. And I read the autobiography, but the prose there is often limp.

Folsom: *In the American Grain*?
Merwin: *In the American Grain* is a wonder—I love that.

Nelson: Much of that is beautifully composed prose—sentence by sentence, phrase by phrase.
Merwin: Yes. Many of the Williamsites seem to ignore the element of composition in that great book, probably the most impressive and imposing single book that he wrote.

Nelson: I reread parts of it every year.
Merwin: There's nothing in it like the really exquisite lyrics, but it's there on the shelf with the great American single volumes. It's on my shelf.

Folsom: When I think of Williams and his experimentation, I think of course of the poetic line. Whitman and Williams and Olson and Ginsberg—all have written so much about the poetic line, and all have theories about its origins, which they all associate with breath. The theories probably culminate in Olson's "Projective Verse." Williams talked of dividing the Whitman line into three parts, coming up with the triadic line composed of three variable feet, and so on. What are your thoughts about the origin of the line in your own work? Where does your line emerge from?
Merwin: I think the line is a matter of absolutely essential importance. If the

line is not that important, why is one writing verse in the first place? One of the meanings of verse after all is "a line." Yet one of the ironies of what you just said about Whitman-Williams-Ginsberg is that, though they talked a lot about the line, their tradition has been involved in the demise of the clarity of the line in a great deal of modern and contemporary American verse. It's one of the danger signs in recent verse. There's a huge amount of talent around now, including some really gifted young people coming out of colleges, but some of them have a very shaky sense of what a line is. This is obviously bad for individual poems, but it's also very bad for the possibility of their development as poets or for the development of anything resembling a tradition—even for the continuation of an Olson or a Williams tradition. You can't go anywhere if you're not fairly clear about what a line is. Yet I'm not even sure that I want to say what I think a line is, though I've thought about it. I'll describe how I've taught the topic, though that may prevent me from doing it again.

With students in certain places I've thought it was valuable to try to force them to figure out what they thought a line was. A year and a half ago I was at Oberlin, where the students were very gifted. I read a lot of manuscripts and said, "I'm not going to do the workshop thing of going over your papers and making little suggestions. I don't think that's really the most appropriate thing. What I'd like to do is go around the room and make everybody who wants to be involved in this try to figure out what a line of verse is." After two hours, we hadn't got very far. They realized that they'd never really thought about it. We left it with my saying, "I think this is what you have to think about the next time you stop a line somewhere. At the risk of losing a great deal of spontaneity for a while, you need to look closely, to figure out what in hell you think you're doing: why you stop it after three syllables, why you stop it after two beats, or why you stop it where you do—what are you doing? Are you just writing prose and saying, 'I like it better this way,' or is there really some reason for doing it?"

As far as they could get spontaneously in two hours, these young people who'd read a lot—mostly in their own contemporaries, but they were addressing themselves to poetry with some seriousness—was to realize that a line was a unit of something. What it was a unit *of* was something they couldn't agree on.

Nelson: Do line breaks seem to come to you naturally as you write, or is that one of the things you have to work with to change?
Merwin: Both. And of course there are two things that a line is doing—it's

making a rhythm of its own by means of stopping where it does; and unless you're doing it wrong, unless it's working against you and you've lost it, lost this *line*, it's making a continuity of movement and making a rhythm within a continuity. It's doing those two things at the same time. And this is something that you don't see happening very often in these limp, unheard little bits of prose—lines just tacked one after the other. And their continuity is the continuity of prose. There's no real reason why it should stop at any particular place.

Folsom: Over the years you've used many different lines. Certainly your lines derive in part from your study of various traditions—I suppose this is one thing that takes you back to Pound, his experimentation with different lines. But does line have any association with breath for you?

Merwin: No, I don't think so. It *can*, but I don't think there's any necessary connection. I think of stopping at a given point as a rhythmical gesture, and also as a gesture of meaning—because where you stop, if the rhythm is working, is going to have an effect on the meaning, particularly if you're not punctuating. But it's important to stop in such a way that the stop itself has something to do with impetus. It keeps the motion of the poem going, both in terms of rhythm, sound, and in terms of meaning, denotative meaning.

Nelson: Your control of line breaks is clearly one of the real strengths of your work over a long period of time. It always seems minutely perfect, yet I have the uncanny feeling that it simply comes to you instinctively.

Merwin: I pay a lot of attention to it.

Nelson: You mentioned punctuation. I don't think you've ever talked about your decision not to use punctuation for such a long period of time. It has always seemed absolutely right. I can't imagine the poetry with punctuation, but have you worked out the appeal and the poetics of abandoning punctuation?

Merwin: I don't know about its appeal, but there are various things that led to that decision. I had virtually stopped writing poetry at the end of the fifties, because I felt that I had come to the end of something and that if I wrote again I'd want to do it quite differently. James Wright went through very much the same process, although we never conferred with each other to know that we had both reached that point at the same time. Of course during the time when I wasn't writing, I was thinking about it. There's a passage from Milosz's *The Captive Mind* about the suddenness with which he had this moment of crisis when he was lying on his face on the cobbles with machine gun bullets going around him and friends being herded into trucks, and thinking, what do I want to remember, what poetry has been most important to me, what poetry do I want now, right *now*, this minute? And I thought, I don't ever want to forget this about poetry again: I want to write something to take with me at a bad time. Because we're going to have a bad time from now on.

One of the corollaries of that is that there's a lot you really don't need in poetry. You have to pay attention to things and see what their function is. If there's really no function, what are they doing there? Why are you writing poetry that includes things you really don't need there? This process of trying to see what was unnecessary, of strengthening by compressing and intensifying, of getting down to what was really essential, led me to write poetry that was farther and farther away from conventional stanzaic and metrical structure.

Of course none of this was quite so deliberate. It was part of practice more than theory, and discontent with what I was doing and wanting to articulate the direction in which I was going. I recognized I was moving away from stanzaic verse, but I also saw myself moving farther from prose. So I asked myself what the point was of staying with prose punctuation. Punctuation is there as a kind of manners in prose, articulating prose meaning, but it doesn't necessarily articulate the meaning of this kind of verse. I saw that if I could use the movement of the verse itself and the movement of the line—the actual weight of the language as it moved—to do the punctuation, I would both strengthen the texture of the experience of the poem and also make clear its distinction from other kinds of writing. One would be paying attention to it in those terms. I also noticed something else right away. Punctuation as I looked at it after that seemed to staple the poem to the page, but if I took those staples out the poem lifted itself right up off the page. A poem then had a sense of integrity and liberation that it did not have before. In a sense that made it a late echo of an oral tradition. All this gave the poetry new rules, a new way of being, and I haven't really changed enough to want to give that up.

Someone was asking me the other day about what they called my "broken back" line, the two-part line. I was writing it for a couple of years, and I would still like to feel it is available. Indeed I would like to have it generally available in English. You know, meter is never something permanently absent. I think that line is related to the Middle English line of *Piers Plowman*, which to me is the basic line of English, overlaid—we talked about palimpsests—overlaid, as I said earlier, by the Italianate iambic pentameter. But the caesura in the iambic pentameter is like a ghost of the old Middle English line asserting itself all the time, saying I'm here all the time. I think it's there under what we hear in iambic pentameter. And as the iambic pentameter becomes harder and harder to hear or to stay awake through in contemporary poetry, I think the other, the deeper, older line is something one, with the slightest effort, might be able to hear again.

The difference between that line and iambic pentameter, I think, is a traditional one. Iambic pentameter, because of the long tradition, developed a flexibility which the Middle English line never did. The flow-on qualities of enjambment in iambic pentameter became incredibly varied, but eventually they played themselves out, so that there's hardly a meter there at all. By the time you get to someone like Conrad Aiken you're writing essentially a kind of vers libre. But the enjambment of the Middle English line never developed that way, didn't last long enough probably. If you take up something that is like a continuation of it, it seems a little stiff, but it can do things that iambic pentameter probably can't. And I don't even think of that line with the heavy caesura as a strict meter in the way Pope would have thought of iambic pentameter, but as a different kind of pattern or paradigm.

Folsom: The caesura obviously controls breath—when you read a line, the line controls your breathing. Maybe this has to do with what you were saying the other day—that one problem with "projective verse" as a theory is not that it assigns too much importance to breath, but not enough.
Merwin: But the pauses in verse are not necessarily the pauses of breath, breathing. If the pauses of verse are exactly the pauses of anything else, it becomes boring. It has to have its own pauses.

I like some of Olson's poems very much, but I never cottoned onto that "projective verse." As I remember it, he talks about projective verse and its relation to breath, but it seems to me truistic: the relation of poetry to breath is absolute. And you can come at it from any angle you want to. He talks about it in a rather limited way—that outbreathing and inbreathing in themselves are a kind of metric. I think it's far more complicated, so I doubt that there's much to be gained in pursuing that particular argument.

Nelson: Different poetry teaches you to breathe in different ways. As you read it there's a learning process; you adjust to it. But I've never seen any way of treating Olson's line as the equivalent of a single breath.
Folsom: Ginsberg is probably the one who has come closest to trying to sug-

gest that that's absolutely true, that he breathes a line and when his breath is out he moves to the next line.

Nelson: But it takes a tremendous effort to pull that off, and when he reads in public it's by no means easy to establish that relationship in any literal way.

Merwin: Yes, and that also rules out something which is inseparable from it and in a sense more interior or inward—the whole role of hearing, listening, both in writing and in reading or listening. The Ear—the fact that the body is the ear. Breathing also is a way of hearing; they're not separate. But if it's just physical breathing, what role do the ear and listening play?

Folsom: What's Olson's physiological formula—the Head, by way of the Ear, to the Syllable; the Heart, by way of the Breath, to the Line. Part of his idea, at any rate, is that the *syllable* is what the ear has to do with, not the line. The line has to do with the breathing.

Merwin: I don't see that at all, because I think one of the things that happen with all units in verse, in poetry, is tension. There's always one element playing against another one, whether or not it's metrical. In conventional verse the line is made of variations on the iambic pentameter pattern, so you have the pattern and the variation playing against each other, and the tension resulting—and that's one way of seeing the vigor and the energy in the line. And I think this is true in every kind of metric, whether it's conventional and regular or whether it's what you could call organic. There are always going to be two sorts of forces playing against each other: an expectation and either an answering, a refusing, or a variant on the expectation. The expectation sets up a sense of repetition. You either fulfill the repetition or you don't. That tension runs through the making of lines or the making of stanzaic paragraphs, for the whole poem.

Folsom: That same pattern of expectation and variation is also apparent in the overall rhythm of each of your books as well. Has there been any single one of your books that has affirmed itself to you as *a* book, as a complete thing, more than the others, or do they all have a similar sense of completion?

Merwin: They all do, particularly since *The Drunk in the Furnace.*

Folsom: Including *The Drunk in the Furnace*?

Merwin: Including *The Drunk in the Furnace.* The first three seem to be much more gatherings, but they too each finish with the end of a phase. Of course I don't feel that close to them now.

Nelson: Still, the idea of putting them all together in a collected volume seems inappropriate. I like them as separate objects, even the first four books. But I certainly don't want *The Lice* in the same volume as *The Compass Flower.* They're separate books to me.

Merwin: I don't really either. What do you think about a *Selected Poems*?

Nelson: I can't think of any reason to do it.

Merwin: Well, I've resisted it, because I would not like to undercut the separate books.

Nelson: It may be that if you grow with the poetry and live through the period of time when the poet is actually writing you have a strong feeling of loyalty toward the individual books. Fifty years from now most readers would probably just as well have a *Collected Merwin.* With Yeats, although I am conscious of the huge differences among the books, I'm perfectly happy to have the *Collected Poems.* People who collected the separate volumes, however, often prefer to read them in that form.

Merwin: Yes, but Yeats has been collected in the only way that it would make any sense to me. If I were ever collected I would want it done that way, where you're very much aware of the books as divisions. And you'd have to do that with Lowell too, you know, although all of Cal's fooling around with *History* and *Notebooks* presents problems. Nonetheless, you'd want his books very distinct—you wouldn't want *Lord Weary's Castle* and *Life Studies* combined into something like a *Collected Browning.*

Folsom: One thing that gives your books each a very separate identity is the titles. You tend not to title your books after the name of a poem that is in the book, although you did with *The Drunk in the Furnace.*

Merwin: "The Drunk in the Furnace" is really the kind of poem that is about everything the book is about. Generally, though, I don't do that. I guess I made up my mind about it in a conversation with Bill Arrowsmith a long time ago. I'm not proposing this for everybody, but for me a title should contribute something important. So that if you took a poem's title away, it would be missing something. The title should not just be a redundancy. Of course the relation between a poem and its title is far more specific and intimate than the relation between a book and its title, but the title of a book should still make a significant contribution.

Folsom: Because of the nature of your book titles, the reader is forced to carry the title through each poem, and to allow the juxtaposition of the title of the book and any particular poem to play itself out. The titles of your books force the reader to come to grips with the book as an interrelated whole. At what point do titles for your books come to you?

Merwin: I think it's been different. Sometimes I've hung around for a while, listening for one to come, waiting for it. I had a superstition, in the days when I was writing plays, that if I got my title too soon, especially if I got the title before I started to write, that I'd never get the play finished. In any case, there's no point in rushing it. I suppose one reason I know the new collection isn't finished is that I don't have a title for it yet.

The title for *The Lice* came fairly early. It jumped out of that passage in Heraclitus while I was working on the poems. *The Moving Target*, on the other hand, came late. I know that I've got several pages of false attempts at that title. I was also a time waiting for the title to *Writings to an Unfinished Accompaniment*, trying to figure out what on earth is the title of this collection. With *The Compass Flower*, however, I had the title before the book was finished.

Nelson: Do you save notes for titles and drafts of poems?

Merwin: I keep all the drafts now. I still have some of the old things I wrote in college, but for a while after that, I destroyed things. Then Graves told me to save everything and since then I have.

Folsom: Can you reconstruct the process you go through to come up with a retrospective title like *Writings to an Unfinished Accompaniment*? Do you think through the poems in some way?

Merwin: I wasn't thinking at all; I was sitting and waiting for the title. I can remember the chair and the room in Mexico. Of course I was doing other things as well, but ten days went by before the title came. When I got back to New York, Adrienne Rich said, "What are you going to call the new book," and I told her, and she said, "That's it, that's what we all want to write." Those were happier days.

A Conversation with W. S. Merwin

Daniel Bourne / 1982

From *Artful Dodge* (College of Wooster) 3.3 (Fall 1982). Reprinted by permission.

Daniel Bourne: Your poem on Berryman last night was interesting. It seemed rather un-Merwinlike, a very traditional focus, little elliptical movement. Is this a kind of departure, something new, or a return to the roots of an earlier literature, with that kind of poem?

W. S. Merwin: I have no idea. I don't have any ideological sense of what is Merwinlike or un-Merwinlike. I'm always happy to find I'm writing a poem which is different from anything I've written before, but I don't think you can really write out a paradigm. To be surprised is to find new directions and new regions you haven't been into yet, to be surprised by your own writing, that's what I would always be hoping for.

DB: Does that poem surprise you more than any other poem you've written recently?

Merwin: No. I don't feel that very much about my own writing. I very much don't want to repeat myself or imitate myself or find myself doing something I've already done before. If anything feels as if that's what's happening, then I try to move away from it.

DB: Do you see yourself coming from any springboard as a poet or translator? Did you start with any first principles? Or how long was it until they developed?

Merwin: Probably very few first principles. I started out realizing I didn't know very much and still don't know very much. At some distance, translation obviously has always been of great importance to me. I went to see Ezra Pound when I was nineteen or so. He told me something that I think I really already knew. He said that it was important to regard writing as not a chance or romantic or inspired, (in the occasional sense) thing, but rather a kind of spontaneity which arises out of discipline and continual devotion to something; and translation is a way of keeping one close to what one is doing, to the possibilities of one's own language. I don't translate very much anymore, but for years I tried to translate all the time, a certain amount, and just how that's affected my writing, I don't know. I didn't try to imitate while I was translating or anything like that. The familiarity with one's medium, a familiarity with language and with the practical details of dealing with tension and language which come out of translating, I think, are of great importance to me in writing. What I've chosen to translate is as much a matter of affinity that I recognize as I went along as it is an influence on what I actually wrote. I'm sure it's worked both ways, but I haven't tried to follow it. Just as I don't really theorize much about my own writing, I don't even pay too much analytical attention to it. What I'm really interested in is not what I've written but what I haven't written, the next poem, if there is one. I don't know if there is a next one. It's the part that doesn't know that I believe it comes from, if it comes at all. I don't do it by forming an idea of what the next poem is supposed to be or what kind of poem it's supposed to be or where it's supposed to go, or anything of the kind.

DB: Are you afraid that there won't be another poem?

Merwin: I feel that it's quite possible there won't be another one. I hope there will be. But I don't understand people who can program themselves to the point where they can predict another one. Of course, you can sit down after years of discipline and years of writing and you can write a poem. What kind of poem is it going to be if it is as deliberate as that? I don't want to sound spooky or romantic about it either. I think that the sitting down and trying to write is terribly important, the regularity with which one works. If you do try to write regularly, you will notice that the results are irregular. There are times when you just can't stop writing. Everything contributes to it. I suspect that everything is contributing to it all the time, but there are long periods when it seems very hard to put words together that are at all satisfactory, that are doing what you want them to do. These things come in waves or cycles.

DB: You said that translation seems to be able to serve as that disciplinary force.

Merwin: An example, I guess, of what I'm saying is that in the late fifties, after *The Drunk in the Furnace*, there was a period when I knew perfectly well I wasn't going to write for a while. There wasn't anything I could write that didn't seem to me to be simply a continuation of what I'd been writing before. I didn't want to do that. It seems to me that I had to come to the end of a way of doing something. And then when I began to write again, I wrote about half of *The Moving Target* in a few weeks.

DB: You said that you translated those works towards which you felt a strong affinity. I noticed that your translations of Jean Follain and Antonio Porchia are definitely not the broad cultural works you translated earlier. (*Merwin: Those were done in the mid-sixties, too.*) Is there some kind of movement from the broader appeal . . . ?

Merwin: No, in most cases they were people whom I found and they weren't very well known. Antonio Porchia wasn't known at all in this country. I found a not very satisfactory French translation of him by accident. That led me to write off and get the Spanish original. I took to carrying it around wherever I went. I was fascinated by Antonio Porchia. Since I couldn't remember some of the Spanish aphorisms, I found myself making little notes in English in the margins, which I could remember for reference. These gradually turned into translations and I found I had translated about half the book. That was how I did the Porchia. Again, there was no schematic or programmed view of what I should be doing. This is one of the problems with a lot of literary history. Critics tend to assume that writers work out some sort of program for themselves, that it (writing) is much more calculated than it is. If it's any good, talent or the gift of somebody is an urgency, a moving force, and all one can do is try to direct it, and hope that it stay there, and keep it fed and alive, and alert, awake. . . . I don't know much about fiction writers, of course. My small experience with writing with the theater is rather different. But with all of them, I think there is a great, I almost said blindness, a movement that begins out of what you don't know rather than what you think you should be doing next. It's not some kind of intellectually calculated program that you conform to. Faulkner says in several places that *The Sound and the Fury* really began with an image in his mind of that little girl's wet panties as she was climbing down out of the apple tree. The whole novel came out of this image. Where did this image come from? Heaven knows . . . Faulkner's own imagination. But the image was first and the whole thing rose out of that. I think if it is too calculated there's something fishy about it (writing). Frost says that about individual poems. If you know too much about a poem to begin with, you'll probably write a phony poem. I think there is a danger in writing a lot of so-called political poetry. I said yesterday I think all poetry is political. But most political poetry doesn't turn out to be poetry in the long run because you have double-guessed about it too much to begin with, you know too much about it. You know what it's supposed to be saying, apart from the poem itself, what its message is going to be. If it arises out of a real feeling for rage or oppression or something that's close to visceral experience, then it saves itself, it becomes a real poem, a piece of propaganda.

DB: You speak so much about sound. Is that the basic unit you strive to transpose in translation? Do you think it's more important than metaphor?
Merwin: I think that's one place where I do believe in being calculating and programmed in translation . . . deciding what aspect it is of translation that one really wants to make in the new language. I think that it is very seldom sound. I think usually the sound itself is pretty obvious although it's missed again and again by both critics and translators. I think really the sound is part of the original language, just as I think the sound plus the form is part of the original language and all the association that goes with it. What one can try to transpose is the *role* of the sound. What is the function of the sound? How important is it? What does it do to the effect, the power of the poem? I see if I can remake that function in the translation.

DB: How close do you think translation of syntax is tied up with translation of sound?
Merwin: I don't know that there is an answer to that because it depends wholly on whom you're translating. In the original, sound and syntax are inseparable, if you're translating a really accomplished and interesting first-degree magnitude poet. But in translation, they're bound to be separate because the sound is part of the original language and the role of the syntax in the original language is not the same as the language into which you're translating. But it's related to the value of translating as an exercise, I think. The ability to have some kind of flexibility of syntax, to recognize the enormous importance of the different syntactical ways of trying to say something, each of which is slightly different, is something that's being lost sight of, I think, in the educational system. Students come to the point where they think they want to write and they have very little syntactical experience, very little dramatic education. They reach a certain point where they feel there's only one way of saying anything. The obvious way, the way one is used to saying it, may not be the right way of saying it. Unless there's been a real education in the grammar of your language, translation helps you to finish your education. Otherwise, the choices that are open to you are much

more limited and you feel they are the only choices. That's too bad. It means you can hear only a few choices, that your ear is closed off to all kinds of possibilities. I don't know the answer to this. It's right there in the educational system and in the fact that English is taught so badly now. It goes along with the way vocabulary is getting imprecise, not just in our speech but in our writing. The example I was using is where "convinced" is used more and more often when the person really means "persuaded." "I convinced him to take the afternoon plane rather than the other one." What the person means is, "I persuaded him to take the afternoon plane."

DB: In a way then, the acquisition of good syntax and varied ways of saying something is almost as important as the image.

Merwin: Well, it's a tool. It's like trying to be a fine carpenter when your only hammer is a six-pound sledge and you have a cold chisel. You're going to have a hell of a time, you're handicapped. I think this is related to the matter of the life of the language coming out of colloquial speech. In real vernacular, in real colloquial speech, there's always the energy of the language and we know of contemporaries, critics, and writers, who insist that one must have the colloquial and not the formal or that one must have the control of the form that the colloquial line is put in. I think these are poles which make the tension in which the language operates and the literature can be written. You can't let go of either one without the tension just all disappearing, one must honor them both, absolute energy of colloquial speech, as long as it has not been totally debased by debasing uses of it, such as advertising, communal abstractions, committee English, and things of that kind, and on the other hand, the honoring of the tradition of the language itself and its formal possibilities. They're both assumptions of the life of the language, into the life of what we can write in the language.

DB: When translating *Lazarillo de Tormes*, were you seeking an idiom, and what do you think of rendering local color in translations?

Merwin: I wasn't trying to imitate or invent any particular locality. I think in some ways it was one of the most difficult translations I ever did. It led me to realize the importance of translating comedy. Translation of comedy is one of the great disciplines I know of, because if you are translating jokes, for example, if you get anything wrong, nothing works. You have to get it absolutely right. Then you realize that all translating is really that way. With *Lazarillo de Tormes*, I was trying to get that. These are several things happening. This was a very literate man who wrote *Lazarillo*, and that's very evident in the book, but also he's writing in the voice of a fully formed and funny character, a kind of much harder, much more difficult Huckleberry Finn. It's sort of the original form from which the other picaresque people descended later. I imagine *Huckleberry Finn* is certainly in this tradition, whether Mark Twain was aware of any of the others or not. I certainly wasn't trying to make him sound like Huckleberry Finn but there's a real closeness between those two characters.

DB: Did that book come before Boccacio's *Decameron*?
Merwin: No, I don't think so. The *Decameron* was earlier.

DB: I thought there was a lot of picaresque in that book.
Merwin: But's there's no single character. *Lazarillo* is the original pica-resque because it's the original role-hero going from episode to episode. The only continuity is one character who goes from one episode to another. I think it's one of the first books in literature which actually does that and has a character who, by the standards of the society around him, is a rogue, in all senses a rogue. He's an outsider and an oddball. Lazarillo is also a very winning and touching character, I think, very funny. The whole book is full of those ironies which Cervantes uses not so very long afterwards in *Don Quixote*, which are also virtually untranslatable. The subtlety of Cervantes's irony is one of the things that is lost in translation. I wasn't trying to make him sound like Huck Finn or something like that. He had to sound like a child, very intelligent, very straight, a very courageous and funny child.

DB: Do you feel that maybe the key in translating that book was the voice?
Merwin: Absolutely.

DB: You mentioned last night about the heavy impact of reading Czeslaw Milosz's *The Captive Mind.* Why do you think that during a period like the sixties (which was very political), the book did not really get any attention?
Merwin: I simply don't know. I think that the only theory that I have about it is that Milosz was so critical of the Communist world and there was a great deal of leftist sympathy in the sixties. For example, the SDS-oriented people felt that Milosz was right-wing just as many Marxists felt about Camus and *The Rebel.* I've always felt that this was wrong, I mean in the sense of being incorrect. There's a kind of outlawry that I have been drawn to all my life which is not doctrinaire, which is neither right nor left. In fact, it's opposed to them both. Every time I come back toward a political stance, I never stay

in one very long, because every time I move toward one, I tend to partake of that anarchy, a suspicion of all their houses. That's the only explanation I can think of as to why Milosz was not accepted more widely and was not read more widely in the sixties. I don't remember when *The Captive Mind* was published, 1958, 1959, somewhere along in there. I know some of my friends read it and were excited about it at the time and it just seemed to disappear. I think it went out of print, too. It's been out of print for a long time because I've tried to get copies of it for my friends and couldn't find it.

DB: The seventies seemed a time of political relaxation, or at least part of it did. Was it for you? Do you think your poetry seemed to turn away a bit . . . ?
Merwin: It depends on what you mean by politics. If you mean concern with the manipulation of human beings by other human beings, if you want to define it that way, you could say that's true. I was trying to say last night that what's happening to the world, what organized human activity is doing to the world, is that same thing it's doing to language and culture around us and to other cultures, to other people and species. The natural world, as a whole, is all the same thing, and to me it's all political. One picks it up where one feels most strongly and most immediately about it. Sometimes I feel more immediately concerned with what's happening to the elements, the sea, the animals, the language, than I do with any particular society. I don't make a distinction. The poisoning of the soil, the imminence of nuclear disaster, are absolutely the same thing. You shut your eyes and you open them and you're staring at the same thing, but the form of it looks different. Here you are at a different movie but it's all the same thing.

DB: Do you think you are influenced or have any sort of affinity for Robinson Jeffers?
Merwin: It's been a long time since I read him, and I may be very unfair and I love some of Robinson Jeffers. But there seemed to me to be a kind of relishing of his misanthropy, a kind of hugging to himself of a bitterness which really, I thought, in the long run, was egocentric, feeling very superior to the world around him, to the human race, a real kind of hatred of it. I don't feel close to that at all. I certainly feel it with a sense of elation or relief but one of great sadness, a feeling that if I stay there it would be a kind of moral defeat. One really has to find a way to move out of there. One doesn't stay in nihilism, I think.

DB: In many ways, both of you seem to be dealing with the same thing or the same perspective, but that you're both attacking in completely different ways.

Merwin: The one thing I feel close to is his sense of our self-importance as a species, which I think is one of the things which is strangling us, our own bloated species-ego. The assumption that human beings are different in kind and in importance from other species is something I've had great difficulty in accepting for twenty-five years or so. To me, it's a dangerously wrong way of seeing things. I think that our importance is not separable from the importance of all the rest of life. If we make the distinction in a too self-flattering way, if we say we are the only kind of life that's of any importance, we automatically destroy our own importance. Our importance is based on a feeling of responsibility and awareness of all life, the fact that we are a part of the entire universe and our importance is not different from the importance of the rest of the universe. We're not in that way the only valuable and interesting thing to have appeared in the universe.

DB: Would you answer the criticism that's been leveled about there not being any people in your poems with the fact that this perspective on your work might arise out of Anne Sexton-Sylvia Plath analysis-type poetry?

Merwin: I don't know where it comes from. I can see where it comes from in some of the poems, I suppose. It seems to me that people who make the criticisms have been reading other critics rather than reading the poet, generally. Are there any people in poems like "Western Wind" or "Ode to Melancholy"? Are there people-less poems? A poem that is made of human language and human perception and refers to human experience has people in it, I think. Whether it has drama in it, whether there are people in the third person is another matter. I think the first and second person are more common in my poems, probably, than the third person. This may be what whoever it was who first said that had in mind. Do you think there are people in the poems?

DB: One of my favorite poems of yours is "A Letter from Gussie." That has people in it. I think it's a very clever and human poem. So I really don't agree with the criticism at all. But I'd like to switch over to talking about the genre confusion that's going on now in poetry and prose and what you have said about it. Recently I was rereading William Burroughs's *Naked Lunch* and I sensed that he was consciously taking the narrative further away from poetry even though he used poetic diction. I was wondering if you could say some more about what you said last night, how you're trying to separate the narrative from the poetry.

Merwin: I wasn't suggesting that narrative is anti-poetic at all. I don't even think of prose as being anti-poetic. What I was suggesting is that I think that the more imaginative intensity there is in poetry or in prose, the more it calls in question the difference between poetry and prose, so that if you get a great deal of intensity in prose, rhythms begin to emerge, powerful rhythms, and various things happen in the texture so that people begin to say it's poetic, whatever they mean by that. If there's great intensity in po-etry, sometimes it leads toward a rhetorical thickening of texture, but some-times it drives the poetry toward a greater and greater surface simplicity so that it begins to seem almost like prose. The example that I was giving was Dante—an enormous freight of meaning and experience and enormous in-tensity. As Eliot said somewhere, if you imitate Shakespeare, you're going to get inflated, but if you imitate Dante the worst thing that's going to happen is that it may sound a little flat. I'm trying to say that from either side great intensity follows this shifting, this undefinable boundary in question. What is the difference between poetry and prose? You can make a definition, but it's not going to be applicable forever in all circumstances. This confusion arises out of the fact that the old categories are getting in the way rather than helping to direct and to provide energy. I don't mean that I think there are never going to be categories, but we're going to have to remake them, or else they're going to form themselves again.

DB: I guess what I was trying to get at was the decisions you made back twenty years or so when you evolved the absence of punctuation and you were doing things that tried to make your work more poem-like.
Merwin: I was trying to do things that I suppose poets always try to do. I was trying to write more directly, and in that sense more simply. One of the ironies of that was, there were critics who immediately and for a long time called poetry hopelessly obscure. They thought it was simply willfully obscure and that I was trying to write incomprehensible poetry. I was really trying to make it more direct but at the same time more inclusive, to make it contain more experience and to transmit it more directly in words and do it in a way that carried more of the cadences of pure language, of speech.

DB: Were there any poetics that you can think of behind why you started using what I call the "gapped-line"?
Merwin: You mean just a few years ago? Yes, we were talking about that yesterday. I realized that the predecessor, not even the predecessor (I think of it as the subterranean tradition) of English prosody is the Middle English line that was overlaid at the time of Chaucer, by Chaucer, a great genius who

brought this Romance meter into English and did it so brilliantly and beauti-fully. It became the classical meter of English. But it is an importation and I think the Middle English line is absolutely native to English and it's been there all along. I think that it is even deeper and older than that. I think it is a manifestation of a parallelism that is the basic structure of verse in most languages that I know anything about. I was simply trying to pick that up and use it in a way that would make it available to me and possibly suggest to others that this was every bit as native to our language and consequently as legitimately useful to us as iambic pentameter, which is rather a weary form when most people use it nowadays. It carries a terrible freight of habit, of mere habit, although I think that students should read an awful lot of it and write an awful lot of it to start, to be able to master it, to be able to hear it, to be able to talk it if they have to. Otherwise these bits of the tradition are liable to come as ghosts and use us rather than our using them. Stevenson used to complain about that, that he couldn't write prose without its being filled with iambic pentameter.

An Interview with W. S. Merwin

David L. Elliott / 1984

Originally published in *Contemporary Literature* 29.1 (Spring 1988), 1–25. © 1988 by the Board of Regents of the University of Wisconsin System. Reproduced by the permission of the University of Wisconsin Press. This interview took place on October 3, 1984, in Merwin's Greenwich Village apartment in New York City.

Elliott: I'd like to start with a brief excerpt from Auden's foreword to your first book, *A Mask for Janus*, where he talks about your "concern for the traditional conceptions of Western culture as expressed in its myths" [ix]. Did you agree with that statement then, and whether you did then or not, do you now think it an accurate assessment of your very earliest career, with the emphasis on Western?

Merwin: Auden was pointing out something that I hadn't thought of as a program, obviously, and I would agree with it now, but my notion of what myth means would be very different from what I thought it meant when I was in my early career. I now think that myth is something like the intuition of a kind of coherent sense of experience, which we can't live without. But it is our own projection. It is real in the sense that it's necessary. To us.

Elliott: Was there then a shift from thinking of myth as something borrowed, something received or transmitted from a past culture, to a sense of the mythic consciousness in one's own mind, which is capable of creating modern myth?

Merwin: Yes. I think that any real use of language is mythic in some sense. Language is myth. Language is the articulation of myth.

Elliott: Did any of the change in your attitude toward myth come from exploring primitive mythology through some of the poetry you were translating?

Merwin: I'm sure it did, but I'm sure that everything contributed to it, and to thinking I had had enough to do with myth and wanted to look in other directions, realizing that mythology really informed everything, that mythology was not merely something you learned in school that the Greeks had to make statues to illustrate a couple of thousand years ago. It is everything that helps us to make sense of the world.

Elliott: Did you come to feel that, for all of its perceptiveness in many realms of life, Greek myth was becoming somehow inadequate as a means of coming to terms with certain problems of contemporary civilization, such as the possible extinction of nature or the extinction of man?

Merwin: Maybe. But I think that all of the mythologies come from a place that is so deep that they really do deal with experiences very remote from their original statements. For a long time, for example, it seemed to me that the myths of Phaëthon and Orpheus were complementary ways of looking at two different attitudes toward the world that we still find around us. One is the Orphic one, which evokes a harmonious relation with the whole living world. And the myth of Phaëthon, of course, is a myth based on ego, envy, and exploitation, in which you try to take the chariot into the sun and drive it whether you can drive it or not, and you end up by destroying what you drive over and being destroyed yourself.

Elliott: Was there a point at which oriental myth became important to you in a way that it hadn't been before?

Merwin: Gradually, yes.

Elliott: Is there a sense in which Buddhism and Zen require a different attitude toward myth from the traditional Western attitude? People are fond of making distinctions between the Eastern mind and the Western mind, sometimes too facilely, but do you find a different approach to myth in Buddhism?

Merwin: Oh, it's certainly different. I'd be shy of trying to describe the difference. And, of course, myths are used differently in different traditions of Buddhism, particularly Mahayana. In Theravada the main myth is the myth of the historic Buddha, whatever we know of the historic Buddha. Mahayana Buddhism is highly mythological but also highly abstract. On the other hand, some of the koans that are used in Zen are myth, are folktales.

Elliott: I'd like to read a passage from your foreword to Robert Aitken's *A

Zen Wave: "there has been no presentation of Bashō's work, and the experience of which it is a manifestation, in terms of the particular cast of Bashō's
religious insight into his world and ours. To underestimate this aspect of
Bashō's writing and his life is to risk missing what he himself evidently took
to be the center of them both, the essence of his nature and his art, and the
secret of the relation between them" (11). Do you feel that the same statement can now or could from the start be made about your poetry?

Merwin: I don't think it could have been made at the beginning. I'm not
even sure it could be now. I think the danger of a statement like that is a
sort of sectarian interpretation, so that you have to understand the kind of
ideology that the poems are coming from before you can really understand
them. Dōgen, for example, refused to call Zen *Zen.* I mean he called Zen
Zen, but he kept saying, "We must not even think of this as Buddhism. It
is the awakened way that we are talking about. We're talking about being
awake." And I think this is really the link between that kind of experience
and the poetry of Bashō or any real poetry that is not simply decorative. One
is trying to project and articulate an insight about experience itself—about
the experience of being.

Elliott: But is the demonstration or assertion of the importance of an awakened vision something you would take now to be central to your work?

Merwin: Yes. I mean I'm trying to make sense of things. It is very easy to get
drawn off into a metaphysical discussion of it, which I don't think is much
help, and I wouldn't want to convey the impression at all that I thought that
in order to understand anybody's poems, including mine, one had to have
a particular point of view. I don't think, for example, this is true of Dante.
One doesn't have to be a Catholic for *The Divine Comedy* to go on inform-
ing one's life. One doesn't need to get any closer to orthodox Christianity
for that to be so, or I don't believe that one does. I feel great obligation and
gratitude to Dante, and I am not a Christian.

Elliott: I understand your point. It would be entirely possible for somebody
to read your work and not have any idea that Buddhism was an interest of
yours, and yet an understanding of Buddhism indicates that there are some
parallels or influence there.

Merwin: But I think that it is there in many bodies of poetry where I, at
least, wasn't aware of it. For example, although it didn't occur to me at the
time I was translating him, there is something of that same insight in the
work of Jean Follain. Whether it had any sectarian nourishment or not, I

don't know—he had a certain amount to do with Trappist contemplatives. But I think it is far more common than one is led to expect. That is one of the disadvantages of making this easy distinction between East and West and then waving a flag over one of them. I mean any time in any of the arts—and after all, this is almost the condition of an art—that you make the absolutely specific and unique instance of something a representative of *everything*, you're giving voice to that insight, and it doesn't matter whether you do it from a Christian point of view or from a supposedly atheist point of view or from a Buddhist point of view or a Hindu point of view. It really doesn't matter.

Elliott: In the poems of *The Moving Target*, *The Lice*, and *The Carrier of Ladders* there seems to be the expression of much suffering—both personal suffering, in statements like "my mind is divided" and so on, and also, of course, cultural, political, and ecological suffering, the suffering of nature. I'm wondering if that was an expression of the frame of mind that was leading you to an interest in Buddhism.
Merwin: Probably, yes. I think it was certainly all part of the same movement. There were personal things that had to do with finding my way through some years that involved quite a number of decisions. I mean some quite obvious ones involving New York and living in the city or the country, but also with regard to America, the alien past and the alien present. And certainly, most of *The Lice* was written at a time when I really felt there was no point in writing. I got to the point where I thought the future was so bleak that there was no point in writing anything at all. And so the poems kind of pushed their way upon me when I wasn't thinking of writing. I would be out growing vegetables and walking around the countryside when all of a sudden I'd find myself writing a poem, and I'd write it, and that was the way most of *The Lice* was written.

Elliott: It seems to have been a prolific time in your life in terms of poetic output.
Merwin: It did happen rather fast, yes. A lot of *The Lice* was written in a couple of years. I don't feel much more optimistic about the historic aspect of our experience than I did then, but people have been saying how the more recent poetry seems more calm. I feel, I suppose, that the place of saying something is a little bit different from what I thought it was then. We're born and we very soon know that we are going to die. That's not a reason not to live with it, however. But the feeling of distress and anger and grief

that is there in *The Lice* is there really through all of the poems. I don't know of any way of shrugging it off. I don't see that our culture and our species are behaving in a more enlightened and gentle and harmonious fashion now than we were twenty years ago. And the cause of the anger is, I suppose, the feeling of destruction, watching the destruction of things that I care passionately about. If we're so stupid that we choose to destroy each other and ourselves, that's bad enough; but if we destroy the whole life on the planet! And I'm not talking about a big bang; I'm talking about something that is happening as we are sitting here talking about it—the destruction of the seas, the destruction of species after species, the destruction of the forests. These are not replaceable. We can't suddenly decide years down the line that we made a mistake and put it all back. The feeling of awe—something that we seem to be losing—is essential for survival.

Elliott: Is the overcoming of your feeling that writing was not to the point or impossible related in any way to that Buddhist paradox: because something is impossible and because you acknowledge that it is impossible, you are thereby enabled to try to do it anyway?
Merwin: It's always impossible in some place. I mean poetry is impossible, speech is impossible, life is probably impossible, but we go on living. The bee can't fly, but it doesn't know it, so it flies happily along. An easier way to say something about it is to evoke a passage from Thoreau. Somewhere in the journals, he is talking with grief about the enclosure of the Concord Common, and he says, people won't be able to let their animals roam as they please, and won't be able to pick huckleberries. It will no longer be a free place. It will belong to somebody. And he is very eloquent, as he always is about that. But then he says the other thing. He says, I was not sufficiently aware of it; I didn't pay enough attention; I didn't love it hard enough when I had it. I think it is possible to pay so much attention to how angry we are that we forget why we are angry; and if we are angry for any reason except because we want to save things that we love and can't pay attention to the fact that we do love them, then we've helped to destroy ourselves at the root.

Elliott: So is it a matter of becoming nonattached to anger? Do you feel that in the sixties anger became so much an end in itself that it was counterproductive and not pushing something forward that might have helped the problems you were concerned about?
Merwin: You always are a little frustrated. The part of you that writes poems hoping that it will make something happen, which is the part of you that's

writing propaganda, is always there. Poetry isn't so pure that it's completely devoid of that. You wouldn't want it to be. Pure poetry is an antimacassar, isn't it? It's a decoration. You do want something to happen, even if it is only to get somebody to move something. When we wrote poems during the Vietnam war, we wanted the poems to stop the war. When you write a poem out of grief, what do you want? We still don't know, but we are trying to complete something that we feel is incomplete.

Elliott: I would like to stay with that period of the sixties for a little while. Does the term "deep image" have any meaning for you?
Merwin: I can remember when Jerry Rothenberg and Jerry's friends talked a lot about deep image back in the early sixties and late fifties. It means something in a historical sense. But I always thought they were loading the term unnecessarily. I thought that what they were really talking about was an image that came from where all real images come from, which is not out of the footnotes or wholly out of the promptings of other poems, but out of the oddities and uniqueness of one's own experiences. A real image always comes from that singular "deep" place, dripping with surprise. Coleridge talked about the difference between fancy and imagination, and I think what Coleridge meant by imagination was pretty much what Jerry meant by deep image, where the disparate becomes one—the apparently disparate is seen as a whole. There is a real moment of fusion, of heat, and of urgency involved.

Elliott: For better or worse, at that time the term seemed to gather into it the connotations of a quasi-surrealism.
Merwin: Yes, that always bothered me a little. I mean I have never been as fond of surrealism as some people were in the sixties. I think surrealism was absolutely essential to read and pay attention to, but it's a place I never wanted to get stuck in. To me, almost all surrealism tends to become very two-dimensional. Some depth missing.

Elliott: There often tends to be a kind of arbitrariness about surrealism.
Merwin: The very thing it says it's avoiding. It used to make me impatient to be called a surrealistic poet. When many critics don't understand how metaphor works, they decide that it's surrealistic.

Elliott: It's almost as if calling it surrealist gives you license to ignore it.
Merwin: Yes. It's a way of shrugging it off by putting it in its category: we

know about surrealism, so that takes care of that. I think a lot of imagery that seems very clear to readers is so because it is familiar, and it is familiar because it is doing something that has already been done, and any new use of imagery sets up resistances and defenses which make it seem incomprehensible, whereas fifteen years later it will look perfectly simple. One of the things that always used to give me heart when I was being described as hopelessly obscure and surrealist was that children were not having any trouble at all reading the poems.

Another reason I think this is happening is because we are living in a more and more artificial world. We are living in a world surrounded by human contraptions instead of living creatures, and I profoundly believe this is something that can't go on. I don't think we can live in a completely human-made world. The imagery continues to come out of the place that requires something beyond human fabrication, beyond the human origin of things. And this, I think, is why even people who don't live all the time in the country, if they are above a certain age, will tend to use imagery that has to do with the natural world, and more and more readers can't understand it.

I remember when Robert Bly came to visit me in France years ago. He was talking about surrealism in my poems and mentioned an image about a fly turning around a statue of nothing and said it was surrealistic. And I said, "It's *not*, Robert," and I took him into a room on the farm and showed him flies going round and round and round in a circle, in the middle of the room.

I can't imagine being able to live without the natural world. I wouldn't want to live in a world that was completely fabricated. It seems to me to be completely out of touch with what I think of as real, which involves the mystery of other forms of life. We need them; I certainly do. I think our destruction of other species is disastrous to our own minds.

Elliott: But despite your feeling that labeling your poetry as surrealist was really not to the point, nonetheless there was a period during which many of the images in your poems seem truly anomalous in the same way as surrealism can be, and recently that's much less the case.

Merwin: Well, there definitely were poems, particularly some of the first poems in *The Lice*, that were a deliberate attempt to use certain surrealist devices to convey the same kind of things the other poems were conveying in other ways. Those really might have been called surrealist, but they were seldom the ones that were talked about. For example, "The Unfinished Book of Kings." But even that poem depends on the kind of dramatic coherence which surrealism very often tries to do without.

Elliott: Much surrealism is very static.
Merwin: Yes.

Elliott: Is that one reason why you've left that kind of poem behind?
Merwin: Well, when you've written something, you don't have to write it again. That's reason enough to leave it behind.

Elliott: The feeling that I get from your poetry in the sixties, and which is something that many people have said about your poetry then, is that it gives the feeling of a world stripped down to essences. Is there a connection between the anger and despair you were experiencing and your use at that time of a kind of imagery that does not look on the page as if it is giving a detailed vision of the phenomenal world, as much of your later poetry does? Is that shift from the imagery in *The Lice* to the imagery of later poetry in some way connected with overcoming or coming to terms with the anger and bitterness and maybe dealing more closely with the things in the world?
Merwin: I wanted to accept more and more aspects of the world. Certain things are no more acceptable than ever, of course; but wanting to be more intimate and closer to things and to be able to take the real day-to-day details of existence and use them, and to have that kind of closeness—that's been the real intent.

Elliott: During that time in the sixties and early seventies some of the images could be characterized as being dark in a negative sense, using a word like "emptiness" with negative connotations of the void in a way that might express a kind of existential dread. And yet there is the Buddhist concept of emptiness which is really a kind of fullness. I am wondering whether the negative emptiness—the way that many Westerners think of the world as empty—seemed to be more appropriate at that time, but now it's emptiness in the sense of fullness that you are interested in.
Merwin: Yes, I think that is probably true. Although I have to keep saying that I don't feel historically much more optimistic.

Elliott: Have you ever thought that in the period of *The Lice*, when your poetry often seemed stripped down and there was much use of silence and space, the interplay between the words and the surrounding space was somewhat like sumi painting? I sometimes get the same feel out of those poems, as if they were just a few brush strokes and not concerned with photographic detail.

Merwin: I wouldn't have made the analogy, but I see what you mean. I really wanted something that was utterly compressed. You know, something that was portable, something you could take with you—and that you might want to take with you.

Elliott: How do you feel about the poems of that period now? Are you somewhat distanced from them? They seem so different from the poems of the past few years.
Merwin: I couldn't write them now. I *wouldn't* write them now, but I don't feel so distant. No. They are all part of a story, and there is no point in trying to erase parts of the story. You can't do it. That was twenty-five years ago almost. So I do feel *that* distance from them. On the other hand, they were a breakthrough into a place which was a perfectly authentic place for me. I had to write them.

Elliott: Looking back, do you feel that possibly you were keeping the world at a greater distance—holding back from it because of the negative things that you saw—and that that was somehow done more compatibly in a poetry that erased the particulars?
Merwin: You know the old problem: if you simply string together a whole lot of particulars, it is not a poem. Particulars do what surrealist images do. They become two-dimensional and there is no shape to the whole thing. There is no reason. It becomes like reading a telephone book.

Elliott: Was the poetry of that period valuable to you partly because of what you were learning about form?
Merwin: About what made a poem have a certain kind of life to it, let's say, and vibrancy, which seemed to me essential, and I would happily have incorporated as many particulars as possible, but just incorporating particulars wasn't going to make it happen.

Elliott: You rarely wrote poems at that point like "Green Water Tower" or "The Sea Cliffs at Kailua in December," for example, in your recent book *Opening the Hand*, where it seems as if they are describing specific places that you are familiar with. Not that you are describing them in great photographic detail, but they seem like real places, whereas so many of the poems in *The Lice* seem as if they could be anywhere.
Merwin: Most of them were about real places. They present a perception about a real place. It wasn't a matter of withholding detail; it was a matter of

trying to do something else with the experience. The particulars were not so much the things that seemed to convey it as was some kind of perception about the experience of a place itself, of being there. At least that's how I thought of it then—and don't now.

Elliott: Another way of pointing to a difference between your poetry in the sixties and early seventies and the more recent poetry has to do with the voice. In the same way that the particularity of the world is more present in the recent poetry, so the particularity of the speaker seems more evident in the recent poems. And in your foreword to *A Zen Wave*, in talking about Bashō, you refer to "the profound intimacy of this poetry into which the postures and qualifications and noise of an I obtrude relatively so little" (Aitken 15). With regard to your own poetry, that statement is no less true of your more recent work than it was for the poetry at the time of *The Lice*, and yet at the same time it seems as if the real historical figure, the writer behind the poem, was somehow again at greater remove in the earlier period.
Merwin: Yes.

Elliott: From what came that act of putting yourself into the forefront of the poem a little bit more?
Merwin: I suppose being able to accept some more things. I couldn't even say what they are. I don't know what they are. It would be very easy to say "accepting oneself," which of course is part of it. But it's something that I always wanted. You can't often write the poems you want to write. You write what you can, and you write closer to things sometimes—often with a sense of surprise.

Elliott: In your career, as with so many other poets there for a long while, were you quite consciously influenced by Eliot's ideas on the impersonal nature of poetry?
Merwin: He was so much around it would have been very hard not to be. He seemed to be present the way Freud would be present if you were talking about psychology.

Elliott: Then there were reactions against that influence in so many different directions: the Confessional poets, the Beats, for example. But one of the things that seemed to be the case with your poetry was that instead of going from the Eliot-influenced impersonal to the very narrowly personal, as some poets did, it was as if the voice in those poems, from *The Moving Target* on, became somehow transpersonal; or if it was going from the objective to the subjective, it was quite radically subjective, so that some people would mistake it for objectivity when in truth it was not. Does that seem to tally with your sense of what you were doing then?

Merwin: Yes. But you know when I say anything about that, it is hindsight, because there wasn't at any point a calculated program of what to do next. I mean with some poets, Bly, for example, there probably was, and with Denise Levertov there certainly was. But I never sat down and thought, "Well, now I should do this, now I should do that, now I should do something else." I finished the poems in *The Drunk in the Furnace*, and I didn't know where I was going next. I knew I wasn't going to do the same thing over again.

Elliott: Toward the end of that book you included those family portraits which seemed to be bringing the autobiographical self into the poem more, and then you left them behind, as if that kind of narrowly personal poetry was somehow not what was needed.

Merwin: I felt that I could come to depend on what could be described as a subject matter, and be stuck, and be defined and define myself by it and feel that I couldn't do anything else. That's very easy to do.

Elliott: And then twenty years later you come back and write about some of the same relatives in *Unframed Originals*, which is unabashedly factual, or at least it appears that way, and also in *Opening the Hand*. But perhaps because of having gone through that phase of *The Lice* it seems now as if the poems in which you are dealing with your family are much more effectively personal than those in *The Drunk in the Furnace*.

Merwin: Just with age, if you are lucky, you may learn how to make that happen. The earlier poems seem to be more distant than what I write now. I wouldn't like to write from such a distance. I made little attempts to write autobiographical things in my twenties and early thirties. I put them all aside. One talks about perspective, which really implies distance from things, but actually one has to arrive at a certain perspective before one really can be intimate about them. Usually, the first autobiographical novel is just a way of getting the arm warmed up for being able to write something else, and later on the writer will come back to that material and be able to do something with it.

Elliott: One of the many associations with the title of *Opening the Hand* in addition to suggesting the poem about your parents' hands, is that it seems a gesture of acceptance to me, a kind of acceptance of the world. I think of the difference in tone between "For a Coming Extinction" and "The Shore." They are essentially about the same subject. And yet the more recent poem seems much more tender. There's certainly no more of an acceptance of the horrible conditions that are creating these ecological changes, but it's as if you and the whale are on more intimate grounds with each other, in terms of the language of the poem, than in the earlier poem, which didn't seem to have so much of a connection with the creature itself.

Merwin: I hope that is true. There is no difference between us and the whales in the last poem.

Elliott: As I was going back through *Writings to an Unfinished Accompaniment*, I noticed more clearly than I had before how many poems are dealing with eyes and vision. It seems to be quite a strong, recurring theme. That sent me back to a stanza in "Words from a Totem Animal": "My eyes are waiting for me / in the dusk / they are still closed / they have been waiting a long time / and I am feeling my way toward them" (*Carrier* 16). There is an interesting progression in *Writings* where the achievement of vision and of eyes capable of seeing seems to be more and more possible. And then there's the poem "The Initiate," which goes one step further to say that we don't even need the eyes, implying an inward vision. But *Writings* seems to represent a transitional period in your poetry from the three books that preceded it, and most of the poems in that book, to what happens in the poetry in *The Compass Flower*, *Finding the Islands*, and *Opening the Hand*, where all of a sudden it is as if the world is let in more freely, is seen with great particularity.

Merwin: That's interesting. I never thought of that, but you may very well be right. It certainly was a time of trying to see and find a way through to just what you have been describing. Whether it worked or not I never thought to look back and see. I never know what the next poem will be. I never even know if there is going to be a next poem.

Elliott: Is there a historical referent to "Finding a Teacher" in terms of your own experience? That poem from *Writings* seems like a little Zen parable.

Merwin: No, there isn't. It wasn't that way at all. That was before I'd ever found any kind of Zen teacher. I'd always imagined that a teacher would be an animal. I still think that's true. I think the animals really are our teachers in many essentials.

Elliott: But to return to the change in your poetry, in relation to the poems

of *The Compass Flower*, it is almost as if those three earlier books, from *The Moving Target* on, were, in anthropological terms, a kind of initiation experience, like a going out into the barren wilderness. There is so much that seems negative in them. Do *The Compass Flower, Finding the Islands*, and *Opening the Hand* feel of a piece to you, in the way that *The Moving Target, The Lice*, and *The Carrier of Ladders* are?
Merwin: I suppose so. *Opening the Hand*, to me, seems to be separate from the two others.

Elliott: I was going to ask that. But it does seem informed by the kind of more detailed perception of the world that those previous two books have. The poems in *Finding the Islands* even resemble haiku in their attention to the details of particular moments. But I have heard you read from that book and you were very careful to say, "These are not haiku."
Merwin: Well, they aren't haiku.

Elliott: No, they aren't. But, on the other hand, they seem to be haiku-informed, so to speak, and doing a lot of the same things that haiku do.
Merwin: I would like them to do some of the same things.

Elliott: And I don't mean just that they are three lines long.
Merwin: A lot of haiku, as you know, were never written as three lines; they were written as one line. I did want to try to do some of the same things that I think haiku do in Japanese, but of course I don't know what haiku do in Japanese because I don't read Japanese, and I'm less than satisfied with most translations of haiku. With many translations of mine, what started me translating was a sense that there was a poem behind the existing translation that wasn't making it into English, and I wanted to try to make a translation into English that did carry it over. I probably didn't succeed any better than any of the other translators, but I tried to do it my own way. These poems aren't translations, but I would have liked them to do some of the things that I imagine haiku would do in the original. I wasn't trying to follow a set of rules, but I was intrigued by the notion of the linked haiku that Bashō and some of his disciples were writing, and that was what made me think of joining a series of them so that they played off against each other and made a larger whole. It made a kind of context.

Elliott: Would you ever consider doing a renga? Have you ever toyed with the possibility?
Merwin: I've considered it, but it never got very far. In our society, it seems

like a game. There was a very interesting article on them as a kind of spiritual practice in the last issue of *Eastern Buddhist.* But I can remember being interested in very short verse forms because of the speed with which they seem to travel and the sort of lightning flash that they are. They're there in quite a number of traditions, some in Spanish—very short poems. I translated some of them back in the fifties.

Elliott: I've noticed in some of the haiku journals that more and more people seem to be taking haiku as a jumping-off point and writing three-line, two-line, or one-line poems that probably would not be officially thought of as haiku at all by the conservative schools of haiku in Japan.
Merwin: I love the thought of haiku as being a jumping-off point, considering Bashō's frog.

Elliott: What did you think of Robert Aitken's including the transliterations of Bashō's haiku along with the translations and then trying to talk the reader through the various meanings of the words?
Merwin: I think transliteration is a very good idea. I'm not talking about Aitken's now, but there are books where the transliteration is much more exciting than the translation.

Elliott: Are the translations you're doing of Dōgen's poetry posing quite a challenge?
Merwin: I'm working with Kazuaki Tanahashi, who knows very well what Dōgen is talking about, and the basic situation with many of his poems we've been translating is very simple. Students of Dōgen's will come to him with portraits of Dōgen and ask him to write a little poem on them; many of them are little poems about portraits of him. And it's a wonderful starting point for Dōgen to make up the poems.

Elliott: Another book that certainly comes to mind in talking about short forms is *Asian Figures.* In the foreword to that book you talk in terms of the "urge to finality of utterance . . . and to be irreducible and unchangeable" [vii], as if such poems are little units that perhaps have an integrity that longer poems begin to lose. But is there the problem, when writing haiku or your three-line poems, that you could fall into just making a little set piece, like one little jewel?
Merwin: I think it is a problem. I think the urge that you are talking about could be an urge to find something that is as near absolute as you can get in

language. I think that's okay, but you don't want to be stuck with that either. You don't want to paint yourself into a corner. Language is articulation of something, but we don't know what it's articulation of. Finally it's an attempt to say what we *are*, to say what our experience is to us, and we can't be absolute about that. So the urge to say something undeformable, unchangeable, irreversible is a very important urge, but it's only one, and the tension is set up by the fact that there is an opposite urge too, which is to be articulate, and to expatiate, to be discursive, to do all of those things. At regular intervals the writing of poetry in general does tend to become extremely prolix, the way traditions get very discursive, very diluted and diffuse, and the other pole is lost sight of. But you can get so succinct that there is nothing left.

Elliott: Did you finally stop writing those three-line poems? You have written short poems at various times in your career, but certainly it seemed as if all of a sudden there were a great many of them and then in *Opening the Hand* probably fewer short poems than in your other major collections of poetry. Have you written out that shortness?
Merwin: Yes. I think the short ones really had all gone into those two collections in *Finding the Islands.*

Elliott: Was there then a tension in your own writing between the more discursive, which comes out in *Opening the Hand*, and that temptation to be as succinct as possible?
Merwin: Probably. There are poems that try to do both, like the questionnaire poem, about the pineapple. Every one of the questions has a completeness of its own.

Elliott: In *A Zen Wave* Robert Aitken says that "like . . . Bashō, we must use words. How should we use them? By playing with them . . . The purpose is to present something, not to mean something. Meaning something destroys it" (127). Is that, you think, one of those difficult lessons that many Western poets cannot come to terms with?
Merwin: You can push that too far and you end up with the postphenomenologists saying that there is no subject and that there is no need for a subject, that the poetry need have no relationship to any subject. The poem is on its own, apart from anything. Something that seems to me fairly obvious is that both things are true: the poem does exist on its own, but that doesn't mean the poem has no relation to a subject. These two apparently contradictory things are actually happening at the same time. The poem is

not the same thing as the subject. The poem would also not exist *without* the subject. The two have an essential relationship; and I really can't imagine being interested in a poem that doesn't have a subject, some kind of subject.

Elliott: How about the Language poets?
Merwin: Well, if you like games just for the sake of games . . . I find them boring after a while—after a fairly short while.

Elliott: Because their subject is just themselves?
Merwin: I really want a poem to make the world stop, for a matter of a few seconds.

Elliott: Why is it, do you think, that such poets seem to be interested in going on beyond the traditional role for poetry, as if saying, "Well, that's been done. For poetry to go forward it has to be doing something completely different?"
Merwin: True originality has to do not with trying to be new but trying to come from the place from which all renewal comes. The meaning of originality has to do with origin, the place where something comes from, not the fact that it is different from everything else. You can't be different from everything else. It's like saying life must do something quite new. It is doing something quite new all the time.

The Language poets clearly want something out of poetry that is different from what I want out of poetry. Why that should be so I can guess, but I certainly don't know. I haven't talked to them about it. I think it's very decadent. It's what you do when you haven't got anything to do.

Elliott: So are we into another fin-de-siécle period, and that's the form of decadence that our poetry is taking?
Merwin: Maybe. I wonder whether there's a certain numbness involved. At a time when there is tremendous urgency, to say there must be no urgency in poetry, of all arts! We don't know what speech is for. Every time we speak we are finding out a little bit more about what the words are for. Speech is for speaking, speech is for saying.

Elliott: In your poetry you refer to names quite frequently, to things "with their names" and other things "without their names." In *The Compass Flower* there are two or three images that are somewhat similar: "The beginning / comes from before / when the words for it were pictures of strangers / it comes on wings that never waited for their names" ("Kore"; 51), or "the rain whose ancestors / with no names / made the valley" ("June Rain"; 69). What is it that naming does?

Merwin: It sets up a concept between you and what you are looking at. The cat doesn't know it's a cat until you teach it that it is a cat.

Elliott: And then by setting up that concept do we feel that we have possession over it?

Merwin: I think so. We feel that we have some control over it. The names are important to us; we can't do without them. But on the other hand you can be trapped in the names and they can keep that barrier between you and things. I don't know his writing very well, but I believe that Heidegger talks about that.

Elliott: Heidegger and Sartre both trace back to Husserl, but Sartre seems somehow to regret and yet accept as unavoidable the distance which naming and language create between us and the phenomenal world, whereas Heidegger and Buddhism go beyond that. Getting back to the Language poets, might they be working out of that frustration with the separation?

Merwin: We can't live without concepts, but it's important to notice that they're concepts.

Elliott: So then when you say things like "with no names," in a sense you are talking about a relationship between you and something else where you are able to perceive the suchness directly; there is no name interposed, no concept of your own which you think somehow draws it into you.

Merwin: Well, there is an evocation of the thing that is there before there's a name, before there's a concept of it. The rain falls whether we know it's rain falling or not.

Elliott: Is it something like the practice of sitting in meditation that gives us what we need to separate things from their names?

Merwin: Then you might notice whether what you are seeing is the rain falling or your idea of the rain falling.

Elliott: It's in images and lines such as the ones referring to names that the parallel between your poetry and Buddhism is evident, but it is put there in terms that do not force the reader to think, "That's Buddhist."

Merwin: I would not want it to be put there in those terms. In fact even in translating Dōgen we are trying to find our way around using words like "dharma."

Elliott: In other words, you would like these translations to exist without a need for a glossary.
Merwin: Yes, without the need for a special vocabulary, which means a prejudiced set of assumptions about it, like "Dharma is a good thing."

Elliott: Twentieth-century poets who come to mind in terms of Eastern influence are first of all Eliot and Pound, both in rather idiosyncratic ways. Are there any other poets in the twentieth-century American tradition who you think have been influenced in a positive way by Eastern thought or Buddhism?
Merwin: I suspect that Stevens was. I don't know that, but poems like "The Snow Man" and "A Rabbit as King of the Ghosts" and "The River of Rivers in Connecticut," a quite late one and a poem that I love, seem to me to be very marked by it. I don't know whether this was deliberate. I don't believe that such insight is the monopoly of any "ism." I think that it's a basic way of seeing the world which Buddhism happened to articulate in a particularly clear way. But it's human. For that matter, it may not even be just human; it may be mammalian. It may be vertebrate.

Elliott: But it does seem as if Western civilization did a better job of repressing it for a long period of time than Eastern civilization.
Merwin: We set up a dualism which obscures it. I understand that Stevens had a Buddha in his study. I don't know what that means. He may have had it there for decorative purposes.

Elliott: I'm glad you said what you did about "The Snow Man" because I think that gets back to what we were talking about a while ago, about how the concept of emptiness has traditionally been seen in the West as something to fear. I've seen many interpretations of "The Snow Man" that tried to turn it into a very negative poem. It does seem more like a Buddhist emptiness.
Merwin: I think it's an exhilarating poem. What happens if one is going to see that poem as a negative poem, as a depressing and finally a despairing poem, is that you start thinking too fast about those last lines before you've really taken them in. You start setting up a defense about them and analyzing them before you've really listened to them.

Elliott: Is there something categorically different about Dōgen's poems when compared to a poem like "The Snow Man"? In other words, is there a way in which those poems are probably going to be more remote to the Western mind?

Merwin: I don't know. I think that late poem of Dōgen's about snow, for example, is no more remote than Stevens's "Snow Man" and is really not very different in its purport.

Elliott: I'd like to see that one.

Merwin: It was written a year before he died, when he was in his fifties. It goes,

> All my life tangled
> in false and real
> right and wrong
> playing with the moon
> laughing at wind
> listening to birds
> year after year wasted seeing
> a mountain covered
> with snow
> only this winter
> I know that the snow
> is the mountain

Elliott: I'd like to return to your recent poetry. Before the publication of *Opening the Hand* you said that you were thinking of removing from the poem "Coming Back in the Spring" a specific reference to IRA hunger strikers (Folsom and Nelson 48). Now, I don't know what you might have taken out, but you mention an IRA hunger striker in that poem.

Merwin: They are all there.

Elliott: So you didn't take anything out? Are you happy with that decision now?

Merwin: I am *now*. But it's not a matter of principle. Some things just don't seem to work. Sometimes it takes a long time before you can tell with any kind of certainty yourself whether they really work or not. My wish to have those things in the poem may not have had much to do with the poem. It may have been from outside the poem. I may have been self-indulgent. That was what my misgiving was concerned with. And then I became finally satisfied that it did belong in the poem, that it did seem to work.

Elliott: But does your leaving those specific references in the poem come from a different response to the present political turmoil than the one you had in the sixties? Is your feeling one of, "OK, here we go again, and maybe this time I should leave in some of the specifics instead of withholding them or not allowing them to enter in"?

Merwin: Well, I would like to be able to write them in such a way that I can feel they belong there. I don't think that just because I've got the particulars I can decide to put them into the poem and it will make the poem good. There is an awful lot of bad poetry written that way. And it doesn't matter how much one agrees with the intent. The poem can still be bad.

Elliott: I wonder if we are not far from a time when, as in the sixties, there are going to be more poets writing topical poems and rallying around some current political causes.

Merwin: I just hope that they and we can make them poems, because the urge to write propaganda is one that I not only understand but that I sympathize with. But I think it is an urge that doesn't make poems very often.

Elliott: But as propaganda, you are willing to let it have its short life?

Merwin: Oh sure. It's better than not saying anything. And the occasional political poem that works is sometimes a very great poem, and sometimes a very funny poem. You know that poem by Ernesto Cardenál about all the dreadful things that are going on in Nicaragua. All the babies are crying and the people are fighting with each other. And the last line is "Somoza is driving through town."

Elliott: There seems to be a listlessness in much contemporary poetry.

Merwin: About political issues?

Elliott: Yes.

Merwin: A listlessness about what's really going on. There is a terrible temptation, a terrible danger of preaching. But there is an awful lot of frivolity too and that sort of fluff—part of that same decadence we were talking about.

Elliott: Would you like to talk about your current writing on Hawaii?

Merwin: We were talking earlier about intent. You never know what you've written, and you forget what you intended. You know at a given time what you want to write, but it's never what you end up writing. I have been thinking about this in the last year, partly because of the great satisfaction and excitement of working on what I've been doing, which seems to me to gather together things that I've been wanting to do since before I could read and write, for reasons that I don't altogether understand in a rational way, having a certain amount to do with the culture of Hawaiian people, and with a non-European, non-literate life, all of it happening at a time indeed when the culture seems to be doomed and disappearing.

Elliott: The Hawaiian culture?
Merwin: Well, what culture isn't? But the Hawaiian culture is under terrible menace. There are no Hawaiians who don't speak English and many Hawaiians who don't speak Hawaiian. Draw your own conclusions. The land has been taken away and the culture has been downgraded and kept in pockets on the islands. But being able to have any closeness and any relation to it— to me it's a great fulfillment. And to realize that that relation has come into direct conflict with the things that I have long been in conflict with myself ... I mean the destruction of the natural world and the destruction of other cultures, the kind of military and technological arrogance of our culture and our time. And in fact it's happening all over the Pacific. The Pacific to me historically is now the focus of history. For years for me it was New York; but now it really seems to be somewhere in the Pacific, probably on the uninhabited island of Kahoolawe, which the Navy is bombing.

Elliott: Just routinely, as practice?
Merwin: Routinely, every year. It is the sacred island of the Hawaiians and is covered with archeological sites.

Elliott: How long has this been going on?
Merwin: Since 1939. They were about to stop it when the Hawaiian people asked to have the island back. But they stepped it up. That's the basis for the story. But in order to write it you have to figure out what the involvement of the Hawaiian people on that island has been right through to the present and then what the involvement of the Navy has been. It's history in a sense, the kind of writing I suppose would go in the same genre with something like the books of Peter Matthiessen. I'm just trying to tell the story fairly straight.

Elliott: And you are tape-recording conversations with people to find out their feelings about this?

Merwin: Their lives as they've had to do with this island.

Elliott: So you see it as a book-length manuscript?

Merwin: I didn't start it that way. I started it as a neat little essay. And there are a lot of other aspects of the situation that I think of as nice essays of about forty pages, but who knows? I mean there is so much of that story that has never been told. When the old people start talking on this, it streams out, they talk so well.

Elliott: Do you see Hawaii as being permanent in your life? You've lived in France, you've lived in Mexico, and New York has always been a sort of coming back place.

Merwin: I feel very much at home there. I love it. One of the other things I've become involved in is trying to grow and save endangered species of trees and plants. That has a history too of its own. Hawaii is unique. The flora and fauna that were there when Captain Cook got there were almost entirely exclusive to Hawaii. They had almost all evolved there. There's no other place on earth where this is true. There is still no place on earth which is as priceless a laboratory for studying evolution as the Hawaiian Islands, and they have been raped and torn apart by large-scale exploitative agriculture.

Elliott: Given the current political and ecological crises, do you feel the impulse to write more occasional pieces of a political nature, such as those you wrote for the *Nation* in the sixties?

Merwin: This enormous thing that I seem to be in the middle of is that. I mean it is political because you can't write about this subject unpolitically, apolitically. I've come to believe that there is scarcely any such thing as the Russian military and the American military. I believe that deeper than that there is the world military, and they are mutually sustaining.

Elliott: Did the people you interviewed in Hawaii seem to have concerns that went beyond simply the concern for that particular sacred island?

Merwin: We were on the island in May. The Navy allows them to go over on a part of the island once a month. The organization is called the Protect Kahoolawe Ohana, which now is the focus organization for the Hawaiian consciousness; and we went over at the end of May with a bunch of people from all around the Pacific, people from Belau, New Caledonia, the Marshall Islands, the Philippines, New Zealand, Maui. This is something which is happening now very fast around the Pacific. There have already been two pan-Pacific conferences organized by the Independent Nuclear-free Pacific, mainly indigenous people saying, "We are tired of being rubbed out and we insist on our own identity, our own culture, and the Pacific nature of our culture, and we don't want to be part of the Russian bloc, the Chinese bloc, or any other bloc; we're Pacific, and we don't want the nuclear threat here in any form: we don't want nuclear missiles, we don't want nuclear dumping, we don't want nuclear tests, we don't want nuclear stockpiling." How far it will go, who knows? But it's growing and the State Department doesn't like it very much. As one of the guys in the diplomatic corps said, "They don't understand that it is unacceptable to our strategy." A nuclear-free Pacific, that is. I had the feeling very strongly on Kahoolawe in May that this was the center, where it was all happening, on this empty island in the Pacific.

Elliott: Much of what you've said brings to mind the concluding lines to "The River of Bees": "we were not born to survive / Only to live" (*Lice* 33).
Merwin: That again has been described as an incredibly bleak and negative point of view. I don't think of it that way.

Elliott: Is losing attachment to survival something that might be needed in order to survive?
Merwin: I think it is important to pay attention to living rather than to surviving, if we can. I mean, surviving doesn't mean very much if your life doesn't mean very much, does it?

Works Cited

Aitken, Robert. *A Zen Wave.* Foreword W. S. Merwin. New York: Weatherhill, 1978.
Auden, W. H. Foreword. *A Mask for Janus.* By W. S. Merwin. New Haven: Yale, 1952.
"Snow." Trans. Kazuaki Tanahashi and David Schneider. Adapted W. S. Merwin.
Folsom, Ed, and Cary Nelson. "'Fact Has Two Faces': An Interview with W. S. Merwin." *Iowa Review* 13.1 (1982): 30–66.
Merwin, W. S. *Asian Figures.* New York: Atheneum, 1973.
———. *The Carrier of Ladders.* New York: Atheneum, 1970.
———. *The Compass Flower.* New York: Atheneum, 1977.
———. *The Lice.* New York: Atheneum, 1967.

W. S. Merwin, The Art of Poetry, No. 38

Edward Hirsch / 1986

The Paris Review 102 (Spring 1987). W. S. Merwin interview, "The Art of Poetry," No. 38 by The Paris Review. Copyright © 1987 by The Paris Review, used by permission of The Wylie Agency LLC. This interview took place in mid-June 1986 at Merwin's home in Maui.

Edward Hirsch: In the past thirty-four years, you have published twelve books of poetry, three books of prose, and at least fifteen books in translation. Yet you said recently that "writing is something I know little about." How is that possible?

W. S. Merwin: The kind of writing that matters most to me is something you don't learn about. It's constantly coming out of what I don't know rather than what I do know. I find it as I go. In a sense, much that is learned is bound to be bad habits. You're always beginning again.

Hirsch: Do you write every day? Ezra Pound once advised you to write seventy-five lines a day. Have you followed his advice?

Merwin: I haven't written seventy-five lines a day, but for years I've tried to stare at a piece of paper for a while every day. It tends to turn one into a kind of monster.

Hirsch: How's that?

Merwin: You have to be rather relentless about pushing other things out of the way. This activity of writing, which has no promises attached to it, comes to be given a kind of arbitrary but persistent importance.

Hirsch: Would you say something about the hymns you used to write for your father? Were those your first poems?

Merwin: I suppose they were. I was about five years old when I wrote them.

I wrote them on my own, and I was very disappointed that they weren't used in church.

Hirsch: You have a highly developed ecological and environmental consciousness. When did it start?

Merwin: I've tried repeatedly to figure out just when and how it began. It's probably impossible to say. Such dispositions come long before most decisions, I think. But there are two things I remember. First, I had a rather repressed childhood. I was brought up never to say *no* to anybody, never to say I didn't like something, never to talk back. But one day—I must have been around the age of three—two men came and started cutting the limbs off the one tree in the backyard, and I simply lost my temper and ran out and started beating them. Everybody was so impressed with this outburst of real rage that my father never even punished me. And the second thing: I was so fascinated by these watercolors in a book about Indians that I began teaching myself to read the captions. The Indians seemed to be living in a place and in a way that was of immense importance to me. So I associate learning to read—English, oddly enough—with wanting to know about Indians. I'm still growing into it. I've never outgrown that. The Indians represented to me a wider and more cohesive world than the one I saw around me that everyone took for granted. I grew up within sight of New York City, and whenever I was asked what I really wanted to do, I would say I wanted to go to the country. I'd been taken out and had seen the country when I was very small and that was what I always wanted to go back to. I'm not sure of the exact origin, but I do know that it goes back a very long way. Feeling that way about "the country" has made me ask questions that I suppose are strange to many of my contemporaries, but they seem to get less and less eccentric as our plight as a species grows more and more desperate, and we behave accordingly. As a child, I used to have a secret dread—and a recurring nightmare—of the whole world becoming city, being covered with cement and buildings and streets. No more country. No more woods. It doesn't seem so remote, though I don't believe such a world could survive, and I certainly would not want to live in it.

Hirsch: Your father was a Presbyterian minister. Do you think you inherited from him a Presbyterian urge to improve the world?

Merwin: I don't think it was an urge to improve the world. It was an urge to love and revere something in the world that seemed to me more beautiful and rare and magnificent than I could say, and at the time in danger of being ignored and destroyed. I think I felt that as a very small child. Though how much of it I owe to my father or his family, I can't say. The world around me did not seem to me to be satisfactory. There was something incomplete about the world of streets and sidewalks and cement—and I did have a very strong sense of growing plants and trees and so forth, and still do. I remember walking in the streets of New York and New Jersey and telling myself, as a kind of reassurance, that the ground was really under there. I've talked and tried to write about that, but I feel that I haven't even begun to say it. But that hunger, that tropism, is something that I don't believe we can live without, even if we aren't aware of what we're missing and by now many of us aren't aware of it. We're missing it just the same. We're deprived of something essential.

Hirsch: Is it some profound connection to the natural world?

Merwin: The connection is there—our blood is connected with the sea. It's the recognition of that connection. It's the sense that we are absolutely, intimately connected with every living thing. We don't have to be sentimental and pious about it, but we can't turn our backs on that fact and survive. When we destroy the so-called natural world around us, we're simply destroying ourselves. And I think it's irreversible.

Hirsch: Do you see a connection between poetry and prayer?

Merwin: I guess the simple answer is yes, if only because I think of poetry as an attempt to use language as completely as possible. And if you want to do that, obviously you're not concerned with language as decoration, or language as amusement, although you certainly want language to be pleasurable. Pleasure is part of the completeness. I think of poetry as having to do with the completeness of life, and the completeness of relation with one's experience, completing one's experience, articulating it, making sense of it.

Hirsch: How about the influence of Zen in your work?

Merwin: When you talk about prayer in Judeo-Christian terms, prayer is usually construed as a kind of dualistic act. You're praying to somebody else for something. Prayer in the Western sense is usually construed as making a connection. I don't think that connection has to be made; it's already there. Poetry probably has to do with the recognizing of that connection, rather than trying to create something that isn't there.

Hirsch: In your memorial poem to John Berryman, you remember that "he suggested that I pray to the Muse / get down on my knees and pray / right there in the corner and he / said he meant it literally" What do you think of the advice?

Merwin: I think it's excellent advice. Writing poetry is never a wholly deliberate act over which you have complete control. It's important to recognize that writing is at the disposition of all sorts of forces, some of which you don't know anything at all about. You can describe them as parts of your own psyche, if you like, they probably are, but there are lots of other ways of describing them that are as good, or better—the muses, or the collective unconscious. More suggestive and so, in a way, more accurate. Any means of invoking these forces is good, as far as I'm concerned.

Hirsch: What did you learn from Berryman during your undergraduate days at Princeton?

Merwin: I tried to put some of that in the poem I wrote about him, some of the main directives that he made. Intransigence was one of them. He taught me something about taking poetry very seriously. He was certainly one of the two or three brightest individuals I've ever known, and his sense of language was passionate and had immense momentum. His integrity was absolute. He was a wacky man, but that devotion was like a pure flame all the time and that was a great example for me.

Hirsch: You've written an affectionate memoir of R. P. Blackmur, "Affable Irregular." Was he an example for you as a writer and an intellectual?

Merwin: I revered Blackmur. He was a kind of mentor and parent, except that the relation was not intimate, and there was a great deal of awe in it. I think that Blackmur had, in some ways, the most haunting literary intelligence I've ever known. He was a critic of a kind I really revered, too, and he was not serving himself with his opinions. He thought of a critic as a house waiting to be haunted. I haven't reread those essays in many years now, and yet things that he said and attitudes that he embodied, I've never forgotten. I know that he had deep uncertainties and yet he was a man of great independence. He reassured me. He encouraged me to believe that my own hankering after independence was okay.

Hirsch: So he encouraged you to follow your own path?

Merwin: I think he did that with many people. I don't know how many people took the advice. I think that even without his advice I probably wouldn't have fit into the academy. I'm very uncomfortable around institutions for any length of time. They make me uneasy. Like a shut-in.

Hirsch: Who were the first poets your own age that you knew?
Merwin: Well, I knew Galway Kinnell at Princeton, but we didn't read each other's poems very much. James Merrill came through once to see Blackmur. I didn't really know the poetry of my contemporaries very well until I came back from England and lived in Boston. I was almost thirty.

Hirsch: So you were already developed as a poet in a certain way?
Merwin: In a certain way. Until then my main influence had been Pound and all the poets of his generation, the great figures of that generation. And Pound turned me toward medieval poetry.

Hirsch: A lot of your early work seems to have followed a Poundian program. How central was he to you as a model?
Merwin: He was very important. Pound's ear was a revelation to me when I was eighteen and nineteen. I mean I really heard something clear when I read him. Many poets since Pound have heard something pure and penetrating in his work. I don't subscribe to a lot of the myths about Pound. I've tried to. Pound is so important to me that I've wanted to admire him very much. The intellectual coherence of Pound's work is something that I don't any longer believe in. I really think he was a very chaotic, fragmented, and troubled man. I don't think it adds up to this prescient and profound, architectural perfection that Hugh Kenner and some people have read into it. One minute I find him dazzling, the next minute disappointing and often exasperating. The example of writing by what you heard rather than out of your opinions—it was funny, he was so opinionated—that was the side that appealed to me. I imagined it was more exceptional than I do now. Now I suspect that all poets proceed by hearing. It was Pound's devotion to language and to poetry, and that incomparable ear.

Hirsch: Would you talk about your visit, which you have called a pilgrimage, to see Pound at St. Elizabeth's in the 1940s?
Merwin: I was staying with friends in Washington, at Easter vacation, when I went over to see him. He received me in this open ward, with people wandering around, flushing imaginary toilets. He sat in a deep chair and held forth. I was eighteen—I didn't have much to say to Pound—and he told me

all about how, when the hundredth canto was finished, the whole thing was all going to fall into place and so on. It would be like putting the keystone in the arch, or the lintel on the doorposts. He was also wonderfully generous and wrote me postcards afterwards. "Read seeds, not twigs E.P.," he wrote. And he gave me a bit of advice about translating, about taking translating seriously as a kind of practice, about learning languages and trying to get as close as possible to the sense and the form of the original. I didn't know what he meant about a lot of those things until I had been practicing for a while, until I had been trying to do it.

Hirsch: What initially attracted you to translation?
Merwin: At eighteen it's very hard to find something to write about. I was writing a lot but it was perfectly clear to me that what I was writing wasn't *about* very much. You have what you think of as your feelings when you're seventeen and eighteen, and they are your feelings, but they're very far from your words, you know, and the words are a mess. With translation, it was possible to actually work on something—and pay attention just to the writing, to the writing of something—and getting the words right, coming at it from the other end, from the "how" side.

Hirsch: When did you begin to translate primitive or archaic poetry?
Merwin: I guess I didn't really start translating it until I was well into my thirties anyway. I had always wanted to learn an oral language, a nonliterate language. I don't know what it was about my education and my temperament and character that kept me so long from doing that. Those Crow versions, for example, which I did about 1970 or '71, were all done from Robert Lowie's work on the Crow in the thirties. And I had very much the feeling about the Crow, along with American Indian poetry in general, and many other nonliterate poetries, too—that even as we talked about it, it was disappearing. And I think of it as of comparable importance to, say, the burning of the library at Alexandria. But I never did set about learning one of those languages until quite recently. I went to Crow country when I was doing those translations. I tried to find out what other work had been done on the Crow since Robert Lowie. It turned out very little work had been done at all. There had been a little bit of work done on the grammar of the language, but no more collecting of material; and Lowie himself only collected a few pages of lyrics. So, from a vast tradition, that's all that's left. It's like having maybe one or two pages of Herrick and one of Donne and two or three of Keats out of the whole of English literature. You know, you're grateful for

them, but it makes you sick to think of what's been lost. The Crow were not the only ones, either. The Crow were one of many great cultures. You look at those Crow lyrics, and you know they are the last of a vast, deep, powerful tradition. We brought about the loss of those things. They're lost; we can't reinvent them.

Hirsch: Do you think your early work, and maybe even your strong interest in translation, indicates any ambivalence about being an American poet?
Merwin: No, I never thought about it that way. There was a time when I really tried to sort that question out. But translation never entered into it—I mean, translation always seemed to be a way simply of expanding the possibilities, you know, of not being stuck. American poetry of the forties, which I grew up in, seemed to me pretty wooden. I mean, it was like living in a packing crate, and I knew I had to get out of that. Trying to figure out what it meant to be an American poet was something I did particularly during the years when I was living in England and very much wanting to get back to America. I certainly knew that I was not an English poet. But what it is to be an American poet I still don't know. It's nice that we no longer have to think about that. We still seemed to have to worry about it in the forties.

Hirsch: How did you come to know Robert Graves? What kind of a relationship did you establish with him when you worked as a tutor in the family?
Merwin: Well, it was a family relationship. The second tutoring job I had was in Portugal with the Portugese royal family. I was paid forty dollars a month. I was given a house and meals and so forth, and there were no expenses at all. During the summer I went across Spain on milk trains and I was determined to meet Robert Graves, so I just went and knocked on his door. I was staying in a house down in the port of Sóller, and Robert arranged to put me up in one of the empty houses in the village there so we could spend some time together. And while I was there, the tutor, who was supposed to be coming out for his son, wired and said he couldn't come, and Robert said, "Would you like the job?" and I said, "Sure." So that's how I got it. Piece of luck.

Hirsch: And how long did you work for him?
Merwin: I worked for him for only a year, but then I went back and lived in the village for part of another winter, translating *The Poem of the Cid* for the BBC. I've been trying to put together some things about Robert since he died. He was not the easiest man in the world to get along with. We didn't

really get along—I mean, not very well. He got along badly with many young people, and especially with other poets, and we didn't part on the best of terms.

Hirsch: What was the problem?

Merwin: It was all a very tiny circle, and when anything was abrasive, it became very abrasive. I tried a couple of times after I left Robert to bridge the gap because I knew there was really no reason not to be friends, but Robert had decided he didn't want to be friends. He said he was born without a reverse gear. I would feel even worse about it all if so many other people had not had much the same experience.

Hirsch: I've felt the influence of Eliot in some of your work. Did you know him?

Merwin: Yes, in the early fifties, in London. Eliot was a very kind man. In those days I smoked and liked French cigarettes, and people used to give him French cigarettes, which he no longer smoked. So whenever I went to see him he would open a drawer and hand me a whole bunch. That was a big thing in London in the early fifties, and I was touched that he remembered. We used to sit and reminisce about America. There was a side of Eliot that was very homesick for the States, and I was feeling homesick in London, too. We had several wonderful conversations—about the Ohio River and about his family out on the Mississippi in St. Louis and about the riverboats. It's very strange to think of him having any connection with that world. He talked about the *Delta Queen*, that steamboat that went up and down the river until a few years ago. He really wanted to take a trip on that. I wanted to write verse plays in those days, when I was in my early twenties. But, after a while, I came to feel that the plays weren't going very well and that the verse certainly wasn't helping them. As long as I had this fixation about verse plays, I wasn't learning anything about writing plays. I talked to him about that. I said I was thinking of abandoning writing them in verse altogether and trying to write them in prose. "Well," he said, "I've thought of doing that, too, but if I were to write my plays in prose, there are so many other people who could do it better."

Hirsch: How important was Auden to you as a poet and as a man?

Merwin: I admired Auden enormously. I love some of his poetry. We never knew each other very well personally. In fact, I think we only met twice. I have a few marvelous avuncular letters from Auden at the time when he did the introduction to my Yale Younger Poets book. But we never became friends. Our paths just didn't cross. I was very much in awe of him. I was shy about intruding on him. I used to see him padding around the Village when we both lived there, but I didn't go over and tap him on the shoulder, which I suppose I should have done. Once when he was away, and I was walking around the Village with Allen Ginsberg, Allen said he had the key to Auden's apartment. He asked, "Shall we go and look around Auden's apartment?" He said, "I hallow that man." And I said, "So do I. Let's go." So we did, and I must say it was the most god-awful mess I've ever seen. Obviously nothing was ever cleaned or dusted. He had some people staying there who were apparently just as messy as he was. Someone had asked him how he would sort out the mess when he got back and he said, "Well, we'll just peel off the top layer and they can take that with them."

Hirsch: Do you think that the way you grew up created a nomadic streak in you?

Merwin: Probably. But I think I always wanted to travel. I mean, when I was very small, I remember the great joy of being in my father's church, being allowed to go up to his study a few times and watch the boats on the river and imagine going to sea. It was the old dream from Sir Walter Raleigh—wanting to ship out. It was one of the things that made me read Conrad when I was fourteen. Conrad was one of the first authors who made me want to write.

Hirsch: You've been criticized for excluding "the apparatus of the industrial revolution" from your work, especially from your early work. What do you make of that criticism?

Merwin: It's probably just. What someone writes about is never an entirely rational or deliberate choice. I've always envied poets to whom the immediacies of history were more tractable than I've found them to be. My difficulty may have to do with the fact that, although I lived in cities as a child, I was never allowed to have much to do with them, and I did feel alienated. I've always felt very different the moment I got out of cities or came back to them. But for many years, of course, this made for a real ambivalence, because I felt the need for the ultimate city, which for me was New York, and yet for the exact opposite, for the country, wherever I could find it, and they were always both pulling at me.

Hirsch: Your fifth and sixth books, *The Moving Target* and *The Lice*, are explosively different from the books which preceded them. On a technical level, they break with the formal tradition of the forties and fifties, breaking up lines and stanzas, loosening diction and syntax. And about two-thirds of the way through *The Moving Target*, you suddenly abandon using punctuation altogether. What happened?

Merwin: In the late fifties, I had the feeling I had simply come to the end of a way of writing. I didn't reject it, but it was no longer satisfying. So there was a period of close to two years when I wrote very little poetry. And then all of a sudden, the first poems of *The Moving Target* came out, I wrote almost half of the book in a few weeks—it was all coming from a different kind of impulse that I had not known was preparing itself. I was in Europe, knowing that if I came back to the States, I would have to get involved in an academic career, or something like that, which I didn't want to do, and yet, not wanting to be in England any more, the tensions of wanting to change my life, and not yet knowing quite how to do it, this all built up, with the result of a release of a new kind of writing, and many of the images and poems of the first part of *The Moving Target.* The second part of that book was written after I did get back to New York and was living on the Lower East Side. Probably the dropping of punctuation was partly the result of many years of reading Spanish and French poetry. Suddenly, they seemed to be a part of a tradition that was mine if I wanted it. Also, I came to believe that poetry has a much stronger relation to the spoken word than prose has. Punctuation basically has to do with prose and the printed word. I came to feel that punctuation was like nailing the words onto the page. Since I wanted instead the movement and lightness of the spoken word, one step toward that was to do away with punctuation, make the movement of the words do the punctuating for themselves, as they do in ordinary speech.

Hirsch: James Wright went through a similar crisis in his work at about the same time. Do you see a connection between what happened to you and what happened to him?

Merwin: Oh, yes. But neither of us knew what the other was doing. A number of people—like Louis Simpson and Robert Bly—were moving in that direction. The Beats were around also. We didn't so much influence each other as feel the same things. It was perfectly clear that the things I had felt as a kind of straitjacket could be broken out of after all. The straitjacket really wasn't there. We didn't have to pay attention to it anymore. The other thing about that time—I don't know that anyone has described it very thoroughly, and maybe nobody can—but all of us were about the same age, and we all went through that at pretty much the same time—throwing out the respectable way of going about things too. We were throwing out all of the apparatus of literary careers and everything, saying, Ah, that's not important; what's important is writing a different kind of poem. And that's wonderful. In some ways I wish that poets younger than us had gone through that experience. I love the idea of dropping—even if it's just for a few months—all of the assumptions about what makes poems and what makes literary careers and what makes any of these things, and living without that for a while.

Hirsch: I wonder how much you think of yourself as belonging to a specific generation of poets who share similar experiences. You've dedicated work, for example, to Galway Kinnell, Richard Howard, Anthony Hecht, and you've written a moving, haiku-like elegy for James Wright.
Merwin: I feel a part of that generation. But I don't feel part of any school or approach or movement or anything like that. I never have. In the late fifties, all of American poetry was supposed to be divided into two camps. That never made any sense to me at all. I've always liked disparate kinds of poets—Robert Creeley and Denise Levertov and Gerald Stern and Richard Howard and Anthony Hecht, and so forth—without feeling that there's any disloyalty or impossibility in that. I'm sad to see other poets and critics who insist that poetry has to be of a certain kind or it's not poetry.

Hirsch: Would you talk about your experiences in the embryonic peace movement and the anti-nuclear movement in the United States and abroad? How politically active have you been? How did it affect your work?
Merwin: I've always known that there were connections. I've tried to find them in different ways, but I've realized that I wasn't doing it very well. I did a bunch of essays about political events back in the early sixties. My involvement began in the fifties. The first demonstrations that I was involved in were in the late fifties and early sixties in the States. One of the first was outside Fort Dietrich, Maryland, where there was a biochemical warfare base. We were glad if there were six or seven of us standing outside the gates on what we called a vigil. Demonstrations in those days in the States were tiny—I mean, sometimes you were lucky if there were twelve people. On the other hand, in 1958, I had been in England, and was on the third Aldermaston march, which was the largest march in England since the Chartists, and very nearly split the Labour Party. It was huge, and the whole of central London at the end of that march was just jammed with people standing in silence. It was unforgettable. I also remember that Ted Hughes and Sylvia

Plath came and watched the end of that. Ted and Sylvia were reluctant to get involved in that kind of thing, but they did come and watch.

Hirsch: *The Lice* is your bleakest, most apocalyptic and agonized book. It's fueled by a savage ecological and political rage. I wonder what your current feelings are about what you call the "overt misanthropy" of *The Lice*.

Merwin: When I wrote *The Lice*, I thought that things were so black, that what we as a species had done was so terrible that there was very little hope, and certainly not much point in writing. The arts really were over; the culture, the salutary role of the arts in our lives—that was finished. There was nothing left but decoration. I'd become more interested in raising vegetables. In some ways, I think it's even worse now. But I don't think you can get stuck with just plain anger. It's a dead end in the long run. If the anger is to mean anything, it has to lead you back to caring about what is being destroyed. It's more important to pay attention to what it is that you care about. I don't want to preach about that, but that is how I've tried to find my way out of that impasse by returning to the things that I did care about. They're still there. I remember, for example, just as I was beginning *The Lice*, the Cuban missile crisis was happening. It was a great shock to me. I'd been working in the anti-nuclear movement, and I kept walking through the streets and hearing people saying that we should drop the bomb on Cuba, that it was high time, that we should have done it years ago, and things like that. I kept waking up in the morning in a real fury. I finally thought, Well, I know all of the things I *don't* want and what's wrong and what seems to be the trouble, and so forth. But if someone were to say to me, What would you think of as a good way to live? I wouldn't have any answer at all. I thought I really should find the answer to that. I had this place to live in France, this little farm, and I thought, I'm going to go there. I realized I didn't know how to grow even one lettuce plant. I'd eaten food all my life and I wouldn't be able to recognize it as it grew. It was about time I learned something as simple and obvious as that. So I went there and spent several years just trying to grow the things that I ate, and to make sense of things of the kind. A lot of *The Lice* came during the time that I was trying to work that out. I still haven't found any eternal answers. What is happening in the world is terrible and irreversible, and that history is probably a doomed enterprise. But in the meantime, it's important to live in the world as completely as we can. In Thoreau's journals he's mourning the closing of the Concord Common. He says people will no longer be able to pasture their cows or go on picking blueberries there. He says, This is terrible. Then he says, I didn't pay enough attention to it while it was free. Thoreau was always saying things that I seem to have been looking for.

Hirsch: Beginning with *The Moving Target*, and continuing through the next few books, your poems evidence radical dissatisfaction and distrust of language, a sense of the inadequacy and failure of speech. Do you still "believe too much in words," as one poem put it?

Merwin: I do. I have a faith in language. It's the ultimate achievement that we as a species have evolved so far. (I don't mean that I think we are the only species with a language). It's the most flexible articulation of our experience and yet, finally, that experience is something that we cannot really articulate. We can look out and see the sunlight in those trees, but we can't convey the full unique intimacy of that experience. That's the other side, one of those things that make poetry both exhilarating and painful all the time. It's conveying both the great possibility and the thing that we can't do.

Hirsch: You once wrote that "absolute despair has no art. I imagine that the writing of poems, in whatever form, still betrays the existence of hope." That seems to be part of a more optimistic and celebratory turn after *The Lice*.

Merwin: As I was talking about these two dimensions of language, I realized that I also think this is true of existence and life, too. We know perfectly well from the moment that we know anything about mortal existence, that it is mortal, in the sense that there's no hope—you're going to die. And yet, we go on, our hope is involved in what happens every day as we wake up and go through it and meet friends and talk and read poems and see the light come and go. Our hope is not a thing in the future; it's a way of seeing the present.

Hirsch: I sense some of the same apocalyptic fervor from *The Lice* in some of your most recent work. In your poem "The Inauguration, 1985" you write, "We have elected the end because we have looked on everything alive with a look that has killed it and we see it already dead." Does that summarize your current political feelings?

Merwin: To a great degree. I write poems of that kind with a considerable amount of doubt. They seem to me to run the risk of preaching or didacticism or rant. But we have to try to write what we feel, if we can. If we have any talent, any use of language that's a little bit out of the ordinary, we have to try to use it. And we have to try to use it in the times when it seems desperately necessary. I don't know that a poem is going to change the course of history, but one can't stop to wonder, to guess about its effects before one does these things. This question came up again and again during the Vietnam War when a lot of us were trying to write poems about it. Did the poems do any good? We'll never know. We certainly wrote, all of us, some very bad poems, and we knew it. But the alternative was not to do it at all, and that seemed unthinkable, and it still does. A bad poem, after all, doesn't do any harm; it disappears in a little while.

Hirsch: You have written a lot more memoirs in the past few years. Is that the sign of coming to a certain age?
Merwin: I've asked myself that. I suppose it is because suddenly it seems possible to write about certain things that may be a way of describing age. But, you know, deliberate plans to write things, as I think back about it, and what I eventually have written, seem to me a little like two people walking along roads where they can sort of wave to each other over the hedge, but not much more. Sometimes I spend three or four years trying to write something, and then all of a sudden start writing something quite different that works, or seems to, whereas the first may not have done so. You know, I spent five years trying to write plays in England, and I wrote five plays, but I didn't like any of them. But out of that, I think, came changes in the way I was writing poems, and I think that out of the poems at the end of *The Drunk in the Furnace* and some of the poems after that came, much later, the prose of *Unframed Originals.* Obviously you have to write one thing to make the next thing possible. You can't have written things in a different order. I think that's the way it should be, too.

Hirsch: When did you first come to Hawaii?
Merwin: I first came here in the late sixties for a reading and I thought it beautiful, but it didn't seem to have much to do with my life at the time. And then I came back in the mid-seventies and it did, and I stayed.

Hirsch: Do you think you'll stay?
Merwin: Oh yes.

Hirsch: Recently you've begun translating chants and songs from Hawaii. What do you find compelling about the poems?
Merwin: I'm just feeling my way. Everything that I ever might have fancied I learned about translation is in abeyance while I try to work this one out. There are no chants in English. English has never been a chanted language, so there is no tradition to draw on or to extend. I have the long-standing

wish we spoke of to work from an oral tradition, and also the urgent feeling that this tradition is part of a culture that is being lost. But I'm an outsider. Putting it into English isn't going to save it, though it may save some kind of link with it, you know, which seems to me to have some point. I feel it is tied to other kinds of extinction of various things too. Several species a week are now becoming extinct, and this is an accelerating process. It's all because of human action, entirely human action. It's natural for species to become extinct, of course, but not at the rate that we have brought it about. Languages, cultures, and our own language are suffering the same fate. These aren't different processes. They're not different books on a shelf; they're all the same book. Any way of trying to turn that process around is useful. The love of what's there and the attempt to articulate it, the attempt to make this connection with it, the attempt to put it into reverent and complete form in our own language, into words that have some of the excitement of the original poetry, is a way of both paying respect to it—a living and enthusiastic respect to it—and maybe keeping it alive a little bit longer, or just keeping oneself alive a bit longer. At the same time, I've been working with the Hawaiian language as well as with Crow, and indigenous poetry even in translation has led me to some doubts about the imperial present of our own language—it betrays our lack of any sense of place. To some, no doubt, this is an advantage.

Hirsch: Recently, you've gotten more and more involved in writing nonfiction. I wonder if you'd talk about the impetus behind your book about Hawaii?

Merwin: I'm writing—trying to write—about what has already happened and what is still happening to these islands. I tried to write essays on political things twenty-five years ago. And I stopped because other people were finally writing about the same subjects better than I could. I don't think I have any particular gift for this. My mind is not a historian's mind at all. I want to write about these subjects simply because they seem to me urgent. The subjects are things that are passing rapidly from these islands and an examination of how and why this came about, and I want to write about it before these things are gone. I want to write about them because they are still, in many cases, vexed questions, and conceivably, by writing about them, one might be able to do something to check the flow. And because I care about the place, and the culture and language of the place. While they're still here. And also, because in each case, each of these subjects seems to be a kind of focus or symbol for things that are happening everywhere in the world. Again, there is always the danger of getting close to writing tracts, and I don't want to do that. But when one is talking, for example, about Kaho'olawe, the sacred island of a culture that has been treated with something like contempt for two hundred years—and this island has been systematically exploited by a different attitude and a different race—when you start writing about this island, it has both a symbolic and a practical significance. When you begin to tell the story to indigenous peoples anywhere in the Pacific, they immediately know what you're talking about and recognize it in every detail. If you start talking to Native Americans about it, they know what the story is all about. There are people all around the world who know what the story is about. It's a story of arrogance, exploitation, and consistent destruction. If the island of Delos were being used as a bombing range, as Kaho'olawe is, there are a great many people of European background who would know what that was about, and they would be outraged. The fact that it is happening to another race is something that makes it seem quite unreal, still, to people of European descent. That cultural obtuseness is something that fascinates me and makes me want to look into it in myself and in the world around me and try to write about it. We try to save what is passing, if only by describing it, telling it, knowing all the time that we can't do any of these things. The urge to tell it, and the knowledge of the impossibility. Isn't that one reason we write?

A Poet of Their Own

Dinitia Smith / 1995

From the *New York Times*, February 19, 1995. Reprinted by permission.

I'd got lost looking for W. S. Merwin's house on the Hawaiian island of Maui, driving along roads lined with palms and sugar cane, then turning into a dense area of ironwood and heliconia trees. It was almost like rain forest here—pink and red hibiscus, ginger flowers filled with rain from the night.

Then, suddenly, there he was, as if he'd somehow materialized out of the rain. He was standing by the gate to his land, looking like a Zen sensei, in a kimonolike shirt. He had slanting blue eyes and wide cheekbones. His skin was a silvery color. He was staring at me intently. "You said you'd be here at 10:15," he said in a precise voice.

I had come to see Merwin because he had just won the $100,000 Tanning Prize. And I had the distinct impression he was not sure he wanted to be found.

For eighteen years Merwin, now sixty-seven, has been living in this remote section of Hawaii, obsessively restoring, inch by inch, an abandoned pineapple farm to its original rain-forest-like state.

In Merwin's poetry, the subject is loss, loss of place especially, the destruction of the environment:

Well they'd made up their minds to be everywhere because why not.
Everywhere was theirs because they thought so.
They with two leaves they whom the birds despise.
In the middle of stones they made up their minds.
They started to cut.

When the Academy of American Poets announced it was giving Merwin the Tanning Prize, some said Merwin's best work was behind him, that since his 1967 book, *The Lice*, a gloomy volume about the destruction of nature, his work had become obscure and abstract. (The critic Helen Vendler once called Merwin "a lesser Eliot," and his poems "elusive pallors.") In addition, Merwin is a chancellor of the academy; the judges—the late James Merrill, J. D. McClatchy, and Carolyn Kizer—were all friends of Merwin's.

Initially, Kizer wanted the prize to go to Gwendolyn Brooks, an African American. "My qualm was it would look like the white male establishment handing around prizes to each other." But James Merrill was chairman of the jury. "We wanted to find a real master," he said last fall. "Gwendolyn Brooks would be very distinguished. But somehow I don't think she's a master." Kizer, herself a potential candidate for chancellor, was outnumbered and eventually voted with the rest. "I revere him," says Kizer. "Thank God it was Merwin, who has such enormous stature."

Merwin—his first name is William, he doesn't like Bill—tries to stay out of literary politics. He would like to be left alone to tend his garden and to write. He never answers his phone. Yet he's ambivalent about solitude. "He's a strange combination of recluse and very convivial," says his wife, Paula. Merwin is always being torn away—especially to receive prizes. A few weeks after he won the Tanning, he flew to New York to get the $10,000 Lenore Marshall Prize. And then a few weeks after that he flew back again to receive a $105,000 Lila Wallace–Readers' Digest Fellowship, awarded over a period of three years.

A Merwin poem is a highly crafted thing. The images seem etched; sometimes they come together with an almost magnetic force. He doesn't use punctuation anymore, and often begins a sentence on the preceding line. His poetry has an onrushing, murmurous quality:

This is what I have heard

at last the wind in December
lashing the old trees with rain
unseen rain racing along the tiles
under the moon
wind rising and falling
wind with many clouds
trees in the night wind

"Everything's got to do with listening," Merwin says. We are sitting on the porch of his house. The house, small and quite dark, is built on the lip of a dormant volcano, Haleakala, that rises 10,000 feet above the sea.

"Poetry is physical. As Pound said, poetry has one pole in reason and one pole in music. It's like making a joke. If you get one word wrong at the end of a joke, you've lost the whole thing."

Merwin admits his work is sometimes abstract. "The word Lowell used was 'history.' I had great difficulty putting the actual, ephemeral, phenomenal fact into a poem—because I was interested in the universality of it. It's the way the fact is heard or seen that counts."

Merwin puts a knife with honey on it on the table. "Watch," he says. Two geckos climb from a hidden place in the eaves, and begin licking the knife with pink tongues.

As Merwin and I talk, sudden, tropical rains come and go. The sun shines, then there's a giant rainbow out over the Pacific. Under the table, Merwin's four chows nap, their doggy smell filling the air. The chows are Merwin's substitute for children. He carries photos of them in his wallet. "I've never had a desire for children," he says. "I'm very sort of egotistical and impatient."

Merwin is a curious mixture of sensuality and reserve. The epithet "pretty boy" has haunted him all his life. *Time* magazine once wrote that Merwin "flutters female hearts." When he was younger, his face was almost faun-like—the eyes wary, trapped. Howard Moss, the late poetry editor of the *New Yorker*, used to keep a picture of Merwin on his wall. "Nobody has a right to be that good-looking," he would say.

Over the years, Merwin has almost reinvented himself in the nineteenth-century Romantic ideal of the poet at one with nature. When he isn't writing, he's down in his forest, trying to restore it to its primeval state. In conversation, he refers constantly to "the environment," to a tree that doesn't belong in Hawaii but was brought here by merchants or missionaries, to a geothermal project on a neighboring island that he's campaigning against. In many ways, Merwin's is a mythic self, far from the little boy who grew up in a family clinging precariously to the middle class.

Merwin was the son of a Presbyterian minister in a poor parish in Scranton, Pennsylvania, surrounded by barren, strip-mined land. His mother had been orphaned as a child; then her brother died; then her first baby, Merwin's older brother. Merwin grew up haunted by this brother, in an atmosphere permeated by grief. (He has a sister, Ruth, two years younger, a high-school teacher.)

Merwin's father almost never spoke of his own family. The Merwins were rough people. Merwin's grandfather was a drunken, violent riverboat pilot on the Allegheny. Merwin's father had violence in him, too. He was "a bully," says Merwin. "I was frightened of him. There was a fair amount of physical punishment. I turned on him physically two times in early adolescence. I thought one time he was getting abusive to my mother. When I was thirteen, I said, 'Never touch me again!'" The theme of violence runs through Merwin's poetry—violence to animals, to plants, to the soil, human violence. Merwin's mother was a committed pacifist. Today, Merwin is a pacifist, too, and also a Buddhist. It's as if Buddhism will somehow overcome the violence in the world—and the potential for violence within Merwin himself. Merwin's father was also mean to pets—and to this day the sight of an animal being mistreated can send Merwin into a rage. "He has a temper," says Merwin's wife, "but he loses it very rarely. It's always been on the occasion of somebody or something helpless."

Merwin's first poems were hymns he wrote for his father. And he is indebted to his father for a crucial lesson: "As long as you are doing something you respect, it's okay not to make money," is the way Merwin defines it. Today, Merwin lives on $25,000 to $30,000. With his resonant voice and dramatic pauses, Merwin is a riveting reader. "He could always just go to a university, stand up, open his mouth—and pick up $2,000," says Moira Hodgson, a writer who lived with Merwin during the late sixties. Unlike most poets, he doesn't teach.

Merwin's parents were uneducated, but Merwin is a translator of Neruda, *El Cid*, *The Chanson de Roland*; he reads and quotes often from Dante and the Welsh sagas. He was a scholarship student at Princeton in the forties—a waiter in one of the university's elite eating clubs. "He was a kind of prodigy," recalls Galway Kinnell, a Princeton classmate, "writing poetry that was so incredibly resonant." Even then, Merwin attracted the attention of eminent older figures. He studied writing with the critic R. P. Blackmur, and showed his poems to Blackmur's teaching assistant, John Berryman. Berryman, literally trembling with passion, would say, "You should get down on your knees to the Muse." Sometimes Berryman told Merwin his poems were terrible, but he was encouraging too, in a "guarded" way. One day, Merwin asked how he could be sure his poetry was any good. Berryman's response was memorable, and later, Merwin wrote a poem about it: "you can't you can never be sure / you die without knowing."

After Princeton, Merwin married Dorothy Jeanne Ferry, a secretary at Princeton. Merwin decided to write verse plays, and supported himself teaching the children of wealthy aristocrats. Eventually the poet Robert Graves hired him as a tutor to his son in Majorca.

Soon tension developed between Graves and Merwin. Graves was flirting outrageously with a house guest in front of his wife and children. "It was quite nauseating," Merwin remembers. "He was treating her as though she were the Muse, flirting and not going to bed with her." Merwin and Graves quarreled. Later, Merwin got back at Graves in a poem: "Opportunist, shrewd waster, half calculation, / Half difficult child; a phoney, it would seem." Another Graves house guest was Dido Milroy, an Englishwoman with literary aspirations. Dido was a powerful figure, fifteen years older than Merwin. They began to collaborate on a verse play. After Merwin left Majorca, he went to London, broke up with his wife, Dorothy, and eventually married Dido.

Merwin's relationship with Dido dominated most of his adult life. She introduced him to English literary figures, helped get him a job translating *El Cid* for the BBC. Yet Dido was a devouring figure who wanted to inhabit Merwin's very existence. "Dido's ex-husband said she always wanted to own a poet," says Merwin.

In 1952, Merwin published his first book, *A Mask for Janus*. The poems are ornate, sometimes mannered—and were good enough to win him the first prize an establishment poet must win, the Yale Younger Poets Prize, judged then by W. H. Auden.

Merwin felt confined by Dido and longed to hear American voices. In 1956, he won a fellowship at the Poets' Theater in Boston and moved there. But Dido resolutely followed. In Boston, Merwin became part of a group who surrounded the charismatic, intermittently mad Robert Lowell, then teaching at Boston University. Lowell could be viciously competitive. One day, Lowell said to Merwin: "You'll always be a good poet, but not a great poet."

In Boston, Merwin abandoned verse plays. He had begun to rediscover his "American" voice and to explore his family's secrets. His 1960 collection, *The Drunk in the Furnace*, is less precious than Merwin's previous work, more in the American vernacular. The title poem is evocative of Merwin's drunken grandfather:

> They were afterwards astonished
> To confirm, one morning, a twist of smoke like a pale
> Resurrection, staggering out of its chewed hole,
> And to remark then other tokens that someone

Cozily bolted behind the eye-holed iron
Door of the drafty burner, had there established
His bad castle.

Ever restless, the Merwins again moved back to England. In London, Merwin was friends with Sylvia Plath and Ted Hughes. Plath idolized Merwin—she wanted to be pure like him, free to just write. At one point, according to a memoir by Dido Merwin, Plath became infatuated with Merwin. But Merwin didn't return her affections. The Merwins were witness to the awful disintegration of the Hugheses' marriage before Plath's suicide in 1963. Today, Merwin won't talk about Plath. Plath is bad karma.

Finally, in 1968, Merwin separated from Dido (though she refused to give him a divorce). She clung to Merwin's beloved house in Lacan, France, about which Merwin has written many poems and a prose collection, *The Lost Upland.*

Merwin began living part of the year in New York with Moira Hodgson, an English writer twenty years younger. Ever reluctant to let him go, Dido befriended Hodgson. "She had a very powerful personality," says Hodgson. "It was a bit like the mother who says, 'Let my son bring his girlfriends home.'" (Dido died in 1990.)

"Merwin was incredibly difficult," adds Hodgson, "but all poets are incredibly difficult. He had a lot of conflicting feelings about leaving France, but he liked the excitement and hard edge of the city. Then he'd say, 'O, God, I can't bear to be here!'"

Merwin opposed the Vietnam War. In 1971, when his book *The Carrier of Ladders* won the Pulitzer, he gave the $1,000 away to antiwar causes in protest.

On a reading trip to Hawaii in 1975, he met Dana Naone, a Hawaiian and an aspiring poet, also younger. "I think William was looking to chart a new course," says Merwin's friend the poet William Matthews. "Dana had a willingness to live in the country and get into the dirt." Merwin and Hodgson broke up, and he began living with Naone.

One thing Naone and Merwin shared was an interest in Buddhism. Early in their relationship, they were invited to the Naropa Institute in Boulder, Colorado, a center for Buddhist studies where Allen Ginsberg was teaching.

Naropa was presided over by a Tibetan guru, Chögyam Trungpa, a tireless drunk and womanizer. At a Halloween party while Ginsberg was away, Trungpa ordered everyone to undress. Merwin and Naone refused. Trungpa's bodyguards tried to batter down the door to their room. "I was not going to go peacefully," Merwin recalls. "I started hitting people with beer bottles. It was a very violent scene." Trungpa's bodyguards stripped them, and the two figures cowered together before the guru like a chastened Adam and Eve.

The incident came to be mythologized as "The Great Naropa Poetry Wars." Naropa became an epitaph for an era, a paradigm of the difference between two kinds of poetry—between Ginsberg's passionate, declamatory style and Merwin's restrained, Western formalism.

Despite what happened at Naropa, Merwin is still a Buddhist. He likes to quote the thirteenth-century Buddhist teacher Dōgen, a contemporary of Dante's: "'You must let the body and mind fall away.'" In his house, Merwin has a zazen (meditation) room, a sparse place with four pillows, where he meditates—forty-five minutes before breakfast, and again before dinner.

After Naropa, Merwin moved to Hawaii for good. He built his house with an inheritance from his mother. Later, he bought additional land with money left to him by George Kirstein, former publisher of the *Nation*. Eventually, he broke up with Dana Naone.

In 1970, Merwin met a blond woman who seemed to him "beautiful, terrified." She was Paula Schwartz, an editor of children's books. Schwartz was married, and they went their own ways. Then in 1982, Merwin (finally divorced from Dido) met Schwartz again at a dinner party in New York. In a poem, "Late Spring," he describes the moment:

> after looking and mistakes and forgetting
> turning there thinking to find
> no one except those I knew
> finally I saw you
> sitting in white

They were married in a Buddhist ceremony in 1983.

One afternoon, in the rain, Merwin takes me on a tour of the garden. "That's a koa tree, what Hawaiian canoes were made from," he says as we trudge along a wet, rocky path. "I put that in as a tiny tree."

We come to an eroded ledge, one patch he hasn't restored yet. "See there, that's what it used to be like. It wants to be a forest!"

As he digs in the garden, Merwin thinks about poetry. Recently Milton's sonnet about his wife came to mind: "'Me thought I saw my late espoused saint / brought to me like Alcestis from the grave.'"

"The fact is he never saw her," says Merwin. "He was blind before he married her. It hadn't occurred to me—his wife appears to him in a dream! I realized 'Jove's great son' was Jesus, who rescues her from death."

Since the restoration of Merwin's land, since his marriage to Paula, his poetry has become more accessible, more celebratory. Now in his poems, you can almost feel the rain in the trees:

> I lie listening to the black hour
> before dawn and you are
> still asleep beside me while
> around us the trees full of night lean
> hushed in their dream that bears
> us up asleep and awake then I hear
> drops falling one by one into
> the sightless leaves

An Interview with W. S. Merwin

Michael Ondaatje, Sam Solecki, and Linda Spalding / 1998

From *Brick: A Journal of Reviews* 62 (1999), 14–19. The interview took place in October 1998, in Toronto, Ontario. Reprinted by permission.

MO: Yesterday, before the reading, you said something about holocausts. Not just the twentieth-century holocaust that we know about but the repetition of holocausts in history. You spoke of the necessity of writing poetry within that reality. Can you talk about how this might have affected how you write now or how you think now?

WSM: It's a huge subject. I guess I've been angry about history all my life. This poem, *The Folding Cliffs*, is related to my inescapable feelings about the Hawaiian people and the rest of life and my heretical relation to conventional humanism, which seems to me kind of like a club with a restricted entrance policy. My feeling about it evolved over the years. I don't understand how we continue to be sexist and racist. I realize that what we're doing to the rest of life is suicidal. It also destroys us morally. This is the great flaw of the human species. We make an image of our social selves and then we defend it violently. It's never perfect, it's never complete. We look for threats to it, because we know that it's fragile. I think racism comes out of that, sometimes. And I think anti-Semitism comes out of that. I think there's another kind of racism that comes out of justifying imperialism, justifying the urge to dominate and to possess, to own, acquire.

You're talking about holocausts and you're thinking as I am of what happened in the Congo, at the same time this story (in Hawaii) was happening. It's pretty well forgotten in the Western world, but there was a death rate in the Congo in one generation that was greater than the number of people killed on both sides in World War I in Europe. Enormous. You know, because of reading Sebald—

MO: And Conrad.

WSM: Conrad, yes. And I hadn't realized before how many people were killed in China in the period just preceding the Opium Wars and during the Opium Wars—millions, millions of people. And the Albigensian Crusade, which was a brutal trashing of southern France. They just went south and took everything, with the blessing of the church.

SS: Zbigniew Herbert writes about that in *The Barbarian in the Garden.* That's a kind of central moment for him—barbarism and culture, side by side.

WSM: He was fascinated by that kind of mechanism in history. He was fascinated by the sack of Rome in his poem "The Longobards." I loved Herbert. I loved him as a man, a very difficult man but I loved him.

MO: How did you meet him?

WSM: I met him in New York. I introduced him and Czeslaw Milosz in New York, at the Y. In '68, '69, I think. Zbigniew was a few years older than I was; Milosz was many years older than I was. Actually, I'd known Milosz before that. He came to see me in France. I think I wrote to him after *The Captive Mind*, which was a very important book to me. I loved Herbert's writing.

SS: He certainly writes about holocausts or genocide, but always indirectly. He can't write about it directly, he can't mention the Katyn Forest massacre, he can't mention the Gulag, and when he writes about history, it's with an ironic tone, with detachment. In fact, your mentioning Milosz is interesting, because one of the things it seems to me you and Miloz have in common is that you may be among the small handful of people who still write a kind of rhapsodic poem occasionally.

WSM: Individual limitations differ as do individual personalities. But I don't think that we, as poets and writers, should ever allow limitations to be imposed upon us. I don't mean just in the totalitarian way, but in the way that every generation tries to do it. A critical stamp is put upon writing and then all of a sudden a particular kind of address, a particular kind of poem, a particular kind of subject—or any subject, or some form or other, or any apparent form—suddenly becomes unacceptable, beyond the pale, as if you've no right to it. I think that one should not oppose it, because if you oppose it, you're being affected by it. The possibilities of the imagination and the possibilities of language cannot be mathematically influenced. They are existentially influenced. There is no reason why any form is impossible or why any subject is impossible. If you can do it. The reason for not doing it should not be a critical/political theory. It should be that it's not within your talent or within your knowledge or within your capacity, but it should not have to do with the mores at the time or with what any critic has to say about it.

SS: Did you ever sense, when you began writing, that the problem of a delimiting criticism was there?
WSM: Probably not. But think how long ago that was! The—what should we call it—wave of deconstruction is not that old.

SS: I'm not talking about deconstruction so much as waves of fashion, what you can and cannot write, what subjects were the subjects of poetry in the fifties and the sixties as opposed to now.
WSM: The limiting apparatus has been there. Think of Randall Jarrell's wonderful essay "The Age of Criticism." That was before any of this stuff got really going, but there already was the age of criticism. The academic structure—publish or perish and all that. There's an awful lot that's published that really shouldn't have been published. People pay a lot of attention to that, especially in the universities, and a lot of the writers are in the universities, for reasons that we all know. Good and bad.

LS: Are poets less political now?
WSM: They're certainly less political than they were in the sixties. In the forties and fifties they weren't really political, but the Beats got going in the mid-fifties, and everybody knew about them by the end of the decade, although their serious political connections didn't really get going till the Vietnam War. That's sort of surprising to me. I never wanted any connection with politics, but I kept bumping into things that I felt somebody had to say something about. It was the anti-nuclear movement in England that really started me off, and having to do with the *Nation* in the end of the fifties. I was in the second Aldermaston march, and then I began to realize that the anti-nuclear ferment and poisoning the earth with agribiz—the whole thing that really got going in World War II—that these were related, and I began to make these connections. That was my political self-education, I guess. Once you make connections, you can't unmake them. Once you really believe that there is a connection, it's very hard to unmake it. And I don't think you should. It's like denying an affection or a talent. You can't turn away from those things.

SS: You're very political now, but in poems like, "Home Tundra" and "The Comet Museum" that appeared last week in the *New York Review*, those concerns might be there, but they're certainly not there in a direct or polemical way.

WSM: Yes, yes. I certainly don't want to preach and I also am very suspicious of it, though during the Vietnam War we all wrote political things, there was a lot of that. And it wasn't all bad. There was some very good poetry. I think that, if the concern for these things is not simply mental but comes to involve you in the place where the poetry comes from, you may very well write a good poem out of it. *The Divine Comedy* is a great, political poem. The greatness of Dante is that he realizes different aspects of his own character and puts them in the poem with the same skill Shakespeare would have managed characters in a play.

Still, I'm very cautious of poetry turning into propaganda. It's also very dangerous to feel that you're right, to start by feeling that you're right about something. I don't think the fact that the didactic and propagandistic and poetry are at odds with each other is a reason why we should not try to engage those feelings, though. I think poetry comes out of the deepest parts and places. It's always a matter of life and death questions. And I say again, I don't think one should be limited. Milosz is a very good example. There's a wonderful political feeling in Milosz. But after all, when he was asked to write a poem about oppression at the time of the occupation of Poland, what he wrote—it was in that series of poems called "The World"—

SS: "A Naive Poem," he subtitled it.

WSM: Do you remember that poem? It's actually a series of poems—I can't remember how many there are, maybe twenty-four very short poems—and they're like songs of innocence. They're really about his childhood.

MO: How do you see Denise Levertov's career in terms of the political?

WSM: I think it was wonderful the way she—it's not that she internalized it, although that's what it looks like. She was trying to find ways of writing about things like indignation, which is one of the hardest things to handle in a poem. Sometimes she wrote weak poems, as a result of the didactic side of it, but that was a risk everybody took. I think some of the best poets of the sixties were quite aware of the dangers of self-righteousness, which is one of the ugliest human manifestations. It really can destroy a poem.

SS: Were you worried about that with *The Folding Cliffs*?

WSM: Do you think there was a danger of that?

SS: Given the subject matter, sure. Here you're writing about a difficult, historical situation—you navigate it very well, both by contextualizing it historically and mythically. But here you've got on the one hand Christianity, one of the worst master narratives of the last two thousand years, and within which the Native experience has unfolded. And on the other hand, you've got Natives who are so clearly victims. You've got characters like Louis Stolz who were representative of a certain kind of evil—what in another poem you call the "shamelessness of man." You're constantly swerving away from easy moral judgments by dramatizing certain things, trying to find a certain detachment, a voice that will not fall into moral categories.

WSM: I try to do it by putting in real characters. Like Judge Kauai.

SS: He's a wonderful figure! In retrospect, it seems to me that the Judge is really the key figure, because he's able to reflect on the situation; he feels sorry, but he sees it as inevitable. It reminds me that you've said that you wouldn't have written this book early in your life.

WSM: Exactly. I don't think that, in youth, one is able to see both sides. It's not that I think there are two sides to the question. I don't. What happened to the "lepers" in Hawaii was unjust and immoral and destructive. But that doesn't mean that everybody behaved all the time out of injustice and destructiveness or that Hawaiians didn't do a lot of destructive things, too. During the takeover by Kamehameha's family of the island of Kauai there was a real pogrom! In ten days they killed every member of the families of the chiefs of Kauai.

SS: When I first saw the book, knowing that you were interested in dramatic monologues, I expected that there would be monologues of various kinds. I also assumed that anybody who writes a long, syllabic-oriented narrative poem would at some point show King James's rhythms. They seem almost inevitable, once you stretch the line out. I was very surprised that neither of those things was happening. That you managed to achieve some kind of tone, a voice that seemed to me unique, that didn't have the Bible haunting it.

Again, you have a way of tightening up lyrics, whenever you want to, with a metaphoric ambiguity often at the end of certain poems. But here, you loosened up and moved into a different narrative mode. I would not have spotted this immediately as you, if somebody had given me a few of the proofs and said, start reading, I wouldn't have spotted the voice, the vocabulary, and the tone. I think it more than a little surprising that here you've gone into a narrative mode—who does that anymore?

WSM: Yes. I was very dubious about writing anything about Hawaii, because I didn't want to start exploiting the Hawaiian material. That's tacky, and I felt very cautious about that. But the story kept nagging at me. Finally, after most of ten years, I thought it probably had to be poem. A history is fine, but it becomes one other essay and gets forgotten. It seems very free, but it actually isn't. I couldn't think of anything else that it could be but a poem. But I thought, what kind of poem? And I wasn't very sure about that. Certainly it couldn't be blank verse. Free verse? It doesn't do it. I think that people like Williams and Pound—Pound couldn't tell a story anyway. Williams tried to do it but he did it by changing the mode all the time; he had to keep doing that to cover the range of the subject. And I thought, that doesn't work, and it doesn't really tell the whole story. But what is the whole story? So I started trying to find out more about the story—really digging into it— and I got into this history. I found everybody who knew anything about it. I spent several years doing that.

Brooding about the facts as they came out, I kept a lot of notes, and out of that I began to think of what kind of poem, what form the narrative would take. I really wanted a line which was close to what was happening in *The Vixen.* It sort of evolved out of that. But I thought, just as in the ancient world in Europe, the elegy and the narrative are not exactly the same thing but they're very close to each other and the one always seemed to reflect the other. I wanted something that could be flexible enough to reflect that tradition in English and in the European past but also could reflect the Hawaiian chant, which I think is untranslatable, and which is a strange mixture of vernacular speech on the one hand and great formality on the other. I wanted something that could move from taking a phrase out of a letter straight into a chant and dialogue—without changing the mode, doing the whole thing all the way through. And then I didn't want to tell the story in the chronological way, because that makes it anecdotal. It's only the genealogical chants that really start talking about the beginning of the Hawaiian Islands.

LS: You've studied the Hawaiian language . . .

WSM: But it's a difficult language to study because of the breaks in time, in history. Hawaiian was forbidden. Thurston, who wrote the biography of Dole and was the minister of education under the takeover, prided himself on how many schools he'd forbidden to use or teach the Hawaiian language.

There were at least two generations, almost everywhere in the islands, where Hawaiians were punished for speaking their own language. The kids got punished and then the parents got to be ashamed for letting children speak Hawaiian. By the late sixties and early seventies, many Hawaiians wanted to have it back, but it's very hard to find it now except among a few very old people.

LS: So the chant itself, except as something heard in English, has almost disappeared. But there's something else going on, I think. I'm very interested in how your work on Dante overlaps with *The Folding Cliffs*.
WSM: Well, I've been fascinated by Dante since I was eighteen.

LS: You hadn't thought there was any connection between the two?
WSM: No. But now that I look back, I realize there are always connections between things. I never thought to translate Dante. I used to lecture about the impossibility of translating Dante. You can prove that it's impossible to translate Dante. But it really arose the same way as Robert Pinsky's *Inferno* did. Dan Halpern wanted to do this project of getting poets to translate *The Inferno*. He asked me to do it and I said, "Do I get to choose my cantos?" He said, "Yes." I said, "Well, I've always been curious about—the twenty-sixth canto is almost my favorite in *The Inferno*. I believe that all the translations have missed it in one place."

LS: You've lived both in France and in Hawaii. Can you talk about the difference in learning from the French landscape and the Hawaiian? Because there was not a real native connection to the French landscape by the time you discovered it, was there?
WSM: There was! Literally, because the peasant world that I found when I went there went back to before the Romans. Not in the form that I found it, but the old inhabitants remembered the Gaulish cemetery, and the actual people living there in the country, the country people were descendants of pre-Roman tribes and they differed. One tribe really lived in the limestone uplands and the other tribe lived in the chestnut forests. They didn't look the same and they didn't behave the same. They knew they were different. There was the sense of real antiquity, of something going a long, long way back to Lascaux and the painted caves, even way back before the Ice Age. There was a feeling of great antiquity. There the peasant world really tried to take care. When they cut wood—when I first went there, I learned all these wonderful things from them. They said, "You only cut wood in the old moon

in the month of August." You wait till the moon changes and that's when you cut the wood. The reason for that is that sap suddenly starts flowing down, when the moon turns. Wood that you cut for building, at that time, seasons fast and never rots. The wood that you cut for firewood at that time dries faster and burns better.

LS: This is not my image of France. I feel that it's completely denatured and—
WSM: France is less denatured than almost anywhere in Europe. You think of Germany or Eastern Europe or even England. But there was also the sense of time and the sense of that being obliterated. The farming village is no longer a farming village, it's a summer village. It's taken me years to come to terms with that. And you know what's happened in Hawaii, the overlaying of tourism and the whorehouse mentality that goes with it and development, the building over.

LS: Isn't there any place in North America where one could still find these connections to the landscape?
WSM: I hope so. I suppose the Hopis are clinging to it. Everywhere the story's the same. The invading, the economic dominance, divide and use the division in your own interest. I don't know. I don't think there's any simple solution. I'm not very optimistic.

MO: Can you talk about other people who were important to you as poets, in the last ten to fifteen years? North Americans tend to look at North America most of the time, and you are someone who—because of all your translations over the years and your awareness of European and Asian writing—can you talk about a few of the writers who have stayed with you and that you feel close to?
WSM: It keeps changing. It's not that I reject people, but I read somebody for a while and I'll read them over and over again and then move on. I read sort of obvious people. I don't know how influences work. I think there are affinities that you discover.

SS: But there are poets who "sound" more like you, whom you've translated. There are moments in the Mandelstam translation that you did with Clarence Brown where a clarity that is there tightens up in a wonderfully ambiguous metaphor or closing image. It's something one often finds in your poems. There's an image of ink and paper at the end of one of Jean Follain's poems, which I had no problem at all in sensing as similar to yours, especially where you're moving in a certain direction and then you take it all back, the way you seem to do right at the end of *The Folding Cliffs*.

WSM: Yes. [Laughs] In translating Mandelstam, I worked with Clarence Brown and I didn't know the Russian and he didn't want me to, and we had to figure out what made a poem remarkable. Mandelstam's own feeling about translation was such that he wanted one to take the heart of a poem and make a poem out of it. He translated one Petrarch sonnet and you can't even find Petrarch in it. With Follain and now with Dante, I try to do something very different, I try to make the English as close to the original as possible. You can't really do it with Dante, of course, but I've taken no liberty— I've tried to make it closer to the meaning of the original than the two great prose translations, Sinclair's and Singleton's. I wanted to have the clarity and the exact meaning. You know we were talking about speed, about poetry being faster than prose, well the flip side of that is that when you start to hear it, it slows you down. You can't speed read it, you have to read it at the speed of the spoken word, so it's slower in that sense. If occasionally you lose the rhythm and have to go back over it, that's okay too. Of course, poetry covers the ground at a speed that prose very seldom can. John Berryman once said to me, Look at four lines of Baudelaire and look at the first line and the fourth line to see how he got from one to the other. Sometimes it's just incredible. Prose would seem incomprehensible if you tried to move that fast.

MO: It's like not having a set in theater. You step into another room just by turning around and starting another conversation. In your more recent poetry, there is an avoidance of punctuation. I think somewhere you may have said that punctuation means prose.

WSM: Punctuation doesn't mean prose. After all, there are wonderful poets, including present company, who use punctuation.

MO: Minimally!

WSM: Minimally, and not always.

MO: Less and less.

WSM: I do feel that punctuation is a sort of protocol, post-Gutenberg. It really doesn't even have to do so much with the written word as with the printed word. It fixes you in time, in historic time, and it fixes the mode *because* it really is dictated by the concerns of prose, prose clarity. One of the assumptions in printed prose is that you don't have to hear it. The point for me was to make the allegiance clearly to the oral nature of poetry. If you don't hear it, it doesn't speak to you. If you don't punctuate, that becomes a form in itself. The formal requirement is that the movement of the language does the punctuation, which means you have to hear the movement of the narrative, you really have to hear it. I believe that none of the original manuscripts of Virgil were punctuated. Homer obviously was never punctuated. The first manuscripts of the troubadours were never punctuated. It's only later on that they started punctuating. Medieval language wasn't punctuated. The Hawaiian language wasn't punctuated.

MO: I remember the first time I heard you read the Peire Vidal poem last summer. In those last lines, "what is not there I have sung its song I have breathed / its day and it was nothing to you where were you" . . . By having no punctuation you can extend that pause or have no pause at all and it becomes a brutal accusation or it could be a plaintive line. The great thing about the lack of punctuation is that freedom, and all the varieties of ways you can reinterpret your own poem after you've written it. By the way you read it out it could be a brutal line or a very sad line. Richard Howard has written that when you dropped punctuation from your poems, he felt that suddenly the images were not so much enclosed or framed as they were displayed, that the openness left them naked among the silences, they moved more easily.

WSM: For me the great example of it in the twentieth century is Apollinaire. There was one line in particular that just hit me, the end of the little poem about his mother. The mother speaking in "La Porte" and at the end she says "Enfant je t'ai donné ce que j'avais travaille." There's no punctuation.

SS: You almost find yourself suspended over an ambiguity in the syntax that has a semantic effect. But what I'm trying to get at is that there are poets you've translated with whom you seem to have a special affinity. René Char, for example . . .

WSM: Yes, and sometimes that affinity has not lasted. I remember reading Char with great excitement forty years ago and recently I went back and read some more and it was as though he were a new poet because I was seeing something that I'd never seen before. But it didn't startle me the same way. It seemed simpler and more comprehensible and exciting, but in quite a different way. And somebody like Neruda—this is an example of what you're asking—I read Neruda first in college because somebody said, This guy is fantastic and he's writing in Chile now. This was *Residence on Earth* and, with the Spanish I had at the time, it was incredibly difficult. I floundered through it for a while. I thought it was quite wonderful but it really wasn't making much sense to me. Later on, I was asked to translate something for the BBC and I did, but it never occurred to me that it could have any relation to my own writing. In fact, there are only certain periods of Neruda that I really like. I love the *Residencia* poems, which he sort of rejected later on in his life. I think because they were too private or something. I don't like the *Canto General* at all. I think it's inflated and kind of self-regarding. I love many of the late poems. But this is a lifelong off-and-on relationship. I always wanted to be influenced by François Villon and it never happened. But in the next book there's a poem that deliberately starts out to echo "The Great Testament," and it's a testament poem.

MO: What was that great story about Dante and Virgil, where he ends the canto in a different poetic language?

WSM: Oh! That's the twenty-sixth canto of *The Purgatorio.* I believe there are connections between it and the twenty-sixth canto of *The Inferno*, the Odysseus canto. The element is fire. The punishment is fire. The suffering is fire. And the temptation of Dante is so great that he nearly falls into the pit. What Odysseus really exemplifies in the poem is the love of knowledge for its own sake. This really is one of the ultimate vanities and a very destructive vanity. Look at the twentieth century, look at modern man: love of knowledge without concern for the deeper reality. And the twenty-sixth canto in the *Purgatorio* is about erotic love for its own sake, and it's the canto of the poets, above all. In Dante's scheme, it's about love that's gone astray. We're not clear in what way Arnaut Daniel's love went astray, but that was why Daniel was there. And instead of falling into the pit, what Dante does, as a great tribute to Daniel, is to have him answer in Provençal. Dante has Daniel answer in a way that is the deliberate echo of one of the greatest and the most personal of Daniel's own poems. It's the first sestina—ending with three of the greatest lines in Provençal poetry. At the end of the poem, Dante has him say, "I am Arnaut who harvest the wind, / And ride the ox to chase the hare, / And I swim against the tide." It takes your breath away. I've read it all my life.

LS: William, thank you for this, from all of us.

Interview with W. S. Merwin

John Amen / 2003

From the *Pedestal Magazine* 15 (April–June 2003). Reprinted by permission.

John Amen: I am extremely excited to be featuring you in the *Pedestal Magazine*. Let me begin by asking you about your writing habits. Do you write every day? In waves or phases? Do you have a set schedule? Or have you, in fact, embraced different approaches at different times?

W. S. Merwin: I think you put your habits into place as you grow up. And your habits may not be of any use to anyone else. I remember, as a student, being fascinated by a number of German writers who lived in a house near where I went to college. I was so impressed by the way these men worked. They seemed to work all the time. Sometimes I would go out at night and take a walk just to look at Herman Broch's house and see the light on in the upstairs window, which I knew was his study. And then when I worked for Robert Graves, one of the marvelous things about that experience was the way Robert worked all the time. Something would interrupt, or someone would come to the door, and Robert would deal with it and then go right back to work. Robert did everything in longhand. I was impressed by the way he worked. He was a wonderful model. One of the great things for Robert was that there was no telephone. Eventually he had a wind-up phone in one of the corners of the house. But for quite some time, if you wanted to get in touch with Robert, you called in town and a message was sent. The telephone is a tremendous distraction. For years I didn't have one, and I don't think I've ever really gotten used to it.

I've found that the best thing for me is to insist that some part of the day—and for me, it's the morning until about two in the afternoon—be dedicated to writing. I go into my room and shut the door, and that's that. You have to make exceptions, of course, but you just stick to it, and then it becomes a habit, and I think it's a valuable one. Flaubert said that inspiration consists of sitting down at the same table at the same time every day, and I think that's the way one should look at it. If you're waiting for lightning to strike a stump, you're going to sit there for the rest of your life.

Amen: Your poem, "Is That What You Are," is a piece that I first read in the 1980s (when I was thirteen or fourteen). This is one of a small handful of pieces that essentially introduced me to modern poetry. In particular, the lines "Standing on the stairs of water," "Hope and grief are still our wings," and "There are feathers in the ice" are lines that helped give me an impression of what was poetically possible. I'm wondering, could you speak a little about this piece? Can you offer any particular comments regarding this poem?

Merwin: "Is That What You Are" is one of three or four poems that are clustered together, and they all arise out of the deaths of friends. At some point, you're startled to find that friends who are older, and friends who are your age, and, indeed, friends who are writers, die. And your relation to them is something you never really worked out. This is upsetting; apart from the grief itself, it's an experience you don't quite know what to do with. When these people go, there's always so much unfinished about the relationship, and it stays with you and continues to trouble you—trying to resolve it in some way, when it can't be resolved.

It doesn't matter who the friends are. Then it becomes gossip. So much of literary history is really a kind of gossip. And gossip is really a distraction; it doesn't tell you about the poem; it tells you about the background of the poem. The relevance of the poem is something that's in the poem itself.

Amen: I suppose, in some cases, if a reader has that kind of background information, it could compromise his or her reading of the poem.

Merwin: I think it can because then attention is paid to the background rather than to the poem. There's a great example of that. Years ago I read John Livingston Lowe's *The Road to Xanadu*, all about the great poems of Coleridge. He went into great detail about what Coleridge had been reading and with whom he had been corresponding, including Wordsworth. He managed to piece together the most incredible background. When I finished the book, I thought, this is marvelous, and now I know a lot about Coleridge's background. But finally there I am, face to face with the poems, and it's the relationship to the poems that matters. Even with the knowledge about the background, still, I'm ultimately back with the poems. And that's what matters, the relationship to the poem.

Amen: I'm wondering, have you ever had times when you struggled with a block or were unable to write? If so, how did you deal with this impediment?
Merwin: I don't know quite how to answer that because, whenever I finish something, it strikes me that that could well be the last poem I'll ever write. You never know where the next poem is coming from, or if there will be a next poem. I try to write every day. That doesn't mean I try to write poetry every day. And I feel very lucky if I know what I'm working on. You know, one has much conflict of feelings about work. I came gradually to find that the actual process of work was something that I simply loved. Getting completely absorbed was something I really appreciated. With the years it has become a real joy, difficult though it may be, just the "intent-nature" of working.

Amen: When you reflect on your development as a poet, what do you consider to be your major breakthroughs? And, on the other hand, what is something related to the creative or compositional process with which you still struggle?
Merwin: Well, I struggle with all of it. I suppose the constant effort for me is trying to bring what I care about into the words and the writing and the electric charge of language itself, and also to convey a certain immediacy of experience. Writers tend to do one or the other better. Some writers are very close to immediate experience, but the language is rather slack. With others, there is great tension and electricity of language, and specific or immediate experience is rather remote. With me, it's bringing the two together that's always been demanding and something that I keep trying to do. But it happens in different ways. Sometimes I'll try to write something, and it won't come to anything, and I'll put it away for a long period, then bring it back out and start working with it again. In the process of rewriting, it may turn into what I wanted it to be months or years before. That's happened a number of times.

When I was about thirty, I really seemed to come to the end of a way of writing poetry (with the end of *The Drunk in the Furnace*). When I finished that manuscript, I thought, I can't imagine that I will want to write in this way any longer. I wanted to write in a different way. This was not a judgment on that way of writing, it was just that I felt I'd come to the end of it. And I didn't know exactly what to do. I wasn't going to *try*, deliberately, to write differently. For a period of time, I didn't write poetry at all. And then one day I was thinking back to the time when I had been writing the last poems in *The Drunk in the Furnace*. All of a sudden, the first poem of *A Moving Target* came to me. It was a totally different kind of writing. In six weeks I wrote about half of that book. The poems came out one right after another. They're all very different from each other and very different from earlier poems. And they were so different that people assumed this was a deliberate and judgmental break with everything that I had written before. I didn't think of it that way. I simply felt that I had finished writing in one way and didn't want to write that way anymore. And if you change the way you write, you change what you write, and this was a "moving on" rather than a "moving away from." I do think there is a continuity to the poems, the shift between the poems in *The Drunk in the Furnace* and those in *The Moving Target*, but I wasn't concerned with the continuity at that time. I thought that would take care of itself, if the change was authentic; if it came from the right place, the connections would eventually become clear. But in the meantime I wanted to do something new, and that first poem, "Home for Thanksgiving" [from *The Moving Target*], seemed new enough.

Amen: Have you had that experience—that desire for a change, for a shifting—at different times during your career?
Merwin: It has happened a few times, but that was one of the most obvious and dramatic examples. It was very exciting, too. Many years later, when I wrote *The Folding Cliffs*, the long narrative poem, something similar happened. I had that story or part of that story in my head for many years. I didn't know that I could do anything with it, but the story kept nibbling at me. I started doing research on the story, but I still didn't know what to do with it. I knew I wasn't an historian, and I didn't know how to write a novel, and I was writing the poems in *The Vixen*, and when I finished *The Vixen*, suddenly it occurred to me that the only way for me to tell the story would be through poetry. I realized that the poems in *The Vixen* had made it possible for me to find a form to tell the story of *The Folding Cliffs*. I was thinking about the characters all the time. I realized the point in the story where I wanted to start. I was thinking about it one night and just started writing. I worked at it for about two years until I had it written. But it was a number of things coming together. I didn't sit down and decide I was going to write a poem, and this is going to be the story, and so on. All of those things connected on their own, in a way.

Amen: How integral is revision to your writing process?
Merwin: Sometimes going over something is a way of entering into a whole new process of writing, finding new layers in a piece of writing. I think of

it that way. Again, one of the people I learned a great deal from was Robert Graves, who felt that going over a piece—the revisions—was almost more valuable than producing an original draft. I think that depends. I write very slowly. I make a lot of changes as I'm writing because I'm listening to the poem and making changes as I go. My manuscripts, I'm sure, are quite unreadable. When they want my manuscript collections in a university, I never know what they're going to do with them. They're not going to make any sense of them; in two weeks, they won't make any sense to me either. But there's so much revision involved before I actually arrive at a form I want to type up. I don't often change too much after the piece is typed up.

Amen: You have done a great deal of work as a translator. Even though you write (your own poems) primarily in English, does your fluency with other languages make certain experiences and mindsets accessible that might not be if you were monolingual? In other words, does familiarity with other languages broaden your experiential horizons and your capacities as an English-writing poet?

Merwin: The only way I can think about that is to remember my early feeling of excitement when reading poetry in other languages. I think of poems in Spanish, poems in old French. And then, feeling the difficulty of conveying something very beautiful in a language other than the original. That was the thing, perhaps, that was drawing me closer to the idea of translation. But it was also making me listen for something in English, some kind of experience, sound, resonance, that I wanted to have happen, that maybe didn't exist in English. And that was a challenge from the beginning, to make something in English that was poetry in the same sense that it was in the original. And it's impossible; you can't do that. One never does that. But still, it's the impossible thing that one strives to do. I mean, what one wants with translation is the original, and it's never going to be the original; it's always going to be something else. But I always wanted translation to convey something of why one wanted to translate in the first place, which is not just the meaning of the original; it's to do with the sound, the electricity, the excitement of the language.

Amen: Some of your earlier work (such as poems in *The Lice* and *The Carrier of Ladders*) reflects, at least in part, it seems to me, a kind of absorption and reinvention of surrealist and/or dadaist elements. I'm wondering, do you consider some of the surrealist and dadaist writings to be texts that had a significant impact on you? If so, could you speak a little about that?

Merwin: Bly said once that every poet is in his time. Definitely all of us, from my generation, have inherited from the surrealists. For me it was not so much the French surrealists as it was the South American ones, and then I came to the French surrealists later. It's not that we became surrealists; it was that reading their works helped us break out of the fix on poetry in English, poetry that had been made by the English. There had been a few English poets who had experimented with surrealism, such as David Gascoyne, but not very many. It hadn't had a great effect on poetry in England, but we were moving away from English poetry. In the generations before mine, that was extremely deliberate. William Carlos Williams worked very hard to break the link with "English English." By my generation, we didn't have to work that hard. There was Auden, who was the link with England, but Auden was heavily influenced by American writing as well. We just weren't paying that much attention to English poetry, and if we did, it was a kind of friendly attention, but it didn't affect us very much. I don't think any of us were much influenced by English writers. We were much more interested in South American writers or European writers, and that was the value for many of us of Bly's magazine, *The Fifties*, *The Sixties*, and *The Seventies*. We were all encountering these writers, and Bly was publishing them, which was very convenient, but we were all discovering these writers for ourselves. I remember during those years reading all of modern French poetry and all of modern Spanish poetry with great excitement and a wonderful sense of discovery.

Amen: During our phone conversations, you mentioned your concern regarding current conditions in the world. The war in Iraq now seems to be escalating and the political/diplomatic situation worsening. Could you speak a little about what is going on in the world and your specific concerns or hopes?

Merwin: Well, I'm appalled by this administration, which I think is an impostor administration. I think the American people have been conned. I mean, the actual liberation of Iraq is a fine thing, but do we have any right to do such things? And in the way we're doing them? I deeply question these things. Some people question whether a poet has any right to speak up. I certainly think one has a right to speak and should exercise that right, because if one does not, as an individual citizen, exercise that right, then it doesn't get exercised. I think it's also important for poets to speak, whether you think of that in terms of poetic talent or political right. Whether a poet *should* speak or not, as a poet, I've always hesitated to say, because I don't want to prescribe to other people. I mean, I find politics boring, and I find going to the voting poll boring too, but I think these things are important, and I think it's important to exercise our rights. I think if one gives it up, as a poet, if one decides, I'm not going to write about it, one shrinks a bit. I think one is always trying to write things that one doesn't know how to write. You never really know how to write a love poem. A poem about public issues is likely to be bad, but once in a while you may write one that's not so bad, and that's true of every kind of poem. We don't know how to write political poems; most political poems are terrible. But if you don't try to expand your gift, I think you shrink. If you feel something, and you don't try to write about it, then your feelings are kept separate from your writing, and what does that mean?

I think compassion and imagination go together. If you give up trying to use your imagination for new things and for expanding yourself, you begin to wither away. And if you begin to draw back from your compassion, you begin to wither away, too. Compassion and imagination—not intelligence—are what make the human species valuable. And that's our gift; that's our great talent, and if we don't live up to it, it will kill us. If you don't live up to your talent, it kills you. That's why I think it's important to include public life, or one's feelings about public life, in one's writing. I've been reading *The Collected Rexroth*. It's a very revealing book. He's a much more important poet than I'd realized. There's a lot in that book that I don't like very much; there's also a great deal that is absolutely wonderful. There are moments where he makes political statements that I think are quite bad, and there other times when he manages to say something that is very accurate and beautiful. And he manages to say it in poetry. You know, Pound makes a lot of political statements, and usually they're total nonsense, and they wreck the entire context of the poem around them. And Rexroth does that sometimes, but it's marvelous to see someone trying to stretch what they can say, and sometimes he conveys thought, feelings, opinions of great subtlety with moving grace and clarity.

Amen: We also talked briefly around the idea of "busyness," how we live in a world overflowing with various stimuli; how the media is constantly bombarding us with information; how it is increasingly important to protect oneself from the sheer volume of external influences. *A Mask for Janus* was published in 1952. I'm wondering, how have changes—societal, technological, diplomatic—over the last fifty years (and especially over the last, let's say, twenty) affected you as a poet?

Merwin: I'm sure I have been affected, and I'm sure I've been affected in ways I don't even understand. It's hard to tell how much of that is the effect of changes in the world and how much of it is related to just getting older. I feel a couple of things about all that. First, I don't feel completely in sync with it; temperamentally, not at all. I like to lead a much quieter life than most of the public life of the twenty-first century is dedicated to. I'm also living in a place where I don't even see another house, which is the way I like it to be. Not all the time. I love going to the city and seeing friends, but I couldn't stand to do that all the time. I think I watch one television program a day, which is the *Lehrer News Hour.* And maybe there will be something else once or twice a week, but that's pretty much it. Maybe I turn on the laptop computer once a week, so I don't have the computer turned on all the time. I don't think this is typical, and I don't wish it to be different either. When we go back to the old farmhouse in France, it's nice to not even have that much contact.

I think everybody, whether he knows it or not, at his core does not belong to history. Everybody has the life which is there in the outer world and is going along with the moment of history he belongs to. And he's part of that whether he likes it or not, but there's the other aspect of him, which is not part of that. And I think when people feel really disoriented, when they have nervous breakdowns, when they go completely adrift, very often it's because they've lost touch with that part of themselves that is not historical. There's a poem of Muso's, in which he says, "Right among the people coming and going / I have a place to stay / I shut the gate even in the daytime." You don't have to get out of the subway in the middle of the city in order to come to a silent place. You have that silent place with you all the time. If that's important to you, it may well be more important than the rush around you, and there is always a connection. And of course, the poems come from both places. They come from that connection, which is never made by an act of will.

Amen: One of the things that is extremely powerful about your work is your ability to combine what I would call enigmatic and imagistic elements. Much of your work has this quality, reflects this interaction, if you will, between the unconscious or personally complex and the more public, the experientially accessible. I'm wondering, how does what I'm saying strike you? Could you speak a little on this issue?

Merwin: I think what you're talking about is what I think of as images. I don't think images are an act of will. Sometimes one sees the world in a way one is not aware of at other times. We're never really seeing the world; we're only seeing a moment's take on the world. This is true of images. Images are a way of seeing the world which you didn't notice before, and something you cannot make by an act of will; it's something that is suddenly revealed to you. The world has layers, and you start seeing that these layers happen all at once; they're all together. I think that's what is startling about images. At the moment of seeing, they seem so obvious. Why didn't I see that before? Mandelstam wrote wonderfully about images. He said some of the things that I've been saying, and I completely agree with him. He said that an image is not an act of will. A real image is something that occurs to you. He said an image is like running across a river on a bridge of boats, and when you get to the other side, you look back and see that all the boats have moved or drifted and are in different places, and you realize it would be impossible to do all over again. That's always seemed like a great image right there.

Amen: In the last issue of the *Pedestal Magazine*, I asked Robert Mezey to reflect upon his own contributions as a poet. I'd like to ask you a similar question: How do you feel about the corpus of work you have produced, in terms of creating a legacy? I mean, when you look at the volume of work you have created, do you feel that you have indeed been able to document life as you have known it, experienced it? Do you have a sense of having been able to describe, document, concretize this thing called life?
Merwin: Well, I always think of the things that remain to be said, that aren't there. Sometimes I go back over something I've written—which I don't do very often—and I'm startled sometimes to see what is there. But then I think, there's so much that isn't there. And there's always something at the heart of it that isn't there, too. Something always seems to have escaped. Albert Camus said that every true writer has two or three images he goes back to, and no more than that. A writer may have a huge output, but he is basically connected to two or three images. Camus was talking about writers like Tolstoy and Chekhov, that there were core images they kept going back to, that they never got to the bottom of. It may be something as simple as an old woman sitting by a fire, but something takes you back to that image over and over.

If you need an example, my favorite poem by Milton is "Methought I Saw My Late Espoused Saint." I suddenly realized after years and years of reading Milton that everything of Milton's was in that poem. His blindness, the wife he never saw, the paradise lost, his whole idea about what is really pure and what is ritually pure and whether they're the same. Almost anything you can think of with Milton is in that poem.

Amen: You have achieved a definite prominence as a poet, being the recipient of numerous awards and prizes. Also, you recently served as a chancellor of the Academy of American Poets. I'm wondering, what were some of the things you were able to do in that position to help further the impact of poetry?

Merwin: I think I'm very bad at all those public things, and I was always very surprised whenever anyone wanted me to do them. I did them largely as a duty. I really have no ambition in that direction; I never did, and I don't particularly like all of the things that are involved. Sitting around a table discussing policies, all those sorts of things, they don't come naturally for me. I don't think I'm doing any of those things any more. The one reason I welcomed these responsibilities was not that I wanted that kind of role or anything like that, but because it seemed important to occasionally be able to bring recognition or even grants of money to people who really deserved these things. It is satisfying to be in a position to be able to do that, which I have not been able to do very often, but a little bit, from time to time. And I think that's the real value of that for me.

Amen: You mentioned before that you are getting ready to do a few readings in various places. I'm wondering, do you have to find some balance between your public appearances and, I assume, a need for privacy?

Merwin: Well, maybe once or twice a year I do a group of readings, usually a small number of them. This spring there are five readings. The biggest circuit I've ever done is about ten readings, and then I didn't do any for quite a while. I think, for me, if I did more than that, I would feel sort of phony, as if I was repeating myself. I don't feel comfortable with that. Usually I don't really plan a reading. If I'm reading for something like Poets Against the War, then I will plan carefully to make sure there is a connection to the event of the moment, but generally I don't really plan. I want the reading to be spontaneous, something that arises out of the feeling of connection with an audience. I've a horror of performance, of performing the poems. When I read, I try to read the way the poems sound. I try to hear the poems, to read them that way. If I read poems and they seem to get through to people, there is a wonderful sense of confirmation, a sense of being linked with people.

Amen: What are you working on now? And, more generally, what are some of the themes with which you are currently concerned? What sorts of issues, experiences, feelings are you addressing now that you might not have addressed in the past?

Merwin: I can't give you a very precise and specific answer to that question because things change from day to day. But one of the things that I've come to realize through my life is that what we write about is nostalgia. As writers, what we have is memory. We're always writing about the past. We're never writing about the present. We may think we're writing about the present, but we only recognize the present because of the past. Language comes out of the past. The past is always with us, and it's partly memory and partly what we make of it. And what you remember is not what happened, it's something that's already changed. Changed in your mind. And then when you are writing, you take what you remember and what you recognize and you invent something else out of it.

Death is the end of memory. And that's what is terrifying, the idea that your memory suddenly stops. But we come to the present with our memory. That's who we are, that's what we recognize. And every day what we remember is different. What I bring to what I write is different every day. I don't know how to talk about that in some generic way; the only way to talk about it specifically is by writing. Balzac said, "A painter should never think about painting except when he has a brush in his hand." That's absolutely wonderful. I've picked up things like that throughout my life that have meant a great deal to me. Sometimes it is marvelous to be working in the garden, apparently not thinking about anything, and then all of a sudden a phrase will come to me. And if I'd been thinking about it, it wouldn't have happened.

It brings us back to the old discussions of spontaneity versus deliberate practice, intuition versus knowledge, and so on, as though there were a choice: one or the other. You need every bit possible of both, obviously. You need every bit of skill or practice or knowledge or linguistic learning and hearing you can acquire. But a poem always comes out of what you don't know. That's where it begins. That's where the sound of it comes from.

Poet W. S. Merwin

Bill Moyers / 2009

From the *Bill Moyers Journal*. Interview aired on June 26, 2009. BillMoyers.com, Public Affairs Television, Inc. Reprinted by permission.

BILL MOYERS: Welcome to the *Journal*.

To persuade a poet to depart from paradise, even if only briefly, requires a special kind of enticement. The acclaimed poet W. S. Merwin spent part of his childhood just across the Hudson River from our studios here in New York, but he lives now on the Hawaiian island of Maui, where every prospect pleases.

W. S. MERWIN: I love the city, but I also love the country and I realize that when I'm in the city I miss the country all the time, and when I'm in the country I miss the city some of the time. So what I do now is live in the country and go to the city some of the time.

BILL MOYERS: What lured him back east this time was an extraordinary honor, the Pulitzer Prize for poetry. It's the second he's won.

LEE BOLLINGER: For a distinguished volume of original verse by an American author, W. S. Merwin for *The Shadow of Sirius*, a collection of luminous, often tender poems that focus on the profound power of memory. Congratulations, W. S. Merwin.

BILL MOYERS: I first heard Merwin read his poetry at the Geraldine R. Dodge Poetry Festival in New Jersey over a decade ago when we were filming a TV series called *Fooling with Words*.

W. S. MERWIN:

My friend says I was not a good son
you understand
I say yes I understand

he says I did not go
to see my parents very often you know
and I say yes I know

BILL MOYERS: Merwin's literary life began at an early age. By the time he was five he was writing out hymns for his father, a Presbyterian minister in Union City, New Jersey. He escaped from his strict and pious upbringing into books and by the time he entered Princeton University was a fledgling poet.
W. S. MERWIN: The idea of writing to me was from the beginning was writing something which was a little different from the ordinary exchange of speech. It was something that had a certain formality, something in which the words were of interest in themselves. And that's the beginning of a feeling about poetry.

BILL MOYERS: At the age of eighteen, Merwin received advice from the poet Ezra Pound.
W. S. MERWIN: He said if you want to be a poet you have to take it seriously. You have to work on it the way you would work on anything else and you have to do it every day. He said you should write about seventy-five lines every day. You know, Pound was a great one for laying down the law about how you did anything. And he said, you don't really have anything to write about seventy-five lines about a day. He said you don't really have anything to write about. He said, at the age of eighteen, you think you do but you don't. And he said the way to do it is to learn a language and translate. He said, that way, you can practice and you can find out what you can do with your language, with your language. You can learn a foreign language but the translation is your way of learning your own language.

BILL MOYERS: W. S. Merwin's first book of verse, *A Mask for Janus*, was chosen for the Yale Younger Poets Prize by none other than W. H. Auden. It reflects Merwin's early work as poet and translator focusing on the myths and legends of ancient civilizations.

Over the past half century, in addition to over twenty-five volumes of poetry, Merwin has earned distinction with nearly two dozen books of translations, eight works of prose; several verse plays, and his memoir, *Summer Doorways.*

On the printed page, each of his poems appears without punctuation, in the freewheeling spirit of an imagination that creates in longhand on whatever scrap of paper comes to hand.

W. S. MERWIN: I can't imagine ever writing anything of any kind on a machine. I never tried to write either poetry or prose on a typewriter. I like to do it on useless paper, scrap paper, because it's of no importance. If I put a nice new sheet of white paper down in front of myself and took up a new, nicely sharpened anything, it would be instant inhibition, I think. "So now what?" I would think and I would sit there—so now what?—for quite a long time. But if it's something, if I need somewhere to write it down it will be on the back of an envelope, or something like that. Then it's okay. It's just to keep it there so I can find out where it goes from there.

BILL MOYERS: Merwin's later verse shares with Walt Whitman's a deeply felt connection to the natural world that makes all the more poignant his despair over our assault on the Earth through war and pollution. In the late 1970s, Merwin traveled to Maui to study Zen Buddhism. He stayed, married Paula Schwartz there, and together they built a solar-powered home on an abandoned pineapple farm and worked to restore the surrounding palm tree rainforest.

W. S. MERWIN: Writing poetry has to me always had something to do with how you want to live. I guess I've done something that many of my contemporaries didn't do. Many of them went into universities and had academic careers, and I have nothing against that. But I didn't think I was made for it. I begin, after about a week in university, I begin to feel the oxygen's going out of the air very fast and I have to go somewhere else.

BILL MOYERS: He does leave his island reverie from time to time to read his work at universities and libraries—and to pick up his Pulitzer Prize. Here's the book that won, *The Shadow of Sirius.* Its author is with me now. W. S. Merwin, welcome to the Journal.

You titled this new book, the one that just won the Pulitzer Prize, *The Shadow of Sirius.* Now, Sirius is the dog star. The most luminous star in the sky. Twenty-five times more luminous than the sun. And yet, you write about its shadow. Something that no one has ever seen. Something that's invisible to us. Help me to understand that.

W. S. MERWIN: That's the point. The shadow of Sirius is pure metaphor, pure imagination. But we live in it all the time.

BILL MOYERS: How so?

W. S. MERWIN: We are the shadow of Sirius. There is the other side of—as we talk to each other, we see the light, and we see these faces, but we know that behind that, there's the other side, which we never know. And that—it's the dark, the unknown side that guides us, and that is part of our lives all the time. It's the mystery. That's always with us, too. And it gives the depth and dimension to the rest of it.

BILL MOYERS: But this is the first poem in the book. Would you read this for us?

W. S. MERWIN: That must be "The Nomad Flute."

> You that sang to me once sing to me now
> let me hear your long lifted note
> survive with me
> the star is fading
> I can think farther than that but I forget
> do you hear me
>
> do you still hear me
> does your air
> remember you
> oh breath of morning
> night song morning song
> I have with me
> all that I do not know
> I have lost none of it
>
> but I know better now
> than to ask you
> where you learned that music
> where any of it came from
> once there were lions in China
>
> I will listen until the flute stops
> and the light is old again

BILL MOYERS: "I have with me all that I do not know. I have lost none of it." How do you carry with you what you do not know?

W. S. MERWIN: We always do that. I think that poetry and the most valuable things in our lives, and in fact the next sentence, your next question to me, Bill, come out of what we don't know. They don't come out of what we do know. They come out of what we do know, but what we do know doesn't make them. The real source of them is beyond that. It's something we don't know. They arise by themselves. And that's a process that we never understand.

BILL MOYERS: And that's true of poetry.
W. S. MERWIN: That's true of poetry. I think poetry always comes out of what you don't know. And with students I say, knowledge is very important. Learn languages. Read history. Read, listen, above all, listen to everybody. Listen to everything that you hear. Every sound in the street. Every bird and every dog and everything that you hear. But know all of your knowledge is important, but your knowledge will never make anything. It will help you to form the things, but what makes something is something that you will never know. It comes out of you. It's who you are. Who are you, Bill?

BILL MOYERS: I would have to write a poem to try to get at that. And it would not be a very good poem. But this line, "The star is fading." What am I to make of that?
W. S. MERWIN: Whatever you want to. I mean, whatever the star is. Your star or the star that has lighted your life. It's also the morning, you know? The star fades in the morning. And you watch the star fade, and finally you don't see it. I say, you know, I can think farther than that. I can think farther than the star. But I forget. Also, you lose—you can think farther. But finally your thought comes to an end. It's lost in the what we don't know and the vast emptiness and unknown of the universe.

BILL MOYERS: What intrigues me about Sirius is that while it appears to be a single star, it is in fact a binary system.
W. S. MERWIN: Yes.

BILL MOYERS: It's far more complicated than a single star. So that in the universe, as here on Earth, there's always more than meets the eye?
W. S. MERWIN: Yes.

BILL MOYERS: Right?
W. S. MERWIN: Yes. Of course.

BILL MOYERS: And poetry helps us to see what we don't see, right?

W. S. MERWIN: Poetry arises out of the shadow of Sirius. Out of that unknown and speaks to what we do know. Oh, Shakespeare does it all the time. He's doing that all the time. Russell Banks had a wonderful device that he used in teaching. Writing and reading for some years. He told me that he would give people a text, Chekhov's short story or Conrad or something. And then he would ask them when they'd read it, "Where does the language leave the surface?" And see who got it, and what they knew about it. And, of course, you can't do that with Shakespeare. Shakespeare's never on the surface. Shakespeare's always below the surface and above the surface.

BILL MOYERS: How so?

W. S. MERWIN: Well look at the beginning of *Hamlet*. The characters on this bitter cold night up there. And there a sound. And the person who is coming on stage challenges, says, "Who is there?" And it's all wrong. Everything's wrong. It's the sentry who is supposed to challenge the other person. But the other person challenges the sentry. And the whole play gets it wrong.

The original Shakespeare, the original *Hamlet* apparently lasted five hours. And people stood and listened to that. Many of whom couldn't read and write. And they were just absolutely hypnotized by that language.

Shakespeare has a kind of mantric quality. You know, where there's something from below the surface that's happening all the time. And even if you don't get every word, if you don't rationally understand every word that's going on and we don't—we still don't, you know, studying and studying and studying—something gets through, and the groundlings, as they were called. Or we know what is happening and the poetry gets through. The power of those long soliloquies in *Hamlet*. Or of Lear on the heath. Or Prospero's speech about "Where such stuff as dreams are made on."

I don't think you need a great education. I mean, I've seen practically illiterate high school children watching a film in which there are a few lines of Shakespeare. And they put down the popcorn and sit up. They've never heard anything like this. He's got it. I mean, he's got some magic that—

BILL MOYERS: Well, I don't understand all of your poetry, but I get it.

W. S. MERWIN: That's the important thing.

BILL MOYERS: So, what makes a poem work?

W. S. MERWIN: I don't know. I don't know. I'll never know what makes a poem work.

BILL MOYERS: But you once said that if a poem works, it is its own form. It doesn't matter what the form is.

W. S. MERWIN: That's right.

BILL MOYERS: If it reaches you, touches—

W. S. MERWIN: Well, one of the things about poetry, and this is different from prose, when a poem is really finished, you can't change anything. You can't move words around. You can't say, "In other words, you mean." No, that's not it. There are no other words in which you mean it. This is it. And if it doesn't work, it doesn't work. But if it does work, that's the way it is. You know?

BILL MOYERS: I find poetry more physical than prose.

W. S. MERWIN: It is.

BILL MOYERS: Is there a reason for that?

W. S. MERWIN: I think there is. I think that poetry begins with hearing. Prose you don't have to hear. I mean, you can read it off the front page of the *Times* and not hear a thing. But you can't read a sonnet of Shakespeare without hearing it because if you do, you miss the whole thing. You think you know, then you hear, "Shall I compare thee to a summer's day." You think, "Oh, that's it, that's different."

Poetry's really about what can't be said. And you address it when you can't find words for something. And the idea is, is that the poet probably finds words for things. But if you ask the poet, the poet will tell you, you can't find words for it. Nobody finds words for grief. Nobody finds words for love. Nobody finds words for lust. Nobody finds words for real anger. These are things that always escape words.

BILL MOYERS: I long ago gave up asking poets, "What do you mean by that?" 'Cause they don't know, right? The meaning is my response to it, isn't it?

W. S. MERWIN: That's part of it. But there are many shades of that meaning. And you certainly must have your own meaning, your own response to it. If you don't, you're not getting anything, are you? Your take on the poem is essentially what it's for. I mean, it is your poem. When you really get a poem don't you have a feeling that you're remembering it?

BILL MOYERS: Oh.

W. S. MERWIN: That you've discovered it yourself? In fact, you might have written it yourself. Even though that's not true.

BILL MOYERS: No, no. You're on to something important. There is a metaphysical quality to your poems. I mean, they make me feel very vulnerable. And at the same time, exhilarating. As if, here at this very late age, I'm connecting to something primordial. I mean, like the mist rising over an ancient lake I once slept beside in East Africa. I hadn't thought of that lake or those mists in a long time. But as I read poem after poem in your book, I was reconnected.

W. S. MERWIN: I'm so happy to hear that, Bill.

BILL MOYERS: Yeah, but how do you explain it? Do you know?
W. S. MERWIN: Oh, I don't explain it.

BILL MOYERS: Does the poem unlock some meaning?
W. S. MERWIN: It does in me. And that's something that I've felt ever since I was a child. I was very lucky. I think it's very important for parents, those children who have parents. And, you know, that's just, it's a dwindling number. It's very important if their parents can read to them. And not just read prose, to read poetry. Because listening to poetry is not the same as listening to prose.

And those children who've grown up hearing a parent reading poems to them are changed by that forever. They have it forever. They always have that voice. They always hear it. Always able to hear it. My father was a minister. And I didn't remain a Christian. But—

BILL MOYERS: Why?
W. S. MERWIN: I found the apostle's creed and it didn't— that wasn't for me. I didn't believe it. But I did listen—didn't listen to his sermon so much. But as a child, I had to go to church several times a week. But I listened to him reading the psalms and reading the Bible from the pulpit. And I was fascinated by the language. I was fascinated by hearing the psalms. I still know many of the psalms by heart and—

BILL MOYERS: What's your favorite?
W. S. MERWIN: Oh, "Have mercy upon me, oh God, according to thy loving kindness." That certainly would be one of them. Of course, the Shepherd's Psalm. You know, the Lord is my shepherd.

BILL MOYERS: The Lord is my shepherd, I shall not want. Is it true you wrote hymns for your father?

W. S. MERWIN: Well, I'm so certain. I even—lost them, yeah.

BILL MOYERS: At age five?

W. S. MERWIN: As soon as I could write with a little pencil, I was writing these little hymns and illustrating them and I thought they should be sung in church. But they never were.

BILL MOYERS: But do you think that's where your first intrigue with language began?

W. S. MERWIN: That was part of it. And my mother read children's poetry. She read Stevenson's *Child's Garden of Verses*. But there are poems of Stevenson's that I still remember, you know?

BILL MOYERS: Robert Louis Stevenson?

W. S. MERWIN: Yeah. "Dark brown is the river, golden is the sand. It flows along forever with trees on either hand. Green leaves a-floating, castles of the foam. Boats of mine a-boating, where will all come home." It's a beautiful poem. I still love it. And I think Stevenson was a wonderful poet. And his last poem that he wrote from Samoa. About "blows the wind today." That poem is a wonderful poem. Homesickness. Poem of great homesickness.

BILL MOYERS: When we confirmed this meeting, you suggested that I read a poem in here called "Rain Light." Why did you suggest that one?

W. S. MERWIN: I don't know, I just—that seems to be a very close poem to me.

BILL MOYERS: Here it is.

W. S. MERWIN:

> All day the stars watch from long ago
> my mother said I am going now
> when you are alone you will be all right
> whether or not you know you will know
> look at the old house in the dawn rain
> all the flowers are forms of water
> the sun reminds them through a white cloud
> touches the patchwork spread on the hill

the washed colors of the afterlife
that lived there long before you were born
see how they wake without a question
even though the whole world is burning

BILL MOYERS: "Even though the whole world is burning." It is, isn't it?
W. S. MERWIN: Yes. It is. It is burning, and we're part of the burning. We're part of the doing it. We're part of the suffering it. We're part of the watching it helplessly and ignorantly. And we know it's happening. And it is just us. It is our lives. We're burning. We're, you know, we're not the person we were yesterday. We're not the person we were twenty years ago.

BILL MOYERS: You remind me of your poem the title of which is "Youth." And it seems you're addressing youth, right?
W. S. MERWIN: Yes.

BILL MOYERS: Tell me about that.
W. S. MERWIN: Well when I was young, I didn't recognize youth. Because I was youth.

BILL MOYERS: You're addressing youth as our youth, right?
W. S. MERWIN: Our youth.

BILL MOYERS: That period of life—
W. S. MERWIN: Yes. Yes. And I say, I was looking for you all the time. And, of course, I couldn't find you, because you were right there. I can't find my own face, you know? I mean, because I can't see my own face. And it was only when I began to lose you that I began to recognize you. And—

BILL MOYERS: There's a line from another poem of yours where—I'll paraphrase it—where you talk about, we no more are aware of aging than a bird is aware of the air through which it flies.
W. S. MERWIN: Yeah.

BILL MOYERS: And that's true of youth as well.
W. S. MERWIN: Yes. Of course, youth is something that we don't under-stand as long as we have it. It's only when we get—but there are many things in life that are like that. I think that there are many things that we hear or we understand, whatever that means. But we hear or see or get some perspec-

tive on because we've moved away from it. And we begin to see them, and of course, we can't touch them anymore. They're out of reach.

Youth
Through all of youth I was looking for you
without knowing what I was looking for

or what to call you I think I did not
even know I was looking how would I

have known you when I saw you as I did
time after time when you appeared to me

as you did naked offering yourself
entirely at that moment and you let

me breathe you touch you taste you knowing
no more than I did and only when I

began to think of losing you did I
recognize you when you were already

part memory part distance remaining
mine in the ways that I learn to miss you

from what we cannot hold the stars are made

BILL MOYERS: "From what we cannot hold, the stars are made." What can you tell me about that line? Where were you when you wrote that? What was in your head?
W. S. MERWIN: Stars are what we can't touch. They guide us. They, in a sense, are part of us. But we can't hold them. We can't possess them.

BILL MOYERS: I remember at the 1964 Democratic Convention, a few months after John F. Kennedy had been assassinated, his brother Robert spoke to the convention and quoted from *Romeo and Juliet.* He said, "When I think of President Kennedy, I think of what Shakespeare said in *Romeo and Juliet*: 'When he shall die, / Take him up and cut him out in little stars / And he will make the face of heaven so fine / That all the world will be in love with night / And pay no worship to the garish sun.'"

W. S. MERWIN: It's that wonderful.

BILL MOYERS: The stars seem to provide us with a glance of immortality, right?
W. S. MERWIN: Well—

BILL MOYERS: Again.
W. S. MERWIN: There's so many myths where the hero or heroine or the God or Goddess who is the central figure at the end is simply translated and becomes a constellation and is always there and is guiding lights from there on forever in the sky.

BILL MOYERS: And Sirius the star for whom you named your book was so closely associated with the Egyptian Goddess Isis.
W. S. MERWIN: Yeah.

BILL MOYERS: Right? I mean, this goes back a long time.
W. S. MERWIN: Yes. One of the great themes that runs through poetry, all poetry, and I think is one of the reasons for poetry, one of the sources of poetry, one of the sources of language, is the feeling of loss. The feeling of losing things. Not being able to hold, keep things. That's what grief—I mean, grief is the feeling of having lost. Of having something being out of reach. Gone. Inaccessible. And I think that that's a theme that runs through much of all poetry. But I think the language itself and poetry are born the same way.

As I said before, you know, I think poetry's about what can't be said. And I think that language emerges out of what could not be said. Out of this desperate desire to utter something, to express something inexpressible. Probably grief. Maybe something else. You know, you see a silent photograph of an Iraqi woman whose husband or son or brother has just been killed by an explosion. And you know that if you could hear, you would be hearing one long vowel of grief. Just senseless, meaningless vowel of grief. And that's the beginning of language right there.

Inexpressible sound. And it's antisocial. It's destructive. It's utterly painful beyond expression. And the consonants are the attempts to break it, to control it, to do something with it. And I think that's how language emerged.

BILL MOYERS: From perhaps the first woman in a cave, who wakes up in the morning, and puts her hand on her husband's cold body. And something is gone.

W. S. MERWIN: Yes.

BILL MOYERS: There comes this need, you say—
W. S. MERWIN: Yeah. Yeah.

BILL MOYERS: To express it?
W. S. MERWIN: Yes.

BILL MOYERS: In a wail and in a word. Well, you've helped me understand why there does seem to be this lament through so many of your poems, even though you're an affirming person. This lament, this grief that's in your poems. For example, the poem we filmed you reading at the Dodge Poetry Festival some years ago. The poem you called, "Yesterday." After we played that, young men said to me they went home and called their father. So, let me play that for our audience again, and let's talk about it a moment.
W. S. MERWIN ON VIDEO:

My friend says I was not a good son
you understand
I say yes I understand
he says I did not go
to see my parents very often you know
and I say yes I know

even when I was living in the same city he says
maybe I would go there once
a month or maybe even less
I say oh yes

he says the last time I went to see my father
I say the last time I saw my father

he says the last time I saw my father
he was asking me about my life
how I was making out and he
went into the next room
to get something to give me
oh I say
feeling again the cold

of my father's hand the last time
he says and my father turned

in the doorway and saw me
look at my wristwatch and he
said you know I would like you to stay
and talk with me

oh yes I say

but if you are busy he said
I don't want you to feel that you
have to
just because I'm here

I say nothing

he says my father
said maybe
you have important work you are doing
or maybe you should be seeing
somebody I don't want to keep you

I look out the window
my friend is older than I am
he says and I told my father it was so
and I got up and left him then
you know

though there was nowhere I had to go
and nothing I had to do

BILL MOYERS: I have missed my father often since his death in the 1990s. But I never missed him more so than when I heard you read that.

W. S. MERWIN: It's wonderful to feel that a poem that I've written connects with somebody else's experience. And that it becomes their experience. That's the way I think it should be.

BILL MOYERS: Your poetry has become more personal in these later years. What's happened to bring that about?

W. S. MERWIN: Oh, I think just getting older. I wanted each book to be distinct from the others. And when I look back at other books, I think I couldn't write that now. And each book was necessary to write the next one. I think they are different. I've always wanted, through all of them, to write more directly and, in a sense, more simply.

And at one time in the early sixties, there were critics who said, "Oh, Merwin is so . . . so impossible to understand. And clearly he doesn't want to be understood." And at the same time school teachers would come up to me and say, "I've been giving your poems to the children." And I said, "What do they make of them?" And she said, "Oh, they get along fine with them." I thought, "Fine, if the children get them." And I said, "What year do you teach?" She said, "Second year." Mostly young children.

I thought, "You know, if the young children get them, that's all that matters. I mean, it's happening. A friend of mine said, "Oh, it'll be fifteen years and then people will think you're extremely simple to read." And I hope that's what's happened.

BILL MOYERS: To what extent do you think the very personal nature of so many of your later poems has been influenced by your embrace of Buddhism?

W. S. MERWIN: I don't know the answer to that, Bill. I don't because I don't know the alternative, you know? Did the aspirin cure your headache? Or would you have got over it anyway? I don't know.

BILL MOYERS: But you do manage to see light even in the darkness. How do you explain that to yourself?

W. S. MERWIN: I think if we don't that's just ultimate despair. And there's nothing to be said. All of these things have been true always. I mean we have been cruel and dishonest. We have been helplessly angry and greedy. Always.

All of our faults have always been there. And all of our failings have been there. And we haven't worked our way out of them. There's nobody, I don't believe in the saints in that sense. That these are people who have suddenly—they're past, all human failings. I don't think we're ever past human failings. And that's all right. And I think that we should forgive ourselves and forgive each other if we possibly can. It's very difficult sometimes.

BILL MOYERS: So, what about this poem in your new book? "Still Morning."

W. S. MERWIN:

It appears now that there is only one
age and it knows
nothing of age as the flying birds know
nothing of the air they are flying through
or of the day that bears them up
through themselves
and I am a child before there are words
arms are holding me up in a shadow
voices murmur in a shadow
as I watch one patch of sunlight moving
across the green carpet
in a building
gone long ago and all the voices
silent and each word they said in that time
silent now
while I go on seeing that patch of sunlight

BILL MOYERS: That patch of sunlight. Where was it?
W. S. MERWIN: Actually it was in the church in Union City, New Jersey, which has been torn down many, many years ago.

BILL MOYERS: Your father's church?
W. S. MERWIN: And I was being held up. And may even have been when I was baptized, you know? Very, very early. I can remember it. I remember the man in a brown suit, who was holding me. And I said this too once to my mother. And she said, "You can't possibly remember something back that far." And I said, "Who was the man in the brown suit, who was holding me? I never saw him again." And she said, "Oh, yes. That was Reverend so and so. And he came for a visit. And he said he would hold you for the ceremony." And I never saw him again. But I remember being held up and watching the green carpet and that patch of sunlight.

BILL MOYERS: You did grow up right across the river in Metro New York, New Jersey, looking out on the skyline of New York.
W. S. MERWIN: Which was silent.

BILL MOYERS: Silent?

W. S. MERWIN: Yeah. New York was silent. That was extraordinary. And that still, to me, is haunting. You know, to be able to think of that skyline that I saw as a child. And you could hear sounds from the river. There was a river traffic, which is gone, most of which is gone. The ferries back and forth, all the time. And ferrying of whole trains went across on ferries, you know, on barges. And I would spend as much time as I could in the back of the church looking down on Hoboken Harbor and on the river and on the city over there. And the city was absolutely silent. Then, of course, you took the ferry over there all the noise of New York was there. And I found that very exciting.

BILL MOYERS: Well, here's one of my favorite poems from your new book. "The Song of the Trolleys." Remember that one?
W. S. MERWIN: I do. There was a trolley car that went right past our house, you know. In Union City.

The Song of the Trolleys

It was one of the carols
of summer and I knew that
even when all the leaves
were falling through it as it passed
and when frost crusted the tracks
as soon as they had stopped ringing
summer stayed on in that song
going again the whole way
out of sight to the river
under the hill and the hissing
when it had to stop
the humming to itself
while it waited until
it could start again
out of an echo warning
once more with a clang of its bell.
I could hear it coming
from far summers that I
had never known
long before I could see it
swinging its head
to its own tune on its way

and hardly arrived before it
was going and its singing
receding with its growing
smaller until it was gone
into sounds that resounded
only when they have come to silence
the voices of morning stars
and the notes that once rose
out of the throats of women
from cold mountain villages
at the fringe of the forest
calling over the melting
snow to the spirits asleep
in the green heart of the woods
Wake now it is time again

That actually is a strange song that I heard in Macedonia. Some young women come and remake that sound. There was a wonderful living musicologist who was going through the oldest manuscripts and notations of music he could find. And he found these notations that someone had made in these mountain villages of this singing without words that women did until fairly recently. In these mountain villages in the very early spring, before they went out to pick herbs and things that were coming through the snow.

And the women would go out—it was like something between a coyote and a yodel. These strange guttural but very lyrical notes that the women— and you've got these three women stand up and start making these sounds. And it just makes your flesh crawl it's so beautiful. It's so beautiful. But it's like no music you ever heard. And they're calling to the spirits, saying, "Wake up. Wake up. Spring is here. Now, let us come freely into the forest."

BILL MOYERS: You seem to have the world in your ear.
W. S. MERWIN: I believe that poems begin with hearing and with listening. One listens until one hears something. Sometimes, and then if you say to people, "it begins with listening," they say, "What are you listening to? And what are you listening for?" And I say, "That's what you have to find out." You know? You have to learn how to listen first.

BILL MOYERS: I had a portent of our meeting the other day. We took our two small grandchildren to the Central Park Zoo. And entering the preserve they have there of the rainforest every visitor looks up and sees a quote from

W. S. Merwin. Did you know that?
W. S. MERWIN: No.

BILL MOYERS: Yeah. It says, "On the last day of the world, I would want to plant a tree." Why would you want to plant a tree?
W. S. MERWIN: It's a relation to the world. It's nothing to do with thinking that the world is going to be there forever. But that's a relation with the world that I want, to be putting life back into the world, rather than taking life out of it all the time. We do a lot of that, you know? I've lived on Maui for thirty-five years. And I feel very, very lucky.

BILL MOYERS: Why do you live there? Why did you go there?
W. S. MERWIN: A mixture of things. The ancient culture. The remnants of that fascinated me. And what I loved about the climate is that I could garden. I could live in the garden. Be surrounded by a garden all year round. And from before daybreak, I love to get up well before daybreak, before the birds are awake. And we live in a silent valley. The whole remains of a very small valley, leading down to the sea. And it's so beautiful in the morning. And these sounds. You know, the sound that people can pick up with mics. Now the sound of a room with nothing in it. Or the sound I can think often sometimes late at night, I just stop everything before I go to bed or as I go to bed. And just listen to the valley.

And you say, "Now, there's no sound in the valley." But there is. There's the sound of the valley.

BILL MOYERS: There is an urgency to some of these poems that I didn't detect in some of the earlier volumes. You think you feel things more urgently now? That time is diminished?
W. S. MERWIN: Whether that's it or not, I don't know. I certainly feel that—you mean personal time. But I think that personal time for all of us is diminished. I mean, the idea of writing for posterity. I don't know what posterity is. Posterity is right now. Posterity is Bill Moyers. Or posterity is the people who responded to "Yesterday" by going home and calling their fathers. That's what I love, to make that connection of experience to experience. So that my experience becomes their experience and vice versa. You know?

BILL MOYERS: What's the experience in here? This is one of my favorite small ones in your book. "The Long and Short of It."

W. S. MERWIN:

As long as we can believe anything
we believe in measure
we do it with the first breath we take
and the first sound we make
it is in each word we learn
and in each of them it means
what will come again and when
it is there in *meal* and in *moon*
and in *meaning* it is the meaning
it is the firmament and the furrow
turning at the end of the field
and the verse turning with its breath
it is in memory that keeps telling us
some of the old story about us

BILL MOYERS: What's the experience there?

W. S. MERWIN: I think we know the experience every time we draw a breath. Whether it's—this unreasoning repetition of something which doesn't ever quite repeat itself. It goes on evolving. Which is mysterious. The basis of our lives. It's there in the beat of our hearts and in our breaths. And in waking up in the morning. And the rhythm of our days. And we think we can measure it, but we know perfectly well with the other side of our minds that we can't measure it at all.

BILL MOYERS: Has it ever occurred to you that this moon you look up to so often and relished was the same moon seen by Hadrian and Ovid and—

W. S. MERWIN: Oh, yes.

BILL MOYERS: And Shelley and Keats and Byron and Neruda. And—

W. S. MERWIN: Yeah. I often think that.

BILL MOYERS: This constancy through the century of our gaze.

W. S. MERWIN: There's a great poem of a Chinese poet of the late Tang Dynasty, who said, "Asking the moon and the mountains." And he says, "Oh, this is the same moon that I saw in Chang An." And Chang An was—there was a moment of rebellion where everybody was getting killed. And he said, "This is the moon that guided me through the streets as I escaped. And that led me to find my way out into the mountains. And here it is." He said, "I ask what can I believe everywhere. I believe the moon everywhere." You know, "This is the moon that"—

BILL MOYERS: And what's he saying? That it's the constant.
W. S. MERWIN: The constant, yes. There this constant thing that light that is always there.

BILL MOYERS: I finished your book very conflicted about this time in our lives. I mean, I realize that I haven't done enough to try to make a different world more likely and that runs through some of your poems. And I find myself tossing and turning at the prospect of the chaos we are leaving behind for our grandchildren, in particular. Are you ever visited by that kind of anguish?
W. S. MERWIN: Oh, yes. Oh, yes. I always feel that. That "Oh, you know, I should have." I'm a very private kind of person. And I like a very quiet and private life. But I also love coming back and being part of something much more public and talking too much. And loving listening to other people. And I always develop the feeling, "Oh, there's so many other things I could have been doing. And maybe I could have been accomplishing more that way." But I know it's not true. I know that being a poet was what I always had to do. It's what I always wanted to do since I was yea tall. And it was what I had to do.

BILL MOYERS: Can you remember a catalytic moment?
W. S. MERWIN: Yes. There are a number of them. But it's just that. And there's a deep association, Bill, between that feeling for words. Feeling about the mystery of words. What made a word a word. What made a word express something. And what made a blade of grass come up between the stones of the sidewalk. And when my mother explained that the Earth was under the sidewalk, I had a feeling of great reassurance.

BILL MOYERS: So that might be why you want to plant a tree, right?
W. S. MERWIN: That's right. But it's also there's a connection. I don't see any distinction between that and the feeling about words. And the background of words which is not the threatening dark, but the nourishing dark. The nourishing darkness. That there's that we all take with us. The dark and that light are always with us.

BILL MOYERS: Do you think often of death?

W. S. MERWIN: Yes. But doesn't everybody? Everybody—I think one thinks of death all the time. I think it's part of one's life. That doesn't mean that one thinks of it with panic. My mother was never frightened of death. And that's a great gift to be given by a parent. That not fearing of those things.

BILL MOYERS: What was it she said to you? When you go to that dark, do not be afraid of what you do not know? I think that's a paraphrase of one of the lines.

W. S. MERWIN: "Even when you do not know, you will know," she said. That's in the poem. I don't—she never really said that. That's in my mind that she said that.

BILL MOYERS: Well, she has now. 'Cause it's in the poem. How long have you and Paula been married?

W. S. MERWIN: Oh, twenty, let's see, twenty-seven years, I think. I was never sure that monogamy would overtake me. But it did when I met Paula.

BILL MOYERS: Well, here's a poem you wrote to her in late spring. Why late spring?

W. S. MERWIN: Well, we were in the old farmhouse in France in the garden over there. I was sitting in the little garden house that I built there years ago, twenty some or more than that, looking out at the garden and Paula was working in the garden. And I thought, "This is it." It never gets better than this, you know?

To Paula in Late Spring

Let me imagine that we will come again
when we want to and it will be spring
we will be no older than we ever were
the worn griefs will have eased like the early cloud
through which the morning slowly comes to itself
and the ancient defenses against the dead
will be done with and left to the dead at last
the light will be as it is now in the garden
that we have made here these years together
of our long evenings and astonishment

BILL MOYERS: And finally, a poem that touched me very much in this book. "Going."

W. S. MERWIN: Oh. I'm cautious about poems that seem to be on the verge of abstraction. I'm very careful about them. So, I hope this one looks abstract and isn't.

> Only humans believe
> there is a word for goodbye
> we have one in every language
> one of the first words we learn
> it is made out of greeting
> but they are going away
> the raised hand waving
> the face the person the place
> the animal the day
> leaving the word behind
> and what it was meant to say

BILL MOYERS: W. S. Merwin, thank you very much for being with me. The book that won the Pulitzer Prize is *The Shadow of Sirius*.

W. S. MERWIN: Thank you, Bill. Great pleasure.

The Progressive Interview

Ed Rampell / 2010

From *The Progressive* 74.11 (November 2010), 35–39. This interview was reprinted by permission of The Progressive, Inc., which first published the interview in its November 2010 issue. www.progressive.org.

Ed Rampell: How did you react to being asked to become poet laureate?

W. S. Merwin: I dragged my feet quite a lot. I said, "I've never wanted to come to and live in Washington, and wear a suit day and night, and do all of the things I'd be expected to do." I don't think I'm particularly diplomatic. I certainly have no wish to be rude to people, but the political situation does not appeal to me at all. Besides, I don't like that kind of attention. One of the lovely things about living in Maui is that people don't know who I am, and that's fine with me. That's the way I like it. I'm just the guy who lives up the road and has some palm trees. I don't want that cover blown.

Rampell: What do you hope to do as poet laureate?

Merwin: I'd like to be able to bring poetry to people by doing readings. Very often people will come up after a reading and say they've "never heard poetry before." One of the differences between prose and poetry is that prose doesn't have to be heard. That's not true of poetry. If you don't hear a sonnet of Shakespeare, it just doesn't make any sense to you. A large number of the people who say, "I don't read poetry because I don't understand it," are simply saying, "I don't read poetry because I don't hear it." Or they are saying, "I'm not used to it, so I don't know what to make of it." But when they hear poems read out loud, they think: "Oh, I see. It's something different."

Poetry uses the same words as prose, but it's physical. In that way, poetry may be the oldest of the arts. It's probably as old as language itself. Its closest relation would probably be music and dance. A number of theorists think it comes out of an inexpressible emotion, something that was just so, so urgent that the forms of expressing it weren't adequate.

Rampell: Why did you decide to forgo punctuation forty-five years ago?
Merwin: It didn't happen overnight. I came to feel that the over-elaborate punctuation of things and the laws of Fowler's English were basically evolved for prose. They were logical and clear. But they assumed you didn't have to hear the language. I thought punctuation nailed the poem on the page. So I started trying to do with less and less of it, and I finally said, "All right, let me try it without altogether." I was fascinated by the differences that could make. The moment you discard a convention like that, you've made a new poem. And if you drop punctuation, you have to find some other way of doing what punctuation does. The other way, of course, is to make you read it out loud, and start listening to it. And then if it's written basically the way it's spoken, you hear it. I didn't think I'd necessarily make a rule of it and adhere to it the rest of my life, but having started it, I was curious because it brought out things in the language you couldn't bring out with punctuation.

Rampell: Why did you get involved in Poets Against the War?
Merwin: Sam Hamill, the man who then ran Copper Canyon Press, started a thing called Poets Against the War. He thought he'd get half a dozen poets to say why they did not think the invasion of Iraq was a good idea. Well, he ended up with something like 18,000 people from around the world sending in these ideas. Then we went and did this reading in Washington. And I dedicated mine to Laura Bush because it was her invitation that brought us all to Washington. She had invited everybody to talk about Emily Dickinson, but the poets didn't want to do that. So she called the whole thing off.

Rampell: In the spring of 2003, you wrote "Ogres," about:

> the frauds in office
> at this instant devising
> their massacres in my name.

Usually, you're not that direct. Is there a risk in being so direct?
Merwin: Yeah, that's true. But I was thinking about the invasion of Iraq, and I was thinking about organized violence: It's always to some degree effected by lies. Because we justify what we're doing, and the justifications, as we keep finding out, are very often not true. There was no Gulf of Tonkin

incident, which was one of the reasons for the Vietnam invasion. And there were no weapons of mass destruction.

Rampell: What other causes have you espoused through your poetry or activism?

Merwin: I opposed the Vietnam War, and I supported the Civil Rights movement. I also marched against nuclear weapons. A lot of people in that movement were Quakers. They'd read Gandhi and Thoreau, and they didn't think violence was a great idea. One of the things about being opposed to organized violence—and I don't think there's a simple solution—is that violence, I believe, leads to violence. It always makes more violence. There's Albert Camus, whom I've admired enormously all my life, and he was in the Resistance, he worked for the liberation of Algeria, but he said in his diary and in the editorials he wrote, "We must break the cycle of violence wherever we can break it. Don't worry about justification; you try to break it. If there's a chance to break it, you try."

You do everything possible to resist it. We're all murderers. We're all capable of it. I think of the day when a boy I knew, who was two years older than me, said something nasty about my mother. He'd always picked on me; I hated it. I was chopping wood for a lady to use in her stove, and I had a hatchet in my hand, and I had a terrible impulse to just take the hatchet to him.

Rampell: The last line of Camus's *The Stranger* refers to "the benign indifference of the universe." Do you feel that the universe is benignly indifferent to humanity?

Merwin: Yes, and I also think that life itself is both indifferent to us and the source of all of our joys and everything that we love. And it's necessary to accept the one in order to love the other. I read about a Japanese writer of the twentieth century who said, "One must go on trying, even if it's like a pigeon trying to put out a house on fire by carrying a few drops of water on its wing, and then going back for more."

Rampell: How did you get interested in the environment?

Merwin: I grew up across the river from New York City. We had a little backyard with one tree in it, and I loved the tree, and if I was unhappy, or if I thought I was unjustly punished, I would go out and stand by the tree. I felt a closeness to the tree.

When I was very small, I remember walking along the sidewalk with my mother. It was spring, and there was grass coming out between the flag-stones on the sidewalk. I got down and felt it, and I said, "Where does the grass come from?" And my mother said, "Well, the earth is right under the stones there." I can remember, as I tell you, the feeling of great relief and pleasure that I had to think that the earth was right down underneath there.

Rampell: An oriole appears in a lot of your poems. Why?

Merwin: Oh, I love orioles. It's a particularly beautiful bird, a mysterious bird. It's brilliant, brilliant: gold and yellow with black wings. And it has this wonderful sound: It warbles. When it sings, you almost never see it. But sometimes you can glimpse this wonderful gold thing going through the trees.

Rampell: What's your response to the BP oil spill?

Merwin: It's just appalling. I mean, it's perfectly horrible. And we should have known better, considering how sloppy it was and how crooked the permits have been. But put it in context: The forests of North America have been cut down steadily, and as a matter of course forever, since the Pilgrim fathers got here. Nobody ever thought there was anything the matter with that.

Then we got into nuclear proliferation since World War II.

And we started agricultural practices that took for granted that we use poisons. The moment we turn over the soil, we start poisoning it, and we go on poisoning it all the way through. There's probably not a river in the United States that doesn't have pesticide poisoning in it. The fish are dying. The seas are getting polluted. The rainforests are going. And global warming is here.

That's what the context is. These are not single cases. These are all part of a general way we've been looking at the world. As long as we look at the world that way, it's going to go on. The idea that the important thing is for some people to get rich while the rest of the people work for them is very deeply dug in.

It's an attitude of superiority. We are superior to the rest of life. The Book of Genesis says: "Increase and multiply and have dominion over the birds of the air and the animals" and so forth. You run it; it's yours; do what you like with it. I don't know how old that text is, but it represents an attitude that probably really got going with the beginning of agriculture. Before that, the hunter-gatherers were gentler. A lot of the North American peoples were very suspicious about digging in the Earth. You were very careful about what you did to the Earth, and you did it with great respect.

Rampell: Is our current economic system sustainable?
Merwin: This is a subject that's liable to get very dark, so I don't know how far you want to pursue it. I'm very pessimistic about the future of the human species. We have been so indifferent to life on the whole that it will take its toll. It's not just the polar bears who are having a hard time; what we're doing is gradually impoverishing and poisoning the whole of the rest of life. Thirty years ago, when I was at [Oregon State University in] Corvallis, where there's a big biology department, a molecular biologist said: "We're losing a species a week." My jaw dropped.

And now—thirty years later—we're losing a species every few minutes. We cannot put them back. If we change our mind and say, "Oops, we made a mistake," it's too late.

Every species is related to every other species. And they're built up like a pyramid. The simpler cell organisms, and then the more complicated ones, all the way up to the mammals and birds and so forth. The whole thing depends on every part of it. And we're taking out the stones from the pyramid.

Rampell: Sometimes it seems that Americans really don't want to know anything about the rest of the world; they just want to run it.
Merwin: I think that's been true; I do think that's been true. The history of taking over the North American continent and of Hawaii is that of colonizing. It's fairly ruthless. Lots of it looks heroic to us, but we're only looking at one side of it.

Rampell: You wrote a very touching poem called "Lament for the Makers." Most of your generation of poets is now gone. Does it make you feel lonely?
Merwin: A little bit. Some of them were people I was very fond of: James Wright, James Merrill.

Rampell: Who among the younger generation of poets do you like?
Merwin: I like a lot of the women poets: C. D. Wright and Linda Bierds and Linda Gregg and Deborah Digges, who killed herself two years ago. I like C. K. Williams. They're all different.

Today, people say to me, "Do you like rap poetry?" I say, "I don't especially like it. I'm glad it exists." That may be the way some people want to hear poetry. It's better to hear poetry any way than no way at all.

And I think poets ought to behave decently to one another. Jealousy is something I've always disliked. In one of my last conversations with James Merrill, who hated jealousy among poets, he said, "I don't care who writes it. But I want to read a poem that lifts the heart."

Rampell: Who do you write for? In "Cover Note" you wrote:

> . . . I have not
> the ancients' confidence
> in the survival of
> one track of syllables
> nor in some ultimate
> moment of insight . . .

Merwin: There are several answers to that one. There's a sense in which you write only for yourself because the only ear, the only way you can hear the language, is the way you hear it yourself. Beyond that I write for everybody; for everybody who uses the language and who's interested. I'd like anyone who wants to read poems and is interested in these things to find that there's something available in them.

We've gone through a period of modernism that pushed aside the late Victorians, who got very, very conventional and were essentially writing for a particular class structure. Modernism brushed that out of the way. But also at the same time it brushed aside the idea that you're writing for it to be comprehensible.

One has to write for right now, and one writes out of some kind of respect for one's ancestors. My son is a novelist, and he said to me once: "I love this thing about poets: You all really feel there's a line connecting you to Keats, Milton, and Shakespeare and all the way back." I said, "Oh yeah, it's right there. We have whatever they gave."

Rampell: You write, in the poem "First Sight," about "late blessings." What are some that you appreciate?
Merwin: I love my wife, and I love my life here. I'm happy to be alive. I feel very lucky to be able to write sometimes and to work in the garden. That's quite enough.

Rampell: In *The Shadow of Sirius* you write about "astonishment." How do you stay open to being astonished?
Merwin: Good question. I think that's a question one should always ask one's self. The act of being surprised is always marvelous. It means that you're opening up; you're not getting sclerotic. Anything that tends to open your eyes and feelings is a good thing.

Rampell: You seem continually astonished by nature, love, and words. What else astonishes you?

Merwin: What else is there?

Rampell: Any advice?

Merwin: Yes, one important thing: Read for pleasure. Read junk. Read every kind of book. But read for pleasure. The reason the Puritans wanted to stamp out poetry was because it gave pleasure. It's about things you love, things that you care about. Sir Philip Sidney, in the generation before Shakespeare, said, "Poetry begins in delight and ends in wisdom." And it will never end in wisdom if it doesn't begin in delight and continue in delight. When you read a poem and you think, "God, that is so beautiful, I don't want to forget that," and you go on saying it to yourself because you love it, that's pleasure. That is real pleasure.

Nature, Conservation, and the Unseen: A Conversation with W. S. Merwin

Hal Crimmel / 2012

From *Weber—The Contemporary West* 30.1 (Fall 2013), 50–60. This conversation took place in April 2012 in Ogden, Utah, where Mr. Merwin had come to give a talk and reading at Weber State University's annual National Undergraduate Literature Conference. Reprinted by permission.

Hal Crimmel: This morning I spoke with my mother by phone and told her I was going to interview a United States poet laureate. An avid reader, she said, "Who?" and I said, "W. S. Merwin." And she said, "Oh, I know him! What are you going to ask him?" And I said, "I'm not sure. He's a poet laureate. He's in the *Norton Anthology*."
W. S. Merwin: You don't want to take that too seriously.

Crimmel: (Laughter) Being in the *Norton* is like being in the Hall of Fame. How do you begin an interview with a Michael Jordan of literature? In that way mothers speak to sons, she said, "Well, I'd like to know what his favorite book is." I promised her I'd ask you that. So: Is there one book throughout the course of your life that you keep coming back to, for inspiration?
Merwin: Well, there are quite a few of those. I think Thoreau's *Walden* is a wonderful book. Thoreau is one of our great prophets, I think. And there's a Chinese philosopher, Zhuang Zhou, from about the fifth century BC; there are some new translations of him—I love him—and he's very remarkable. The more I think about it, the more books there will be. Of course, I always return to Shakespeare. Shakespeare only gets better as you get older. What a genius he was. He was barely over thirty when he wrote *Hamlet*. He wrote

most of the great comedies in his twenties. Between the richness and the genius of it all, it's a constant joy to read Shakespeare. But it's that spirit, wherever you find it, whether in a poet, in a writer, in a musician, or in a painter, you find it in the arts. You find it in people's voices. Sometimes only a few words are enough to stick with you for the rest of your life. It's that sound, when you hear it, you get it for certain.

Crimmel: *Walden* is my favorite book, and I always come back to it. Each year familiar lines suggest new meanings. Speaking of *Walden* and the perspective on nature it provides, last week we hosted Peter Kareiva, who's the chief scientist for the Nature Conservancy. He gave a talk that he has been giving around the country—there was actually an op-ed piece today in the *New York Times* about it. The article applauds Kareiva's critique of the environmental movement. He claimed the movement is built on a flawed foundation, meaning that our infatuation with Thoreau's *Walden* has led us astray because Thoreau didn't tell the whole story. One of Kareiva's comments was that "Thoreau's mother was out at his cabin every week doing his laundry"—as if that undercuts the message. Focusing on his laundry seems irrelevant and purposefully distracts from Thoreau's message. I mean, so what?

Merwin: It didn't matter. Some talk as though Thoreau's whole life had been spent in the little cabin out at Walden Pond. Walden didn't belong to Thoreau at all, it belonged to Emerson—Emerson let him stay there. Thoreau had built the little cabin, but he makes it very clear, it wasn't a lifetime. He spent parts of one winter, parts of another year, and he wasn't all the time out there, but it offered a way of looking at the world. And that's what the whole thing's about, that's what *Walden*'s about. It's not about how he moved away from society. He just shook off the dust of civilization. At the end of the book he says that he went about his life again. He was playing with the infinite possibilities of life. *Walden* was simply the core of a way of looking at, and imagining, a way of life which was independent and in tune with all of the kinds of life around him. He questioned all the assumptions. You live in a so-called "civilized" human place, and the things that everybody takes for granted simply aren't so—the great self-importance of the human species—as if the whole universe was centered on us.

I have a friend on Maui who has a laboratory on the mountain, Holi Alcoa—the national park is on two different islands, also on the Big Island—and they're putting up a huge telescope there, and this is the last step toward placing radio telescopes on satellites. Those guys are working at the very edge of what's known in astronomy. We visit all the time and see what they're doing. We go right into their laboratories to get the latest discoveries. Nobody uses a telescope to look through space anymore. They're all done on a computer. You'll go into their laboratories, and while you are talking, they've found another star. So, when they found these 12,000 planets, I said, "Wasn't this exciting?" And he said, "Oh, sure, it was exciting, but we already knew they were there. What nobody realizes is that the universe is unimaginably greater than we realize and we keep finding things all the time." And I said to my friend, "What about the 'known?'" because that is of huge importance to human beings. To me, that's always been B.S. He said, "What we know is that it's a speck of dust," which is a great image, because it was one used by a great Chinese master years ago, to address the same thing, that the universe is a speck of dust, a hair floating in infinite space. The unknown is where it all comes from, the unprovable.

I think this is the basis of the arts; it's the basis of what's remarkable about us, about every living thing. That's the thing that I don't share with most organized religion—I don't believe that we are that important. I think that life itself is enormously important, but I don't see a great difference between killing a man and killing an elk; you're just taking a life, and life is unique. But that does not make ours or theirs more valuable. I think viewing the world that way is much more real than the way we go about it. I guess that's the real basis of what you asked. It's something that really troubled me when I realized that I felt that way, until I realized that I have felt that all my life. I don't believe in losing your temper, I've done it very few times in my life. I have come very close when I see the abuse of the helpless—of children or animals. If I see it happening, I want to stop it, quickly if possible.

Crimmel: I spend time thinking about the most effective perspective for considering our relationship with nature—and one of the main debates is between biocentrism, which is really the foundation of deep ecology, and this new idea that Peter Kareiva, the Nature Conservancy speaker, is advocating. He said it makes more sense for conservationists to look at nature purely anthropocentrically because this allows us to make a better case for preservation. The whole idea of a wilderness-based conservation ethic, he said, has alienated people from nature and so forth. So I'm not sure I am quite ready to accept the anthropocentric argument, you know?

Merwin: That's still making humans the number one priority and goes back to the whole self-importance thing. I don't think that works in the long run. One of the arguments for why we should preserve the rainforest is because there are all these new medicines and things that come out of the rainforest. Clearly, there are many more things there that we haven't begun to discover. But still, the attitude behind that view remains one of exploiting the rainforest: it's there for our use and we are going to save it because it might be useful to us. But the fact is, apart from the fact that that is a very arrogant way of looking at it, those healing medicines were there long before there were humans who had those diseases. They're part of another balance that we don't know anything about, and we don't know what they are there to restore, what they are balancing out. It shows how very ignorant we are and how important it is to find out what that balance is. If we don't help regain that balance, we're finished anyway.

At the rate we're going now, I think that we have embarked, without knowing it, on what I would call terminal acceleration. Everything is going faster, everything. Human population reached 1 billion in 1813, now it's somewhere around 8 billion and climbing. It's not a gradual incline, it's a steep curve.

Crimmel: Seven billion thirty million. The world's population crossed the seven billion mark in November 2011. Worldometers.info keeps a running total of births, deaths, and rainforest that's being lost, soil lost to erosion, and so forth. This idea of massive loss appears in your poem "For a Coming Extinction," which was written a year after I was born, in 1967, so you were clearly thinking about these issues a long time ago . . .
Merwin: Actually, it was published in '67 and written in '63. Because I had heard then that the Mexicans planned to build a bridge from the Baja Peninsula to be able to get salt to the mainland more cheaply.

Crimmel: The Sea of Cortez that separates the two is a major breeding ground for whales.
Merwin: That bridge would have kept the whales from getting to their breeding grounds. So that's what this was about. It didn't happen then, but the threat is still there—Money, Money, Money. Once you do those things, you can't undo them. Whales are endangered all through the Pacific largely due to our efforts, but not entirely. Global warming is not entirely human. It is a cyclic thing, but we have excited and aggravated it and made it worse. What we are doing, from the numbers you mentioned, is that the loss of the wild is growing all the time, and even the semi-wild is disappearing and being turned into airports, shopping malls, and parking lots—just asphalted over.

Our land, when I got the conservancy of land, I got three acres back in the seventies, before my wife and I were together, and then in '85 these two older ladies sold us fifteen acres upstream. So we had the whole headwaters of this small stream down to the sea, and it was ruined land. It was, a friend said, wasteland, agriculturally useless wasteland. It had been deforested, overgrazed, and burnt over. They had tried to plant sugarcane on it, and that wouldn't work. Finally, they wanted to have a pineapple plantation and so they dug both sides of the valley; they plowed vertically, so they lost all of the topsoil. It was like trying to plant on a dirt road. Now, the soil is back, the trees are on it and the canopy is coming back. You can keep the sun off the soil and manage the leaf litter so that after thirty years, things will grow there. I try to plant trees every day.

You can't plant a forest, only a forest makes a forest, because a forest is not just a few trees. It's a huge ecosystem of many related things that we can't even begin to understand. It changes. Thoreau was writing about that on his deathbed. The life in the soil and everything begins to come back. There's a point where it begins to take over and do it itself. That's so moving when you begin to see that. Most people don't even recognize that is what is happening, but that's what's happening. It's there, the earth has it.

What I mean by our human arrogance is that we think the universe somehow owes us eternal life right here on earth, and that's not so. The universe doesn't owe us a damn thing; the universe doesn't even notice us. This can sound like a depressing viewpoint, but I think it's an exhilarating viewpoint. Accept your place in this incredible, incomprehensible richness of life, but also accept the unknown in the universe. We're part of it and it's miraculous. How did it ever happen that we should be here?

Crimmel: You feel part of that larger ebb and flow of all life. Students can find it depressing that the universe doesn't care about them. But I suggest it is exhilarating. To accept that nature is ambivalent about your survival causes you to see the world differently, as part of that greater ecosystem. You can change how to live your life accordingly.

Some students get that and some don't. Maybe that is a function of experience in nature, and you have plenty of that. Given your connection to the land, do you think your hands-on restoration of the Hawaii property has influenced or changed your poetry?

Merwin: Well, I don't know, I could never tell you that. But I know that restoration is part of the same thing, it's not part of something else. It's nice to have a garden; I wanted to do that since I was a tiny child. I remember, I must have been about three, when I saw blades of grass coming up through cracks in the pavement, and I said to my mother, "Where's it coming from?" And she said, "Well, the earth is right under the stone," and I remember feeling this great joy that the earth was under that stone. If you think of our species as alien—what a weird idea to think that we're alien to the rest of life and to the whole of the unknown universe—if you go out and look at the night sky, are you depressed, or are you exhilarated? I think it's natural to be exhilarated and to be consoled. I had a great friend who lost his wife after a long and happy marriage a few years ago, and he said, "The only thing for the terrible, inconsolable grief" was to "go outside and lie down and look at the night sky." Why? I mean, we think we have to explain everything. We don't know why, but you're part of this whole thing. The night sky is there like a parent looking at you. You win and lose some, but you're still a part of it. Why can't we accept it? That's the depressing thing, we can't accept it.

Crimmel: One of my earliest memories, I grew up right on the Canadian border back in New York State, is of being out in a nearby swamp with my mother and falling through the ice—just enough to get my boots full of water. It was winter and it wasn't a particularly dramatic landscape, but this image remains—similar to your story of the blades of grass poking up through the sidewalk. I have often thought this memory grounds my belief that a broader environmental consciousness emerges from a connection to a particular place. There's an essay in a book I edited about a teacher from Pennsylvania who loved Robert Frost, but moved to Hawaii for a teaching job.

He used the same Pennsylvania syllabus, and when November rolled around he got out Frost, and he asked the Hawaiian students how the air smells when the first snow of the year falls. (Laughter) He said the students thought he was from another planet. If you were raised in the Northeast you might tend to think of Frost as a poet who speaks universally about place-based experiences. Certainly for the two of us, since we are familiar with that climate, if I say to you, "April day, Pennsylvania," there's probably some image that quickly comes to mind, but how does a Hawaiian relate to Frost, who is so tied to a radically different place? Given the way place shapes so many writers, could you speak to the degree to which your writing emerges out of a particular place?

Merwin: I think that always varies, but it's always true when you are trying to read the poetry of other places. They're deeply rooted in place, but it's true of time too. It's very hard to bring back the circumstances. There's a passage in Thoreau's journal where he goes out and climbs down into the swamp and he spends an hour or so standing in the swamp with his head above the water, just watching the swamp. He ends the passage by saying, the trouble is, you forget all the important things that happen in a time like that. He was wonderful, there's nobody like him.

There's a lovely book of long essays by John Fowles called *The Tree*. It is really about trees and places. The great thing about a tree—and I am not talking about rows of Christmas trees, planted as though they were corn—is that the moment a tree is in the ground, it makes a place, that's its place. The tree and the place are two words for the same thing, and will be as long as it's there. For the tree, the tree is the place, the place is the tree. I said to E. O. Wilson, when I met him at Harvard years ago—nice long conversation we had, we had a little bit of wine to drink and dinner—I said, "I'm going to say something very silly to you. It will seem very silly to a botanist, but I had a very repressed childhood, and I would go out in the backyard where there was a poplar tree, and I would sometimes think, as a very small child, that this tree was my best friend. I could stand by the tree, and I could trust the tree, and I wanted to try to listen to the tree. I thought that the tree wanted to tell me something." He said, "That's not so strange at all. I think a lot of scientists have felt that way without daring to say it. The tree's DNA is much older than yours and the tree's not withholding anything from you. It's you who has to try to find out how to listen to the tree." The first time I lost my temper was when these guys came with a saw to start chopping boughs off of the tree to clear the way for their telephone lines, and I screamed and ran out of the house and started beating on the men, saying, "Let that tree alone!" They just came back later when I wasn't around. (Laughter)

Crimmel: In the selections of your poetry that are in the *Norton*, that theme of loss is omnipresent. Whether it's in "For a Coming Extinction," "Losing a Language," or "Lament for the Makers," something or someone is being taken away from us every day. Is the tone of "Lament for the Makers" melancholy or hopeful?

Merwin: The original poem that mine is modeled on comes from William Dunbar, a Scottish poet, who wrote a poem called "Lament for the Makers"—the Makers were poets—and he goes through all the poets he's known and valued in his lifetime, including Chaucer, and it's a lament for them. It's there in his last line, "Timor Mortis conturbat me"—the fear of death troubles me. So, that's my poem. It's not exactly modeled, but it's very closely modeled on that Dunbar poem. People assume that I knew all these guys, but that wasn't so. These were the poets who were alive in my lifetime and who had meant something to me, including two who nobody reads anymore, and it's a real shame: Edward Mueller, who's a wonderful Scottish poet, and David Jones, who I think is one of the truly great poets of the twentieth century. I think he's as great as Eliot, but his poetry is as difficult to read as *Finnegan's Wake*. The great voice of David Jones comes from the early Welch poetry. There is an incredible voice—little bits of the Aborigine left in it—but you know how great it was. His poem, "A Refusal to Mourn the Death, by Fire, of a Child in London," is the greatest war poem I've ever read. It's a refusal to mourn; it's a refusal to take in war, too, without the ability to withdraw from it. That's what we do; I think there's a war going on all the time.

I look at war and I think, it's not just human depravity, it's human stupidity. What can be more stupid than to put that amount of your life, and your attention, and your energy into killing each other? How dumb! Of course there are too many of us, but it's going to take care of itself. (Laughter) The world will take care of that. Wherever you look, there's a war going on, we're killing each other. Of course, I think we are descended from the wrong ape. Chimps are not peace-loving.

Crimmel: The book I am reading right now discusses their warlike nature.

Merwin: They invented war, we didn't. They wage war; the really aggressive, warlike apes are the baboons and the chimps. If we had descended from the bonobos, or the gorillas, or the orangutans, or the gibbons, it would have been a totally different story. I've known a couple of chimps growing up; the problem is, they are very smart. They're sweethearts until puberty; after that, you never know. They are not to be trusted. They are very violent— they love violence—that's the funny thing about us. The great canines don't love violence; none of them do. And they are carnivores, so they will kill to eat. I said to someone, "We are the only cruel species," and they said, "What do you mean? All animals cause pain." And I said, "Sure, they cause pain, but they don't do it for their own pleasure—they do it to eat, or for some other reason. They don't do it because they get a kick out of it."

Crimmel: You mentioned E. O. Wilson before, and I think he wrote that our great brains might be an evolutionary mistake, and the very thing that we have used to distinguish ourselves from the rest of the nonhuman world might be the very thing that results in our undoing. That's disturbing and fascinating.

Merwin: There were two brothers named Wustall, who won the Nobel

Prize for genetics, and they wrote a wonderful book about genetics and its evolution. Their theory—this is 1909–1910, something like that—focused on the idea that *Homo sapiens* are not the peak of evolution as we like to think. They said, "It's not an accident that the larger skull of the Neanderthal—which we think of as unshapely—has greater brain capacity than its *Homo sapiens* descendants." They believed that the peak was always Neanderthal. I've always thought that the old theory about Neanderthal was completely wrong—that he was so inferior to Cro-Magnon Man, and that Cro-Magnon Man simply wiped Neanderthal out. But that's simply not true. They lived together for 15,000 years and had children together. Our ancestors were neither of the Paleolithic ones; they went across when the ice age came back, into Spain, where they both went extinct together. There was a new wave of only Cro-Magnon that came up from Africa and Asia Minor, quite a few centuries later; they were our ancestors.

Years ago, while my wife and I were in France, we lived very close to the Lascaux Caves, and I used to visit them often, because I wanted to be somewhere where people had a much deeper sense of animals than we do currently. We visited all of the newly discovered caves, and I then began to think that the Cro-Magnon Man learned a great deal from Neanderthal. It was a different kind of brain. It was not as school-book intelligent as Cro-Magnon Man, but was intuitively far deeper. Neanderthal had a far deeper grasp of, and a far closer connection with, the rest of life and the other dimensions of life, including the ones that we now debate whether they exist or not. There are very ancient carvings a mile or so down these long dark tunnels. This was a vision quest for them. Today we can take a little train and get down there; it's no big deal, but not in those days. You went into the cave and it was cold, and you had nothing to eat and nothing to drink. You had a little lamp that would last forty-five minutes—you could try to relight it, but it really didn't work—then you were in the dark. These drawings and paintings were done in the dark. They were done in places where nobody was expected to see them. It was an experience between the person who was there and this being that they found in the dark. The dark and the wall were still that person; the person became one with the place.

Crimmel: Like the tree.
Merwin: Yes, and when the person came out, they were changed. They knew the other dimension was there, and they took it with them for the rest of their lives. I think that's what it was. But it came from the animals. These were not the animals that they hunted, though they might have killed

them occasionally. It wasn't the cave bear which was already gone by this time. In a lot of the paintings, the animals have no feet; they're the great elders, they're the dimension of time. The Neanderthal realized that they are the new arrivals, and they don't know anything. These animal elders are the ones who know the world. That's my theory. I read all the books and I thought, nobody knows. This is all speculation. A poet's speculation is as good as anyone else's. I think they were learning from the elders, and learning is part of realizing your connection to these things and that we are not separate from these things. In embryology, there is a stage in which the human fetus, very early at the beginning of formation, goes through all of the different forms of animal life—fish, insect, bird—until it becomes a mammal and they lose a tail, and we go through all of this in a week, but we've done it, we've done it in our own lifetimes.

Crimmel: Utah has a lot of rock art (though some object to that term).
Merwin: I don't know much about its age and connection, but the indigenous people were here very early. But they couldn't travel, and so the great migrations were subsequent to the Paleolithic caves that came later. That was the time when the first wolves were becoming dogs—they were choosing us just as we were choosing them. The genetic thing was happening that allowed for dogs to happen. Dogs made a great deal possible: new hunting techniques, migrations, pastoral culture with its flocks, and food storage places with guard dogs. People couldn't have crossed the Bering Strait without dogs. We've always mistreated dogs, but dogs are our great link to everything. People are lucky who have that feeling about dogs. The connection with dogs, if we are open to it, offers a huge amount that we can learn. I feel very lucky to have had the dogs I have in my life.

Crimmel: Let me ask you a question on a different topic, namely, Sylvia Plath and Ted Hughes. You knew both quite well. Students are fascinated by her short life. *Letters Home: Correspondence 1950–1963* contains Plath's correspondence with her mother. Historically critics claimed Plath's depression was related to the relationship with her father, but this new collection suggests that it had to do with her mother. Was there any connection between the relationship with her mother and the reason why Ted Hughes destroyed Sylvia's journals?
Merwin: She destroyed his.

Crimmel: So it was an act of revenge?

Merwin: She was jealous of Ted. Ted was angry at her, but he wasn't jealous of her. They were very close friends. I just put together a collection for the University of Illinois archives, and there was one letter from Sylvia, written the last winter of her life before she killed herself. She was up in London and so was Ted, but they had broken up. She wrote this letter, the first in a whole series of letters. She started writing to me every day, sometimes two to three times a day. It was all about Ted and the breakup and this whole new emotional charge that she felt in herself. This of course led to all of the new poems. All of the Ariel poems in the book appear in their original format and also with the changes that she made.

She told me that my former wife [Dido Milroy] and Ted were having an affair. I knew it wasn't so, but I wouldn't have cared if it did happen. Ted and I used to walk all over London every day. We took long walks and we were close friends. I had proposed the situation that caused the suspicion. I said, "Your mother just died; she left this big empty apartment on Montague Square, and Ted hasn't got anywhere to live in London. Why don't you let him stay there for the time being?" So she did. Sylvia had spied on them coming and going from the apartment, so that was that.

Anyway, it was an extraordinary correspondence. When I left, I sent all of the letters to my former wife in London and said, you should read these because of what Sylvia is saying. I never saw them again. She gave them to somebody else to take to France, to keep away from me—there was anger and spite. I think they were destroyed because the woman who had the letters broke up with her husband and headed back to Spain. After she died, the attic was cleaned out and I think the letters were probably thrown away. They may turn up, but I don't think so. Awful. They would have been much more interesting than the letters to her mother. Sylvia was a troubling person. She was very destructive—she was self-destructive, and she was jealous of Ted. I realized there was something about her that made me uneasy. I just didn't trust her.

Crimmel: They were certainly celebrities in a way not many authors are today. I was reading *The Hemingway Women* and the book described Hemingway's visit in the 1950s to London, where he was mobbed on the streets by fans. When my mother was a young woman in the 1940s, authors were celebrities. Everyday people read books and discussed them. That doesn't happen so much anymore. How do you think this change has affected society?
Merwin: I can't think it's a good effect. I think the current love for the microchip is one of these miraculous things, but everything has a price. I think

it points to the real difference between poetry and prose. What prose does can be done in other ways. Prose is about something; prose is much more recent than poetry. Poetry is as ancient as language. Poetry is declining just as language is declining. We speak less. Look at Twitter. People are going back to hieroglyphics. People are illiterate and they don't have any vocabulary. They can't express themselves. Language began as a way of expressing inexpressible things—great grief, or great anger—just making a roar or a whine wasn't enough. You tried to make something more articulate. Articulate is exactly what you did. That's the beginning of language and it's also the beginning of poetry. Poetry is there not to provide information, but to say what can't be said—to express love, grief, anger—these feelings that are inexpressible. We are becoming more unable to express things. This is simply going to become part of the acceleration of violence. What happens when you can't say it at all or can't find a way of saying it? Words fail you and you turn to violence. That's what we are doing.

Crimmel: I have greatly enjoyed our conversation and wish we had more time to talk, but I know you have a reading this evening.
Merwin: Yes. Somebody sent me a photograph of my poem that was in the *New Yorker*, called "The New Song," which I am going to read tonight. Someone made a big copy of it and tacked it to the telephone pole. Isn't that nice?

Crimmel: Most people only share things online these days.
Merwin: That's the funny thing. More people read poetry than one realizes. There was a piece about that in the *Wall Street Journal* not so long ago, and the topic is always treated as though poetry were marginal or disappearing. But there is far more of it than we believe, though it's not mainstream media. Somebody asked me to comment on the documentary film called *Louder Than a Bomb*, and how I feel about "rock poetry" and "rap poetry." I said, "I think it's just fine, poetry is about pleasure. There always has to be pleasure, and if there isn't, there isn't any poetry." So, I think however you come into poetry is fine. I wouldn't spend a whole evening listening to rap poetry, but I wouldn't mind listening to ten minutes of it—it's sometimes quite wonderful.

Additional Interviews

Academy of Achievement. "W. S. Merwin Interview: Sweet Memoirs and Uneasy Dreamscapes." July 3, 2008. http://www.achievement.org/ autodoc/page/meroint-1.

Brusate, Tony, and J. Scott Bryson. "'This Absolutely Matters': An Interview with W. S. Merwin." *Limestone: A Literary Journal* 6.1 (1998): 1–8.

Davidson, Peter. "Swimming Up into Poetry." *Atlantic.* August 28, 1997. Transcript available at: http://www.theatlantic.com/past/docs/un bound/poetry/antholog/merwin/pdmerwin.htm.

Davis, Jordan. "Talking with W. S. Merwin." *Nation.* May 16, 2011. http:// www.thenation.com/article/160239/talking-ws-merwin.

Flint, Roland. "Roland Flint Talking with W. S. Merwin." Howard County Poetry and Literature Society's "The Writing Life." 1994. http://www .youtube.com/watch?v=DYgiBlyS_Jw.

Gross, Terry. "The Poetic 'Shadow' of Memory, Mortality." *Fresh Air* (WHYY, Philadelphia and distributed by National Public Radio). 2008. Transcript archived at www.npr.org/templates/transcript/transcript/ php?storyid=98326584.

Jackson, Richard. "Unnaming the Myths." In *Acts of Mind: Conversations with Contemporary Poets*, 48–52. Ed. Richard Jackson. Huntsville: University of Alabama Press, 1983. Originally published in *Poetry Miscellany*, 1981.

Lynn, David, and David Baker. "A Conversation with Poet Laureate W. S. Merwin." *Kenyon Review.* November 2012. Transcript revised by David Baker for *Talk Poetry: Interviews and Poems by Nine American* Poets, 78–92. Fayetteville: University of Arkansas Press, 2012.

Myers, Jack, and Michael Simms. "Possibilities of the Unknown: Conversations with W. S. Merwin." *Southwest Review* 68.2 (1983): 164–80.

Parisi, Joseph. "Poets in Person: W. S. Merwin." *Contemporary Poets and Their Lives.* The Modern Poetry Association. 1991. Audio cassette.

Pettit, Michael. "W. S. Merwin: An Interview." *Black Warrior Review* 8 (Spring 1982): 7–20.

Silverblatt, Michael. "W. S. Merwin with Michael Silverblatt." Lannan

Foundation. April 18, 2012. Video available at http:www.lannan.org/
    events/w.s.-merwin-with-michael-silverblatt/.
Weisner, Ken, and Kevin Hearle. "Interview with W. S. Merwin." [on
    Merwin and Neruda]. *Quarry West* 25 (1988): 76–82.

Index